The Contract Scorecard

The Contract Scorecard

Successful Outsourcing by Design

SARA CULLEN

GOWER

Published by
Gower Publishing Limited
Wey Court East
Union Road
Farnham
Surrey, GU9 7PT
England

Ashgate Publishing Company
Suite 420
101 Cherry Street
Burlington,
VT 05401-4405
USA

www.gowerpublishing.com

British Library Cataloguing in Publication Data
Cullen, Sara
  The contract scorecard : successful outsourcing by design
  1. Contracting out
  I. Title
  658.4'058

  ISBN-13: 978-0-566-08793-6

Library of Congress Cataloging-in-Publication Data
Cullen, Sara.
  The contract scorecard : successful outsourcing by design / by Sara Cullen.
      p. cm.
  Includes bibliographical references and index.
  ISBN 978-0-566-08793-6
  1. Contracting out. 2. Contracting out--Evaluation. I. Title.

HD2365.C85 2009
658.4'058--dc22

2008040985

Mixed Sources
Product group from well-managed forests and other controlled sources
www.fsc.org Cert no. SA-COC-1565
© 1996 Forest Stewardship Council
FSC

Printed and bound in Great Britain by
MPG Books Ltd, Bodmin, Cornwall.

Contents

List of Figures

List of Tables

Foreword

Why do contracts disappoint; when do they succeed? There are no silver bullets – people hate us saying this, but there it is. The major contributors to success are detailed preparation, having the right internal retained capabilities in place, contracting to encourage the right behaviours, and well applied, detailed post-contract management. With these in place, you stand a higher chance of choosing a supplier with the right capabilities and motivations to work on your case. But wringing value out of contracting arrangements is basically hard work on a daily basis, for all parties.

In this context, the Contract Scorecard concept comes into its own. Adoption and use of a Contract Scorecard is the expression of a maturing ability to manage commercial arrangements. An effective scorecard is also the product of a healthier win–win set of relationships between an organization and its suppliers. Even 5 years ago, each for their different reasons, both clients and suppliers resisted such things as Contract Scorecards. Clients preferred to fall back on more traditional, if less helpful, assessment processes. Suppliers feared being held to account on so many criteria that stretched into business outcomes, over which they often felt they could have all too little influence. But nailing down the key outcomes you want should be the starting point, not the end point, in using suppliers. Losing focus, or having multiple inconsistent objectives in the first place, have been among the more obvious ways of losing the plot in contracting, expressed in hidden costs, indifferent service and deteriorating relations between the parties. In contracts, as in life, if you do not know where you are going, any road will do. Working up a contract scorecard in the ways in which this book effectively details is a more productive way of keeping control of your supplier and your business destiny.

But the Contract Scorecard should not be a fire-and-forget missile, a one-off upfront effort. To be successful, the retention of a mutually agreed dynamism on those outcomes, and working with the Contract Scorecard as an ongoing technique, has to become part of the very management fabric of any sourcing arrangement.

What I have always respected in Sara Cullen's professional work is its sheer practicality. This book is a no-frills ride through how to get yourself up to speed on using an eminently practical approach to focusing attention, and to work only on what matters. It is tried and tested, and it works, but only where management see staying on course as a daily responsibility, see assessment as a way of learning and optimizing performance and relationships, and do not see the scorecard as an opportunity to replace management knowledge and action by a fetish of technique and measurement. Ingrain the contract scorecard concept into your managerial behaviour and that of your supplier and look forward to a less bumpy, more directed ride.

Leslie Willcocks
Professor of Technology Work and Globalisation,
London School of Economics

Preface

This book will help you design and drive successful contracts. Different people have diverse beliefs as to what successful contracts are. Some would consider a contract successful if it did not end up in court. Others believe it to be successful if they did not need to manage the contractor too much. In this book, success means that the people in your organization got the results they were seeking – not that failure was avoided.

This book is more than a 'feel good' management book; it is a systematic guide to success full of practical advice and examples using the concept of a Contract Scorecard. Not only is the Contract Scorecard concept explained, but also the crucial implementation activities such as the development of performance measures that work in practice, sound Service Level Agreements that make obligations clear and effective, and a Governance Charter that ensures both parties will adopt successful management techniques.

There are a number of case examples presented throughout this book, highlighting what can happen when long-term success is not kept in mind when designing and managing contracts. Some of the cases might astound you, as I have been continuously astounded throughout the decades I've been practising. These were all smart folks, but just did not have an in-depth understanding of the ramifications of what they were doing at the time. As these cases will demonstrate, it is too easy for us all to lose track of why we are doing things in our rush to get things done – particularly contracts!

You will need to make an upfront investment into design and manage successful contracts – something many organizations do not do. Even a minor investment in the better design of a contract's success will yield a superior return on that investment. As so many clients have told me, the number one thing they would do differently in all their contracts is to design them better – not from a legal perspective, but from the business perspective. This book is all about making the business goals the focus of a deal and making sure your desired outcomes happen.

Sara Cullen

Introduction

'We are drowning in information and starving for knowledge.'

Rutherford D. Roger

About this Chapter

This chapter takes you through the basic purpose of the Contract Scorecard and explains some of the underlying research behind the concept as well as its predecessor concept – the Balanced Scorecard.

Purpose of the Contract Scorecard

Organizations that are veterans at contracting know that the success of a deal is not just about cost, but that the quality of the work matters too. They also know it is more than just getting value for money; it is about making sure that the relationship between the parties is productive and not dysfunctional. Furthermore, they know that having a contract is not an end in itself – merely a means to achieve a desired goal or goals.

Success can rarely be defined by only one criterion, and never from only one person's perspective. While some people in your organization prefer things cheap, others will want them fast. Some will forgo both to get better quality. Yet others will prefer to work with providers they can trust. Success is multifaceted and everyone has a different opinion. So how can you balance all your stakeholders' needs and still drive results-orientated contracts?

A Contract Scorecard is a very useful tool if you want to focus your contracts, and your stakeholders, on results. It enables you to articulate the myriad of different outcomes that different stakeholders want and then ascertain the degree to which these have been achieved.

It does this by ensuring that the parties not only establish how the quality of the work will be evaluated, but also what the financial outcomes will be judged by, how the relationship is conducted between the parties and if the deal achieves its strategic aims. In sum, a Contract Scorecard defines and then measures the overall success of the deal from a holistic view.

As such, the Contract Scorecard provides you with a key instrument for guiding the details of the contract to put in place the vital contractual provisions. It further expresses these goals in a measurable form so that they are not merely idealistic thinking, but instead are outcomes that are regularly tracked and assessed. As people who are experienced with contracts know, active management of the desired goals delivers results, not the contract itself.

Research Base

The Contract Scorecard was developed as part of my PhD examining 107 contracting arrangements over the last decade and categorizing the key attributes in which success was sought. That research focused initially on examining what success is, and then looked at how organizations achieve it.

The 107 cases are contract initiatives in which I worked with in various organizations (client and providers) across 51 countries covering Asia-Pacific, the Middle East and Europe. These deals represented over US$11 billion annual spend. The largest was US$1.5 billion per annum and the smallest was worth US$0.2 million per annum.

The cases included the full spectrum of outsourcing initiatives, ranging from information technology and communications (IT) outsourcing, to business process contracts covering such areas as human resources, corporate property, call centres and accounting, and many operational contracts, dealing with maintenance, construction, logistics and so on.

Of the case organizations, 60 per cent were in the commercial sector and 40 per cent in the government sector. Within the commercial sector, over 60 per cent of cases were in the finance (insurance, banking, stock broking and so on), ICT (information, communication and technology), or utility (water, electricity and gas) industries. Within the government sector, the cases were chiefly state government agencies and departments, followed by federal government agencies and departments, then local governments (that is, city councils).

As you would expect, the research I conducted involved examining many sources of evidence including systematic analysis of the related working documents (plans, contracts, reports, evaluations, minutes, reviews, audit findings and so on). It also included regular interaction and discussion with 20 different types of stakeholders and participants, ranging from Managing Directors and CEOs, CFOs and CIOs, to employees and advisors (for example, legal, financial advisors, probity and consultants of all kinds).

The Contract Scorecard was created from both my direct involvement in these cases, when working as a consultant, and from what I learned by observing and discussing the experiences of stakeholders and participants when I was an observer (for instance, when conducting detailed case studies on behalf of clients). It consists of four quadrants (see Figure 1.1), each of which contains one aspect that must be addressed by anyone who wants to design a contract that delivers what their organization really wants. By addressing all four aspects or quadrants, you will be able to design and drive the best possible outcomes for your contracts. These quadrants are: 1) quality; 2) financial; 3) relationship; and 4) strategic, and they are fully described the next chapter.

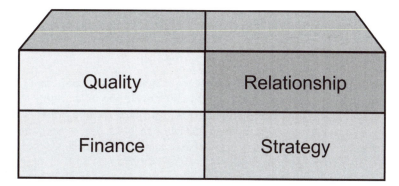

Figure 1.1   Contract Scorecard – quadrants
© The Cullen Group, 2008

Roots of the Concept

The basic idea of a scorecard is, of course, nothing new. People and organizations have been 'scorecarded' for years. The concept hit the corporate scene in the early

1990s, following development of Balanced Scorecard by Robert Kaplan and David Norton. The Balanced Scorecard was the result of their study, which set out to capture and measure the attributes of successful US companies (Kaplan and Norton, 1992 and 1996). They categorized success attributes as: 1) financial results; 2) efficient internal business processes; 3) learning and growth of staff; and 4) satisfied customers. The Balanced Scorecard has since proliferated into many forms and spawned an entire global consulting industry. As I wrote this, a search on Google for 'Balanced Scorecard' yielded 2 670 000 results!

If your organization is employing a form of the Balanced Scorecard for its internal operations, that is all well and good. However, if your organization pays a large portion of its expenditures to external parties, you may be leaving a great deal of your structure unscored, as illustrated below.

A REGIONAL BANK SCORES ONLY PART OF THE PICTURE

A fast-growing regional bank had a decentralized management style, empowering staff to contract with whom, and how, each staff member saw fit. These contracted expenditures were not systematically tracked or controlled – it was up to the buyer to manage whatever they bought in whatever manner they saw fit.

An insightful manager, after gaining substantial cost savings from better design and management of the contracts in their area, thought the techniques they employed could be useful in other contracts in the bank. Their initial guess at external spend with suppliers was approximately 30 per cent of the bank's annual outgoings. A brief assessment of the accounts payable ledger found that the actual spend was about 80 per cent.

The bank had been investing very heavily in a minor component of its outgoings including staff, but nothing on its major outgoings. It had a very large human resources (HR) department and employed many leading HR techniques such as 360-degree evaluations (a performance evaluation that includes an assessment by staff, colleagues and supervisors), leadership training and capability assessments, mentoring programmes and the like.

Meanwhile, it had no contract management area, no 'informed buying' capabilities, and didn't track any form of results from the over 400 providers it engaged.

While the Balanced Scorecard is a useful tool for your organization's internal operations, a different scorecard is required for your organization's contracted operations. With regard to contracting arrangements, the Contract Scorecard is a method used to evaluate the success of the arrangement in a similar holistic manner to the Balanced Scorecard – the technique encourages organizations to think more strategically about what constitutes success, go about setting up measures, and then drive them.

Structure of this Book

This book is intended to help you understand the concept, design the scorecard that you want for each contract, develop practical key performance indicators that will work, select your options when performance is good or bad and develop the key contractual schedules that underpin the scorecard.

Chapter 2, 'The Quadrants of the Contract Scorecard', takes you through each of the quadrants of the Contract Scorecard. In doing so, different ways of measuring each quadrant are explored and 23 different example Key Performance Indicators (KPIs) are given.

Chapter 3, 'The Steps in Developing KPIs', takes you through each of the seven steps that develop KPIs that will work. A note of caution – seven steps sounds easy, but each will take more time and effort than you might think.

Chapter 4, 'Schemes for the Consequences of KPI Performance', takes you through possible incentives and disincentives (the 'carrot' and 'stick' options) that you might choose to invoke if KPI performance is good or if it is poor. These are not just monetary options; non-monetary options are given as well.

Chapter 5, 'Planning the Contract Scorecard', takes you through some key planning considerations including choosing your Contract Scorecard quadrants (each contract does not necessarily require all of them), designing your Scorecard Blueprint (where you intend to specify your chosen quadrants in the contract) as well as the best time in the contract lifecycle to prepare your scorecard.

Chapter 6, 'The Quality Specification – The Service Level Agreement (SLA)', helps you design the contract schedule that specifies the work (what you want for your money) including both parties' work-related accountabilities, the detailed specifications, reporting and the quality KPIs. The chapter appendix includes an example schedule.

Chapter 7, 'The Financial Specification – The Financial Schedule', helps you design the contract schedule that is all about the money. This addresses costs, reimbursables, invoicing, payment, charges, benchmarking and the financial KPIs. The chapter appendix includes an example schedule.

Chapter 8, 'The Relationship Specification – The Governance Charter', helps you design the contract schedule regarding the inter-party relationship by imposing a commitment on both sides to manage the deal in a diligent and agreed manner. It covers the management roles and responsibilities of each party, the meetings and reviews, and the processes surrounding issue, dispute and variation management – all of which are critical to the success of your deal. The chapter appendix includes an example schedule.

Chapter 9, 'The Strategic Specification – Unique Contract Schedules', helps you design the contract schedule(s) that articulates the strategic goals of the deal and details the provider's obligations in assisting you to achieve them. As these schedules can be quite large and varied, only a few examples have been included, one for each type of strategic goal (innovation, business contribution, alignment and underlying business practices).

The last chapter, Chapter 10, summarizes with a few thoughts.

2

The Quadrants of the Contract Scorecard

'The whole is greater than the sum of the parts.'

Euclid

About this Chapter

Too often, organizations are disappointed with some or all aspects of their contracts, because their expectations are not being met. Many of these organizations tend to assume that the provider will adapt easily to their needs without the appropriate financial return. And it is these organizations that usually fail to articulate their expectations in a commercially astute manner, as well as neglecting their own responsibilities to make the contract work. Yet, they always seem to blame the provider for the ensuing problems.

Furthermore, because of inappropriate measures (not measuring the right things), providers can actually believe they are doing a great job, simply because they have achieved a specific KPI within the contract, while at the same time the organizational stakeholders are dissatisfied, and some may even hold the provider in contempt. The lesson? The benefits you seek to gain from any contract will not inherently result from the mere act of signing it. Any benefits you seek to achieve must be clearly specified, and then you must put in place the underlying management processes to ensure the benefits will occur.

The onus is on your organization to articulate what will satisfy its expectations and articulate what is most important to your stakeholders, in terms of how they will perceive success. Leaving it to the provider is not a good solution, as this can have surprising and unwelcome results, as the following case clearly illustrates.

AN INTERNATIONAL ACCOUNTING FIRM GETS THE GUARANTEE BUT NOT THE EXPECTED PERFORMANCE

An international accounting firm had an equipment contract with a global provider. The firm knew that its members around the world depended on the computer equipment to arrive as quickly as possible. Otherwise, its staff would not be productive, or not even chargeable to its clients. Every day a staff member was without the equipment was one day lost in revenue.

It sought a guarantee within the contract from the provider that the equipment would be delivered within 10 days of an order. After a bit of negotiation about which countries this guarantee would cover, the provider agreed. Satisfied, the firm announced this guarantee to their clients in those countries and told them to start placing their orders.

However, the firm's expectations were not in line with what the provider actually intended to measure. Because the equipment was being sold in each country through the provider's resellers and not the provider itself, the guarantee covered the turnaround time from the factory to the delivery dock in each country. From that point, it was up to the resellers to get it to the firm's offices. It was still taking up to 30 days for the resellers to get it from the dock to the various offices in the countries.

The client lived with this situation for 3 years until the contract expired. Then the firm took the performance measures into its own hands, now knowing that only it can make sure the contract meets its needs. The new measurement of the minimum delivery time? Ten days from date of order to the location of the office that placed the order. The former provider wasn't successful in the retendered contract because it couldn't meet this performance standard as its resellers were just too unreliable.

This chapter takes you through each of the quadrants of the Contract Scorecard. In doing so, different ways of measuring each quadrant are explored and 23 different example KPIs are given. These examples are only illustrations of how to think about performance measures, and are by no means definitive. My KPI catalogue has thousands of examples of ways in which organizations have decided to define and measure success. Yours must work for you.

Please note that the KPI examples used in this chapter have a particularly good practice format that includes not only specifying the KPI, but also how frequently it is to be calculated, and the formula and source of the data that must be used in calculating it. How to develop good practice KPIs is the subject of Chapter 3. This chapter is about 'what' you might want to measure; the 'how to' is covered next.

Quality Quadrant

The quality of the scope of work delivered, whether it is services, assets, goods or a combination of these, is paramount to your organization's perception of success. Getting something cheap that does not work can hardly be called a successful deal, at least not for the buyer.

However, quality is a relatively amorphous word – it means many different things to many different people. For some, quality means on-time delivery. For others, they would rather have it meet the specifications even if it arrives a bit late, and they are happy to trade some time to get it right.

On time and to specifications are just two of the many interpretations of quality. In fact, what defines quality is really made up of any combination of five dimensions. These are listed below:

1. **Precision** – the degree to which work is error free and done in full.

2. **Reliability** – the degree to which the work is consistently dependable.

3. **Speed** – the swiftness in which the work is performed.

4. **Effectiveness** – the degree to which an end result is achieved that is outcome-focused as opposed to process-focused.

5. **Satisfaction** – the degree that users, customers or other stakeholders are pleased with the work.

Any number of measurements will come into play to determine the overall quality of the work under the contract. Table 2.1 gives examples of the things that one might find in each of the five dimensions of quality measurements. Each one will now be discussed in turn.

PRECISION

Precision measurements seek to quantify the degree to which the work was performed accurately and in compliance with the rules set up under the contract.

Table 2.1   Quality dimensions and examples

Precision	Reliability	Speed	Effectiveness	Satisfaction
• accuracy/ error rates • compliance to standards • fit to specification • completeness of work	• deadlines • availability • abandon rates • failure/ fault rate • rework • shrinkage • recalls	• response rates • resolution/ rectification time • cycle time • queue time • processing time • volumes/ throughput • turnaround time • backlog clearing	• utilization • vacancy levels • call reduction • customer retention/ return rates • sales	• end users • external customers • other stakeholders

The first rule might be the specification. Specification-related performance measures typically begin with an assessment as to whether the work was conducted, the product delivered or the asset built in accordance with the specification, statement of work or to a specified standard.

An example of such a compliance KPI is shown in Figure 2.1. This KPI was set up to ensure that all equipment ordered by the client was delivered as per the purchase order.

One KPI relating to accurate performance often included in contracts is an assessment to which the work/item meets a specified standard such as that published under the International Standards Organization (ISO). The ISO has 17 000 standards on a variety of technical subjects as well as on generic management systems such as quality management and environmental management.

If you want the provider to follow your specific policies and procedures, you might consider another common KPI that assesses the degree to which your organization's policies and procedures were followed in conducting the work. All of these compliance-orientated KPIs operate as a pass or fail KPI, or one scored by your organization. An example of this type of KPI is shown in Figure 2.2. This KPI was set up to ensure that the provider at least partially complied with the policies and procedures specified in the contract and in place within the client.

| KPI | KPI Minimum Standard | Calculation | | Source Data |
		Frequency	Formula	
1 Delivery accuracy	No delivery errors	Monthly	Delivery error = any variance not authorized by the Client from the Purchase Order*	Service desk

Figure 2.1   Example KPI – delivery to specification

*   All the KPI examples in this chapter use terms that have been defined in the glossaries of the various contracts from which the examples were taken. These contractual defined terms are denoted by the capitalization of the first letter in each word of the term (in this case, Purchase Order).

| KPI | KPI Minimum Standard | Calculation | | Source Data |
		Frequency	Formula	
1 Compliance with Contract and Client Policies and Procedures	Minimum score of B	Quarterly	A = compliant B = part compliant C = non-compliant	Client audit report

Figure 2.2   Example KPI – compliance with policies

Other precision-based KPIs involve an assessment as to accuracy or error rates. For example, a data entry service would likely have a maximum allowable error rate regarding the inputted data, as assessed through regular audits. An invoicing service would also have a maximum allowable error rate, as well as a maximum allowable duplicate invoicing rate (which is often zero). A payroll processing service would do likewise, with a maximum allowable error rate, as well as a maximum allowable duplicate payment rate (which again is often zero).

Figure 2.3 shows an example of a KPI regarding the accuracy of records. This KPI was set up to ensure that the asset and related warranty registers were accurate – important to the client since the provider was managing thousands of assets. In this particular case, the client decided not to have a regular audit, but instead recorded any inaccuracies it found in an issue register. This was used to record not only register issues, but other quality issues as well.

RELIABILITY

Reliability measurements seek to quantify the degree to which you are able to rely on the work. This can be measured in a number of ways.

| KPI | KPI Minimum Standard | Calculation | | |
		Frequency	Formula (if applicable)	Source Data
1 Accuracy of Asset and Warranty Registers	100% accuracy	Quarterly	Register error = any inaccurate data (for example, serial number, model, under warranty, and so on)	Client's Issue Register

Figure 2.3   Example KPI – accuracy of records

The degree to which deadlines are met is important in many time-driven organizations that need certain things done by a certain time or date. For example, a property management contract would have a number of deadline-based KPIs involving lease renegotiations, valuations, make good (returning vacated property to no less than its original state), rent payments or collections, budget preparation and financial reconciliations – to name but a few. A programme of work that has a series of milestones would specify the due date of each and have a measurement regarding the percentage of milestones meeting the due dates.

An example of this is shown in Figure 2.4. This KPI was set up to ensure that the provider completed milestones on the due date. Since the milestones did not all occur every month, a quarterly measure was set up.

Another common reliability-based KPI is an obligation regarding the minimum required availability of staff and/or systems, possibly with different availability requirements during working hours versus non-working hours. With regard to systems, this is measured in terms of *minimum scheduled uptime* (or the opposite, *maximum unscheduled downtime*).

| KPI | KPI Minimum Standard | Calculation | | |
		Frequency	Formula	Source Data
1 Milestone completion	Completed on scheduled date	Quarterly	scheduled date = per Services Plan	Service Plan
			completion date = notified date to Client by Contractor	Contractor notice

Figure 2.4   Example KPI – meeting milestones

An example of this is shown in Figure 2.5. This KPI was set up to ensure that the most important items of equipment were nearly always available. The client had a regulatory obligation that was the same availability, on a rolling 24-month basis. To ensure that obligation was never in danger, the client set a rolling 12-month basis for the KPI.

The failure or fault rate of a product or an item of work is imperative to assess the reliability of the provider in many contracts. In the case of a product, the KPI might be the pass rate of a sample of items subject to a stress test or materials composite test. The reliability of maintenance work might be measured by the frequency of rectification calls within a specific period subsequent to the maintenance being conducted. This is often called *rework*, and the KPI would specify a tolerable limit regarding the amount of rework. For example, only one rectification might be allowed within 3 months of an item of equipment being reconditioned.

Figure 2.6 shows an example with zero tolerance for delivery of equipment that failed to work, which the client termed 'dead on arrival'. This particular client ordered about 5 000 items of equipment per year and needed each item of equipment to be operational immediately.

Where a provider is delivering inventory or products, *minimal shrinkage* is an important measurement (for example in a logistics/transport contract). Shrinkage is defined as the undocumented loss of inventory that can be due to spoilage, spillage or evaporation, but can also be due to theft. A shrinkage KPI would set a maximum tolerable percentage of each shipment that the client will allow before seeking remedy; this might be set, for example, at 2 per cent.

KPI	KPI Minimum Standard	Calculation		Source Data
		Frequency	Formula	
1 Equipment availability	a. Category 1 at least 99.8% available	Rolling 12 month	Availability = percentage of hours per year that each item of equipment is correctly functioning other than by fault of a third party	Client's equipment fault records
	b. Category 2 at least 99% available			
	c. Category 3 at least 97% available			

Figure 2.5   Example KPI – equipment availability

		Calculation		
KPI	**KPI Minimum Standard**	**Frequency**	**Formula**	**Source Data**
1　DOAs (dead on arrivals)	No DOAs	Monthly	DOA excludes Peripherals	Service desk

Figure 2.6　　Example KPI – reliability of equipment at delivery

SPEED

Speed measurements seek to quantify how fast the provider does something for the client. As with all quality KPIs, this can be measured in many ways depending on what you want. Speed-based KPIs can include:

- queue time and call answer time for inbound call centres;

- rate of throughput per specified time period (for example, per hour) for any processing, manufacturing or mining function;

- restoration turnaround time for data backup services.

In most contracts that have a service component there would be a measurement regarding the response and resolution rates of the provider in responding to calls, faults, problems and the like. The first measure is how quickly the provider responds after a notice has been given (for example, how long before they are on-site) and the second how long it takes to fix the issue after a notice has been given. Obviously, these are two very different measures, but it is very common to see scorecards with detailed response rate requirements but without any specified rate for the resolution/rectification of the initial problem.

Figure 2.7 shows examples of both. The first KPI acts as the response KPI and the second as the resolution KPI. The client referred to its fix notices as 'trouble tickets', and each one was assigned a priority either 1 (high) or 2 (low). It did not consider any problem fixed until the provider had entered all of the data regarding the fix solution – a process that the client termed 'closeout' – into the system.

KPI		KPI Minimum Standard	Calculation			Source Data
			Frequency	Formula		
1	Response	a. For Priority 1 Trouble Orders, Contractor on-site within 1 hour of Trouble Order being placed	Monthly	Number of Priority 1 on-site responses within 1 hour/Number of Priority 1 on-site responses required		CIS++ report
		b. For Priority 2 Trouble Orders, Contractor on-site within 4 hours of Trouble Order being placed		Number of Priority 2 on-site responses within 4 hours/Number of Priority 2 on-site responses required		
2	Resolution	a. Closeout of Priority 1 Trouble Orders 100% within 15 minutes of job completion		Number of Priority 1 Closeouts within 15 minutes/Number of Priority 1 Closeouts required		CIS++ Trouble Order system
		b. Closeout of Priority 2 Trouble Orders 100% within 30 minutes of job completion		Number of Priority 2 Closeouts within 30 minutes/Number of Priority 2 Closeouts required		

Figure 2.7   Example KPI – fault response and resolution

The speeds of cycle times are important for many financial functions. For example, an accounts receivable service would always have a cycle measurement over the time it takes to issue an invoice and collect payment. Likewise, an accounts payable service would always have a cycle measurement over the time it takes to receive a bill and make payment (ideally, to get early payment discounts if that is the client's wish, and most certainly to avoid any late fees or interest). Of course, cycle times are not limited to financial functions; for example, a recruiting function might have a cycle time between placing an advert for a position and filling that position.

The following figure (Figure 2.8) provides an example of order fulfilment from the time the order is placed until the product is delivered. In this case, the client believed it was very important to know that its purchase order had been received as well as ensuring that the equipment was delivered on time.

KPI		KPI Minimum Standard	Calculation		
			Frequency	Formula	Source Data
1	Purchase Order confirmation	Confirmation received by Client within two (2) hours of Contractor receiving Purchase Order	Monthly	Confirmation time = time Purchase Order email sent per Client's date and time stamp	Order system
2	Delivery days	Equipment delivered at the Client site within ten (10) Business Days from Purchase Order date		Delivery days = Delivery date minus the Purchase Order date	

Figure 2.8   Example KPI – order and delivery cycle time

EFFECTIVENESS

Effectiveness measurements seek to quantify an end result that is important to the client's business. These measurements have a direct impact on the business activities. For example, two effectiveness measures of a helpdesk are to record: (1) a reduction in repetitive/recurrent calls and (2) the 'first-call resolution rate' (the percentage of calls resolved by the helpdesk operator at the time of the call). In the case of the former, a business saves money if there are fewer calls to a helpdesk, thus requiring fewer operators. In the case of the latter, that of the first call resolution rate, it aims to minimize the total time that the caller needs to invest in getting the issue resolved and thus increase productivity.

Let us say that the client sets a minimum call reduction KPI regarding repetitive issues (for example, excluding calls related to a new system for which there would always be a surge of calls for an initial period) of 5 per cent per year. To reduce calls the operators will need to take more time to teach the caller how to solve a problem, or provide feedback to the training section regarding the need for caller training in problem areas.

Such proactive steps will have a negative effect on any speed measures, and so will not occur naturally unless there are effective KPIs driving the desired behaviour. For example, let us assume there is a speed measurement on call duration (number of minutes per call), as well as on time to closeout the call (number of minutes to resolve the call) – both of which are common. The operators will be motivated to end the call as quickly as possible, often telling the caller to try something and if that does not work to call back. Not only is the call fast and resolved quickly, if the caller calls back then a new call can be raised, thus potentially increasing fees if the contract charges per call. Without counterbalancing KPIs on effectiveness, an operator being assessed on speed will only focus on speed, even if this is actually detrimental to your organization.

Let us next assume that the first call resolution rate was set at 70 per cent of all calls, only 30 per cent of calls would need to get further assistance than the operator can provide (known as *second-level support*). In order to meet this KPI, a provider would need to ensure that knowledgeable operators are staffing the helpdesk, and not operate the *first-level* helpdesk as purely a call-logging function.

Of course, effectiveness measures of a helpdesk would be in addition to the speed measurements including response time, queue time and the reliability measures including availability and abandon rates, and satisfaction of the caller's experience.

Other effectiveness measures include:

- utilization (for example, of a recreational centre by its members);

- vacancy levels in the case of property management;

- customer retention/return visits in the case of a front-line, food or retail service;

- the number of sales in the case of an outbound call centre or other contracted sales activity (an example of which is given in Figure 2.9, in which the provider was in charge of sales regarding a airline's club scheme).

SATISFACTION

Satisfaction is a 'soft' measurement of quality. This is because these are opinion-based measures (based on perceptions) as opposed to the earlier 'hard' measurements that are fact-based (based on systemic independent evidence).

Soft measurements can be erratic and unreliable because they can be influenced by timing – for example, a satisfaction survey first thing on a

KPI	KPI Minimum Standard	Calculation		Source Data
		Frequency	Formula	
• Completed calls	Twelve (12) completed calls per day, per Account Manager	Monthly	Complete call = at the point at which there is document-agreed course of action and all fulfilments completed (for example, bookings made, brochures mailed, and so on)	Account Register
• New members	Two (2) new corporate memberships per Account Manager per week		New membership = at the point at which the Trust Account shows a receipt of membership payment by non-member organization	Bank's Trust Account statement
• Sales revenue	$10 000 per week in sales revenue per Account Manager		Sales revenue = at the point at which the Trust Account shows a receipt of payment other than memberships	

Figure 2.9   Example KPI – effectiveness of sales function

Monday morning can yield worse results than on other days (for those who hate Mondays). They can also be influenced by non-related events – for example, if the person being surveyed had crashed their car on the way to work, causing them to be more ill-tempered than usual. Pity the provider on the other end of that particular satisfaction survey!

Given the degree to which satisfaction assessments are inherently loaded with the emotions of the respondent at the time, it is more useful to use these measurements as an indicator of the validity of the 'hard' measurements. If both are tracking on the same trend-line, the hard measurements are probably measuring what they should be.

However, if the satisfaction measure is going down, while the hard measures are going up, there is a problem. The parties are not measuring what the stakeholders care about, or the stakeholder expectations are out of alignment with what the contract has been designed to deliver.

In the first case, it would be the result of measuring what is easy to measure, and not what is important to the stakeholders. Accordingly, an initiative to identify what the 'hard' measurements are not measuring is required.

In the second case, let us assume that the client signed up for a fantastically cheap deal, but it will take twice as long for delivery. The first question is whether the client has fully informed the stakeholders and the second question is, are the parties managing these stakeholders so that their expectations are aligned with the nature of the current deal. If not, satisfaction results will be declining even though the provider has done nothing wrong. In this case, an initiative to align stakeholders' expectations is in order. The case below highlights just such an event that occurred, and how the parties resolved it.

KPIs ARE BEING MET BUT DISSATISFACTION CONTINUES TO GROW

An international airline had outsourced its IT support services (LANs, desktop fleet management and helpdesk). In this case, stakeholder satisfaction surveys were yielding poor results and there was a general feeling of dissatisfaction with the provider. Yet, the KPIs were showing reasonable performance, certainly of a standard that didn't warrant the animosity exhibited.

A root cause analysis determined that the major contributing factor was that both the provider's sales staff and its operational staff were making unwritten promises to various client personnel and not carrying them out or following them up. These promises included access to global research, technical briefings and facilitation of special interest groups, to name a few. Therefore, the client had immense expectations that were not articulated in the agreement, yet were the major source of dissatisfaction.

Neither party maintained records of the discussions or had correspondence, thus an initiative was undertaken to gather all the unrecorded promises. Once this process was completed, the provider realized it couldn't meet these expectations and keep within its profit margins. The first step was to prioritize the promises and determine which the provider could perform at minimum cost. From among those it couldn't, the client was invited to choose those that it was willing to pay extra for. Lastly, to stop this problem from occurring again, the provider instituted a 'no promises unless supported with a variation' procedure and instituted a minute-keeping and review procedure for all meetings.

Now let us take the opposite case where the satisfaction ratings are going up but the 'hard' measurements are trending downwards. Obviously, something is making the stakeholders very happy and the 'hard' measurements are not influencing their opinion. Again, we could be measuring things the stakeholders do not care about and must query why we are investing in a measurement system that does bear any relation to stakeholder satisfaction.

Alternatively, perhaps the risk/reward system (see Chapter 4) regarding the total KPI portfolio is so skewed towards satisfaction that the provider gets a better return on investment by letting the 'hard' measurements go and focusing on satisfaction instead. In that case, we would need to examine whether the motivational factors used to drive the provider's performance are being skewed towards an unbalanced result.

Any organization will find it quite insightful to examine the trend of perception versus fact in regard to their contracts, and to assure themselves that they are measuring what is important, that everyone has realistic expectations and that no trade-offs are occurring that were not intended.

Figure 2.10 shows an example of the client satisfaction KPIs for five sport and recreation facilities, operated by a provider on behalf of the client. In this case, the client wished to measure satisfaction with particular items, not just

KPI		KPI Minimum Standard – average good to excellent rating					Frequency	Source data
KPI		Site 1	Site 2	Site 3	Site 4	Site 5		
1.	Overall experience	average over 90%					Monthly	Feedback Surveys for the month
2.	Booking process and information	over 90%						
3.	Facilities and equipment range and quality	over 90%	over 75%	over 80%	over 80%	over 75%		
4.	Meal quality and quantity	over 90%						
5.	Staff friendliness, responsiveness and professionalism	over 95%						
6.	Indoor facilities comfort and climate (heating/ cooling)	over 80%						

Figure 2.10   Example KPI – customer satisfaction

have a generic single satisfaction indicator. You will note the format varies from the 'hard' KPIs, which is not unusual with satisfaction indices.

Financial Quadrant

Financial measurements reflect the monetary outcomes that your organization is seeking as part of the contract. In a very simple contract, getting the work/item at the cheapest price offered is very straightforward and does not require a scorecard to design and manage that outcome – merely getting competitive quotes will do the job.

However, complex and long-term contracts can have an array of any of the following four types of financial measurements:

1.   **Historical** – current cost compared to previous periods or a baseline.

2.   **Budget/target** – current cost compared to planned or targeted expenditure.

3.   **Market** – current cost compared to current market rates.

4.   **TCO (total cost of ownership)** – contribution toward reducing the entire supply chain, total asset or total technology costs.

5.   **Invoicing and payment** – degree to which the payment cycle is effective.

Table 2.2 gives examples of the KPIs you might find in each of these dimensions of the financial quadrant.

HISTORICAL

Historical financial measurements compare amounts paid to the provider to past fiscal points. These past fiscal points can be either past periods, such as the previous month or year, or the specified baseline costs that would typically be what the work had cost under the previous service-delivery regime, such as when the work was conducted by your organization (this is known as *insourced*), or when the work was conducted by a previous provider.

Table 2.2   Financial KPI dimensions and examples

Historical	Budget/target	Market	TCO	Invoicing and payment
• Maintain costs to a percentage under historical baseline • Ongoing reduction each year or a limited increase such as CPI (Consumer Price Index)	• Percentage goal under/over budget • Within a percentage of agreed target figure	• No less than a specified percentage of agreed benchmark • Within a specified quartile of the benchmarking sample	• Portion of total cost represented by the contract • Impact of contract performance on downstream processes/asset life	• Invoice accuracy • Submission timeliness of budgets and/or invoices • Payment of subcontractors • Penalties and fines

These historical measurements usually specify one of three things: 1) that the prices must decrease by a specified percentage; 2) cost no more than the previous fiscal point; or 3) cost no greater than a specified percentage.

Figure 2.11 is an example of a KPI that specifies a 5 per cent reduction from the baseline costs (the cost of the last year when the function was operated in-house). The percentage reduction, in this case, was offered as part of the provider's bid when the contract was competitively tendered.

However, you must be careful about setting cost reduction KPIs, because they may work against other KPIs you want to achieve in the scorecard. For example, getting ongoing cost reductions as well as continuous improvement or innovation may be unreasonable to expect, as the case opposite demonstrates very clearly.

BUDGET/TARGET

Budget or target financial measurements compare actual costs to a budgeted or targeted amount, as shown as in Figure 2.12. In this case, only 80 per cent of the hundred or so information systems change requests need to be completed on budget, but the rest had to be within 20 per cent of budget.

A DEAL MOTIVATING THE PROVIDER NOT TO IMPROVE

An insurance company had a 7-year outsourcing contract for its entire IT infrastructure. The contract had a 12.5 per cent mandated annual cost reduction, a capped profit and a capped provision of labour. By the end of the 7-year contract, the entire IT infrastructure and related practices were obsolete and not supported anywhere in the industry (for example, the desktop fleet had not changed in the 7 years. In order to meet the financial obligations imposed by the insurance company, the provider was pushed to drive down costs by retaining obsolete technology, making no investments and by ensuring that all work practices were focused on cost reduction, disallowing any improvements or innovations that didn't result in immediate cost reductions.

KPI	KPI Minimum Standard	Calculation		
		Frequency	Formula	Source Data
1. Baseline reduction	5% reduction in Baseline Cost per year	Annually	Baseline Cost minus actual costs/Baseline Cost	Actual cost per Contractor's invoices
				Baseline Cost per Client Baseline Report

Figure 2.11   Example KPI – cost reduction

KPI	KPI Minimum Standard	Calculation		
		Frequency	Formula	Source Data
1. Change Requests	a. At least 80% delivered within agreed budget	Monthly	Percentage delivery to budget = total number of Change Requests invoiced within agreed budget/ total number of Change Requests implemented	Budget per Change Request
	b. Remainder delivered within 20% of agreed budget			Invoiced charge per Contractor's invoice
				Change Requests implemented per Change Request Log

Figure 2.12   Example KPI – meeting budget

The concept of meeting a budget is quite easy to understand. Either the provider meets, or fails to meet, the budget/target figure. However, it can be difficult to measure in practice. This is because budgets usually change over time as your organization's needs change, its financial situation changes or as better or more accurate information arises after the original budget was prepared. Accordingly, the measurement may need to be in relation to the most recently agreed budget rather than the original budget, with a KPI regarding budget accuracy on the original budget also incorporated to encourage less variance.

MARKET

If your organization wants to compare prices to a market rate, it is most commonly performed through *benchmarking*. This allows you to demonstrate to stakeholders that you are actually getting value for money. On the other hand, if you are not so worried about price, it provides targets, and possibly techniques, that can improve the deal's value-for-money equation.

In the example given in Figure 2.13, the volatility of prices in the market was quite high. To ensure prices were in line with the market's movements, the client performed quarterly benchmarking which it issued in a report to the contract managers of both parties. It required the provider to be no more than five cents above each quarter's benchmark, which in the industry was measured as a price per minute.

KPI			Calculation		
Minimum Standard	**Target**	**Frequency**	**Formula**		**Source Data**
1. Contractor price per minute not more than five cents above benchmark price per minute.	Contractor price per minute five cents or more below benchmark price per minute	Quarterly	Contractor price per minute = average per the three monthly invoices		Monthly invoices
			benchmark price per minute = as determined by Client's benchmarking team		Client Market Analysis report

Figure 2.13   Example KPI – within-market benchmarks

Your approach to a benchmarking exercise can be as economical as you can afford in time and/or money. There are three fundamental approaches to benchmarking:

1.   an independent consultant;

2.   partner organizations; and

3.   your own database of competing providers.

First is the use of independent consultants. This is a popular approach, but it is also the most expensive. There are a number of benchmarking consultants in industries where there are mature markets.[1] The key to getting value for money will be how you scope the benchmarking exercise. There are two special considerations when using consultants: 1) whether they must disclose the individual data sets (as opposed to merely aggregate or average numbers) to your organization as well as the provider (albeit keeping the names of the organizations confidential); and 2) whether fees include any dispute resolution processes resulting from the benchmarking exercises. If your agreement with the consultant does not mention either of these two items, you may not have access to the data and you may have to pay extra if your provider disputes any of the findings and the consultant needs to be involved.

Because consultants are the most expensive option, many organizations choose a few select organizations that they will 'partner' with. Your goal would be to collaborate with client organizations from the same, or similar, industries as yours. However, if this is not possible, choosing a reasonably similar scale and scope of contract is a common practice. While there will probably be fewer data points than a consultant's database, the data you collect is likely to be more meaningful to you. It allows your team to do a detailed 'apples-to-apples' comparison, as well as investigate detailed explanations of differences and solutions.

Lastly, some organizations create their own database using supplier panels or multiple suppliers for the same services. This is typically seen in applications development where it is not unusual to have dozens of, if not a hundred, developers on a panel. By not guaranteeing work and having a reasonable number

---

1   A mature market is one that has been operating for a reasonable length of time, has many providers with competitive equal price/performance offerings, and has standardized goods/services.

of providers compete on a regular basis for various contracts or work orders over a defined period, you are in effect continuously benchmarking each contract.

Expecting good data as an *inherent* result of a benchmarking exercise is a common mistake made by 'first-timers', as the following case illustrates.

LACK OF MEANINGFUL BENCHMARKS IN A UTILITY COMPANY

An electric utility company's CIO had believed benchmarks were readily available and simple to apply; it was merely a matter of finding a consultant. He asked the consultants who were working at the company at the time if they had benchmarks and what it would cost. Happy with the answer, the CIO set the benchmarking project in motion.

Upon receipt of the voluminous report, the CIO struggled to find any meaningful information. When he queried attributes of source data (age, industry, location, and so on) and the method of scope alignment, the consultants told him that all that information was confidential. Having no way of knowing if the benchmarks represented current data in his industry, with comparable scope, let alone whether any of the benchmarks were from international or local sources, he threw the report out. Nevertheless, he still had to pay the $100 000 for it. Here, the benchmarking yielded nothing but a strong desire not to go through it again.

At this point, I should raise a cautionary note about benchmarking between contracts, because this is a bit more difficult than benchmarking between internal operations. This is because you must consider that each contract has unique constraints that lessen benchmarking comparability (for example, insurances, liability levels, warranties) in order to achieve an 'apples-to-apples' comparison.

To ensure your benchmarking exercise delivers the expected amount of meaningful information, and particularly to manage an independent consultant as your benchmarking agent, the most important aspect is to get the scope of the data to a best fit against your organization. Defining what you believe would be apples-to-apples is the only way you can be assured of even getting something that is even vaguely fruit-related.

For example:

- Give detailed scope instructions – how old can the data be? If you do not specify this, the data may be much older than your benchmarking consultant.

- What geographic regions can the data be sourced from? If you do not specify this, do not make any assumptions about what country the information was sourced from, only that it may not be the countries where you operate. Does your organization's success really depend on knowing how long the average Peruvian waits for an ATM transaction to clear?

- Will it be tax inclusive or exclusive? Exclusive is a better approach to normalizing data from other countries and/or states. Even the best tax accountants would struggle here.

- Can it be insourced or only outsourced operations? If you do not specify this, the exercise could result in comparing your contract to internal operations of other organizations. Which is fine if you are considering backsourcing (bringing the work back in-house), but in-house operations do not operate under a contract that imposes legal obligations and liabilities.

- What industry can the data be from? If you do not specify this, it is possible that little of the data would be from your industry. Did you want to compare to a local government body? To offshoring mining operations? To a city ad agency?

- How large and small can the organizations be? If you do not specify this, the data may come from very small to very large organizations, which may not be meaningful to you at all.

TCO (TOTAL COST OF OWNERSHIP)

Another type of financial measurement that can assess the impact of contract performance on the overall costs to your organization is known as Total Cost of Ownership (TCO) or its variants (total cost of asset, total costs of supply/production, and so on). In effect, this measurement attempts to assess all the financial consequences of owning an asset. In addition to the initial purchase price, this typically includes maintenance, accommodation charges, opportunity costs, training costs, consumables, internal and external support, interest on capital, and so on. In supply chain management, the TCO of the supply delivery system is the sum of all the costs associated with every activity of the supply stream.

Very few organizations have the sophisticated data collection processes necessary to assess the impact of the contract on the TCO, supply chain and/or asset. Those that do will often have the financial measurements, calculation techniques and effect of results specified in a separate contract schedule as well. Total cost to your organization, not just monies paid to the provider, is well worth considering, as highlighted in the case shown below.

A MAJOR RETAILER GOES FOR LOWEST PRICE/HIGHEST OVERALL COST

The IT department of a retailing company had recently been reorganized to report under the Corporate Services division. The division had a general manager with a background in procurement. It was her belief that commodity functions should be outsourced so that the division could focus on adding value to the operational business units. She targeted the 'commodity' IT services and went to tender for the IT data centre operations, charging $500 to potential bidders to receive the RFT (Request For Tender) to 'weed out non-contenders'. The emphasis was placed on the price, as she believed the services, and service providers themselves, were undifferentiated. Accordingly, the lowest-priced bid was awarded the contract, rather than any sort of assessment of value for money. This bid was 30 per cent below the nearest bid.

Things began to go awry very quickly. Variations were the norm; in fact, a person within the retailer had to be dedicated to variation management. Service quality KPIs (set up as targets and not as minimum standards in the contract) were rarely achieved as there was no incentive to meet the targets, nor was there recourse if the targets were not met. In addition, the service provider had capped the number of resources they would provide in the contract and the general manager had to hire specialists to work in the data centre to raise service levels back to what they had been. Within a year, the total costs were higher than the highest bid, higher than the in-house baseline and the division's remaining IT people were focused on 'firefighting' and not on adding value.

There are some simple TCO-type measures, such as setting a KPI in which the cost of repair must not exceed a specified percentage value of the replacement cost (see Figure 2.14 for an example). In this case, if the cost of repairs exceeded three-quarters of the replacement cost, the client would prefer to replace the item instead as it was cheaper in the end to buy a new item rather than keep repairing an old one.

INVOICING AND PAYMENT

Invoicing and payment measurements are primarily designed to motivate the provider to bill accurately and on time. Contrary to the beliefs held in some

KPI	KPI Minimum Standard	Calculation		
		Frequency	Formula	Source Data
1. Cost to repair	Repair cost per item not to exceed 75% of the cost of replacement	Monthly	75% × Replacement cost	Repair cost per Contractor's invoice
				Replacement cost per Contractor's Catalogue as of data of repair

Figure 2.14   Example KPI – replacement cost

quarters, client organizations really do want providers' invoices on time so that their accounting staff can close out accounts and/or projects. Very few organizations actually look forward to receiving surprise invoices when the books have been closed. Many clients have reporting getting invoices years after the work has been performed. It is also imperative for all kinds of organizations that they get invoices on time for budget purposes.

If the provider is subcontracting any of the work, you may want to ensure that these subcontractors are also paid on time. This is not only to ensure that the subcontractors stay solvent, but also because in some countries there are laws that may allow a subcontractor to seek compensation from the client if the provider does not pay them.

Examples of invoicing and payment KPIs are provided in Figure 2.15, where, in this case, the client's finance people were adamant about making sure all invoices were on time, were accurate and that no outstanding liabilities might exist regarding payments to subcontractors. Accordingly, the client set up three related KPIs to ensure finance would be satisfied.

Relationship Quadrant

A contracting relationship replaces many of an organization's traditional human resources assets – people and their expertise and knowledge – and becomes an asset itself. In business-to-business arrangements, the well-being of the relationship between the parties has been shown in many studies to affect success (for example Kern and Willcocks, 2001).

KPI	KPI Minimum Standard	Calculation		
		Frequency	Formula	Source Data
1. Invoicing deadline	Invoice received by the 4th day of each month	Monthly	Received date = date stamped by Client's accounts payable	Client's accounts payable records
2. Invoicing accuracy	No inaccuracies		As determined by Client's accounts payable function	
3. Subcontractor invoices and payment	All Subcontracted work is invoiced by the Subcontractor and paid by the Contractor no later than one (1) month after work is completed		Invoice date = date on Subcontractor's invoice	Subcontractor's invoice
			Payment date = date payment cleared Contractor's bank account	Copy of payment advice submitted by Contractor

Figure 2.15   Example KPI – invoicing and payment deadlines and accuracy

A relationship need not be an inadvertent effect of a contract; rather, it can, and should, be a key part of the overall strategy.

UNDERSTANDING POWER-BASED VERSUS PARTNERING-BASED RELATIONSHIPS

Getting the right values and cultures between the parties is often one of the most difficult aspects of a contractual agreement. One natural instinct is to make sure there is a watertight contract so that the provider cannot reinterpret or escape – one that your organization intends to impose in every, excruciatingly minute detail.

You must understand, however, that onerous contracts can severely damage your commercial relationships. The contract is a clear fail-safe device; it is there to be used, but one finds that in practice it cannot predict and cover every eventuality. Active relationship management on both sides is what sustains effective contract performance. Poor contracts can make for poor relationships, if one is not careful, as the following case clearly demonstrates.

A MANUFACTURER CREATES A LOSE-LOSE SITUATION

During a particularly difficult negotiation regarding the outsourcing of the information systems function, the manufacturing client agreed to a contract clause stipulating that 'all costs of transfer of software licensing agreements will be borne by the client'. The account manager at the provider needed the clause in the contract if he was to make any money at all since the transfer costs were not known at the time and he had made no allowances in the price.

The first few transfers cost relatively little, but the next ten virtually eliminated the client's cost savings from the 5-year deal. The client felt that he had been tricked and sought to get money back from the provider any way he could, using any clause he could. The provider, wanting to protect his margins, argued every point and raised further breaches that the client had made. The two sides then proceeded to beat each other up over every ambiguous clause they could find for the rest of the contract's duration.

Academics who study contracts have recognized that it is not the contract, or contract law, that is really worth studying, but relational theories about people's behaviour (Vincent-Jones, 2000; Stinchcombe and Heimer, 1985; Campbell, 1997; Collins, 1996). Legal rationality has been marginalized by the recognition of the complexity of relationship behaviour. Fundamentally, while the contract plays an important part in developing behavioural norms both within and between the parties, the actual practice itself forms the total contracting behaviour.

In fact, a study by Oxford and Melbourne Universities of 235 Australian client organizations credited good relationships as the third most important factor just behind the supplier delivering to expectations and good contract management by both parties (Cullen et al., 2001). In that study, a good contract per se was not mentioned, although good relationship management techniques were – such as flexible working arrangements, the ability to change, and open, frequent and effective communication.

As Figure 2.16 demonstrates, the contract is an important, but superficial, driver of day-to-day behaviour. The deep behaviour drivers are the underlying values and attitudes held by the individual parties and the people involved in the agreement (Cullen and Willcocks, 2003).

The underlying, or deep, drivers of behaviour are underpinned by the orientations of communication, conflict resolution, relationship, strategy and values. These determine whether the relationship will exhibit more power-

Figure 2.16   Underlying drivers of behaviour

based or more partnering-based characteristics, as shown in Figure 2.17. In most cases, you will want a balance between the two extremes of a completely power-based relationship or one based solely on trust. Extremes of either kind are rarely useful for either party.

Power and trust (as earned through partnering behaviours) are alternative means of minimizing risk and securing cooperation (Deakin and Wilkinson, 2000). Power-based relationships use the negative threat of sanctions that might be applied to gain compliance. However, power is really an inferior substitute for earned trust because of the higher transaction costs involved with monitoring and imposing sanctions. Therefore, relations capable of generating trust stand to gain an important competitive advantage over those that do not.

DEFINING THE RELATIONSHIP BEHAVIOURS YOU WANT

Most organizations believe that the contract, in effect, designs the relationship. However, a successful relationship cannot be guaranteed by a contract alone. Organizations that want effective relationships set up and measure the relationship through KPIs that represent the desired partnering values, rather than just assume the desired behaviours will naturally occur.

Relationship KPIs measure the behaviours exhibited by each party as seen through the eyes of the other party. Eight typical types of relationship measurements include:

1.   **Communication** – the degree to which the parties communicate frequently and honestly.

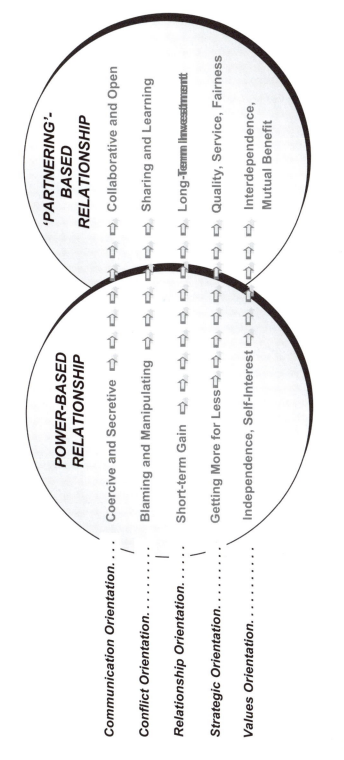

Figure 2.17   Power vs partnering relationships

2.   **Conflict resolution** – the degree to which the focus is on fixing problems, not apportioning the blame.

3.   **Creative solutions** – the degree to which the parties continuously search for better ways of doing things.

4.   **Fairness** – the degree to which the parties act fairly toward each other.

5.   **Integration** – the degree that the services value chain appears seamless to the end customer.

6.   **Positive interaction** – the degree to which the parties enjoy working together and have respect for one another.

7.   **Proactivity** – the degree to which the parties are proactive to each other.

8.   **Time investment** – the degree to which the parties provide management time and focus for each other.

Table 2.3 gives examples of the KPIs you might find in each type of relationship measurement.

Table 2.3   Relationship KPI types and examples

Communication	Conflict resolution	Creative solutions	Fairness
• Frequency • Openness • Correct method and protocol	• Problem-solving focus • Collaborative style • No blaming, no abdication • Personality independent	• Idea generation • Continuous improvement mindset	• Empathy to other party • Win/win mentality
Integration	**Interaction**	**Proactivity**	**Time investment**
• Seamless supply chain • End-to-end focus	• Enjoy working together • Display mutual respect • Strong interpersonal relationships	• Anticipate other's needs • Early notices and warnings	• Provision of management time • Demonstrated dedication • Appropriate prioritization

Like satisfaction (which was discussed in the quality section of this chapter), this is a 'soft' measurement, in that the parties agree that the measurement is concerning the *opinion* and *perceptions* of the other party. This Contract Scorecard quadrant differs from the others in that both parties provide their opinions on the other. A commercial relationship results from the interactions of both parties, who need to exhibit the desired behaviours, not just from the provider. In this sense, analogies that liken the contract to a marriage may be appropriate, and, as many of us know, it takes two to have a good marriage and to make it work.

The purpose of the relationship assessment part of the Contract Scorecard is to prioritize what needs to be addressed in the relationship, not to debate the score itself. Thus, no disputes are allowed. The relationship quadrant is measuring the opinion of the other party and they are entitled to their opinion, just as you are entitled to yours.

To gather these opinions, organizations that design and track the effectiveness of client/provider relationships have adopted a form of agreement called a *Relationship Values Charter* or *Code of Conduct*. This is typically set out in the Governance Charter schedule of the contract (see Chapter 8). It specifies the behaviours that all parties must exhibit during the course of the contract and details the mechanisms used to score them.

Many organizations know that a dysfunctional relationship often leads to increased costs or deteriorating service, but they are unsure as to how to make the other party behave well. Through proactive action, such as a Relationship Values Charter, both parties position themselves to ensure results and have commercial relationships functioning in an effective manner.

Figure 2.18 provides a brief example, from a maintenance contract in the utility industry, of specified behaviours and the scoring system used to assess how well those behaviours were exhibited.

Note that this approach is different from the one found in one-sided agreements, where only the provider's behaviour is detailed and the client has no explicit obligations. However, the goal of the relationship quadrant of the Contract Scorecard is not to identify which parties behave better, but rather to identify which aspects of the relationship are working and which are not working, and then to agree on a process for fixing those areas that need improvement.

CODE OF CONDUCT

1   Overview

1.1   **(Purpose)** This Code of Conduct identifies the behaviour that the parties agree to exhibit during the course of the Term of the Contract. The parties have agreed that if the Contract is to operate effectively, both parties must drive towards a 'partnering' style of relationship. To achieve this, the parties have set out their common goals in this Code of Conduct that are to operate during the Contract and shall use this as a process for relationship review and improvement.

1.2   **(No effect on legal relationship)** The parties agree that their legal relationship must always be governed by the Contract. Nevertheless, the parties have identified that this process needs to be implemented to enable both parties to operate effectively without the Contract being relied on in every instance.

2   Conduct to be Demonstrated by the Parties

Conduct	Description
1. Accuracy	Information provided; reporting; and data entered will be accurate.
2. Communication	The parties shall communicate frequently, openly and honestly with each other. An environment of 'no surprises' shall be sought.
3. Continuous Improvement	The parties shall constantly search for better ways of doing things.
4. Financial	Both parties desire to apply the Profit Program and not incur Work overruns. Each party shall achieve its financial goals: Organization – to reduce cost over time and have competitive pricing; Provider – to have reasonable profits.
5. Industry Model	The parties desire the relationship to be seen as an a leading model within the industry.
6. Meet Needs	The parties shall be both proactive and reactive to each other's needs.
7. Perform Responsibilities	Each party will perform its responsibilities to the standard expected by the other party.
8. Problem Solving	The parties shall focus on rapid solutions to the problem, not apportioning blame or responsibility. Issues shall be resolved at the lowest level appropriate.
9. Resource Reinvestment	The parties wish to have recognized leadership in the Services through continuous reinvestment in human and capital assets.
10. Site Cleanliness	The parties shall maintain a clean and orderly site environment.

3   Scoring the Code of Conduct

3.1   **(Survey)** Each party will conduct a survey of 50 per cent of its staff every six (6) months. The 50 per cent of staff not surveyed in the first survey shall be surveyed in the second survey. Each party shall conduct its survey at its expense.

3.2   **(Scoring)** The parties agree to score their perception of the other party according to the following:

1	2	3	4	5
Unacceptable	Below expectations	Adequate	Above expectations	Delighted

3.3   **(Target score)** The parties seek an average score for each party of at least four (4) for each period.

3.4   **(Analysis)** Each party shall provide the other with a justification of each score given, improvements deemed desirable, and proposed solution for incorporation into the Improvement Agenda.

3.5   **(Report)** The Provider shall provide the combined trend analysis and report for each survey.

Figure 2.18   Example relationship scoring system

Once you have defined the behaviours you believe are important for this contract, you use them throughout the Contract Lifecycle (explained in Chapter 5, 'Timing in the Contract Lifecycle'). For example, when conducting customer reference checks, you ask the referees whether the provider has exhibited the behaviours you are seeking rather than just ask open-end questions regarding how happy the referee is with the provider. In this way, you will be better placed to select a provider that demonstrates it really lives the values you believe are important, which may differ from the referee's values. For example, a referee could be very happy with a provider that never talks to them because it would be considered a nuisance. However, you may want someone who does talk to you, because you want to be continuously informed.

In addition, when you design the contract management function, the individuals you select to fulfil the function should already be displaying the behaviours that you have committed your organization to display or your previous investment may be for nothing, as in the next case.

RELATIONSHIP INVESTMENTS NEED TO BE ONGOING

A telecommunication company made a large investment in a relationship during the bidding and negotiation process. They had conducted a similar relationship diagnostic as part of the transition acceptance and both parties scored reasonably well. However, the contract management function was not involved in the earlier stages of evaluation, negotiation or transition. The client's contract managers, when they were handed the deal to run day-to-day, were traditionally adversarial and stayed that way – disputing all claims for out-of-scope work, disputing all bonus claims, disallowing any requests for excusable delays, and so on. Accordingly, the supplier quickly changed tack and set up its defences. This included not performing work until a variation was signed off (a very long process in the telco), refusing to scale up KPIs that were being achieved with little effort and reporting only the minimum information that was explicitly defined in the contract, not the plethora of information available in the system (unless the client paid handsomely).

Strategic Quadrant

The last quadrant of the Contract Scorecard is that of strategic goals. These KPIs can take many forms ranging from the results from the commercial relationship (for example, to enable an increased focus on core business, increased commercialization of joint research activities or the inclusion of a additional sales channel) to development of local industries or employment for the long-term benefit of your organization, to aligning the provider's demonstrated business activities with the values of your organization, such as environmental sustainability, or community/social contribution.

Strategic KPIs measure results that go beyond the letter of the agreement and represent more of an alliance-type situation. Most deals leave strategic goals unarticulated, perhaps only mentioning them in background information contained in the tender documents. Strategic goals mentioned so casually rarely have any chance of actually occurring.

There is a wide range of potential strategic measurements that an organization may apply, especially if the deal is more than a basic fee-for-service exchange.

Examples include the degree of:

1.   **Innovation** – introduction of new technologies, business practices and/or processes that add value to the client organization.

2.   **Business contribution** – the parties have achieved more out of the deal beyond the fundamental exchange of money for services (for example, joint product offerings to the market, R&D initiatives, knowledge transfer).

3.   **Alignment with corporate initiatives or goals** – the extent to which the provider conducts business in line with your organization's broad corporate goals (for example, the use of local companies, workforce gender balance, environment policies, philanthropic initiatives, and so on).

4.   **Underlying business processes** – the management of the underlying resources and business practices of the provider used to fulfil the contract (for example, workforce management and safety).

Table 2.4 gives examples of the KPIs that one might find in each type of strategic measurement.

INNOVATION

Most client organizations expect that their providers will continually innovate the work under contract, even if it is not a clearly articulated requirement within the contract. And most organizations are bitterly disappointed when there is

Table 2.4   Strategic KPI types and examples

Innovation	Business contribution	Alignment with corporate values and initiatives	Underlying business processes
• Improved practices • Enabling online applications • Research and development investment	• Greater focus on core business • Refocus internal staff on high value/strategic activities • Level of knowledge transfer provided • Number of mutual business initiatives created and completed • Number of joint product offerings created, royalties earned	• Use of SMEs (small to medium enterprises) • Employment created (direct and indirect) • Positions filled by minorities • Environmental contribution • Societal contribution	• Safety (loss time injuries, workplace incidents) • Workforce management (turnover, replacement, and so on) • Standardization

no innovation, feeling that the provider has misled them or let them down. But where was innovation specified? When was it agreed to be implemented?

If you want innovation, you must ensure it will occur, firstly by setting KPIs such as the example shown in Figure 2.19 and secondly by ensuring that other KPIs and the contract itself do not conflict with this goal. As an example of the former, a case example was looked at earlier (see the case study on page 29), whereby the KPI regarding cost reductions overrode any possibility of innovation. In that case, the insurance company had double digit cost reduction KPIs. To make the KPI, the provider did not invest in any technology although innovation was mentioned as a throwaway line in the contract. By the end of the seven-year contract, the technology in use at the client was well and truly obsolete. As an example of the latter, it is unreasonable to expect innovation to happen if the contract vests all created intellectual property rights to the client. If the client retains ownership of the created intellectual property, the provider is motivated to ensure that no innovation occurs at all. This is because the ability of the provider to use the intellectual property in their business with other clients has been removed, and thus it cannot gain efficiency or commercial benefits. Accordingly, such clauses act in direct conflict with any innovation expectations, unless of course the provider has been adequately compensated.

| KPI | KPI Minimum Standard | Calculation | | Source Data |
		Frequency	Formula	
1. Feasibility Studies on time	At least 90% of Feasibility Studies are completed by the due date	Annually	Feasibility Studies due date = as specified in the Innovation Program Schedule	Innovation Program Schedule and log
	No more than 10% of Feasibility Studies are completed later than one month of the due date		Completion date = date each Feasibility Study received by Client	
2. Feasibility Study results	At least 90% of Feasibility Studies achieve the projected results		Project results = per Feasibility Study	Feasibility Study
			Actual results = as calculated in the annual Feasibility Study Review conducted by the Client	Feasibility Study Review Report

Figure 2.19   Example innovation KPI – feasibility studies

BUSINESS CONTRIBUTION

Client organizations may want providers not only to do the work specified under the contract, but also to help improve the business, or contribute to business issues that the client believes they are capable at doing. The case shown below illustrates this very well.

A LOGISTICS PROVIDER KEEPS ADDING VALUE

A maintenance and logistics contract with a Pacific Rim client also had a requirement that the logistics provider seek tenants for vacant space at the client's premises. The provider was responsible for running all the facilities of the client, in addition to maintaining inventory of uniforms, equipment, materials and supplies. The provider was able to decrease the scale of required real estate for warehousing and operations as part of its re-engineering process (driven by an innovation KPI). However, this left the client with 30 per cent of its land and building holdings unutilized. As a result, the parties derived a gain-sharing arrangement whereby the provider was granted a 5 per cent finder's fee for finding subtenants for the properties. The client had no staff available to manage the subtenant search and the provider was better placed with many possible contacts in the area.

An example of a strategic contribution KPI is shown in Figure 2.20, where a technology provider and its client set up a gain-sharing arrangement whereby the provider was to develop approximately 30 new applications per year. Of these, at least one application was required to be commercialized in accordance with a royalty agreement the parties had included in the contract. This royalty agreement gave the provider a 30 per cent royalty in return for its investment in bringing an application to the wider market. The client did not want to assume that the royalty payment was enough as the sole motivation, and so included the goal in a strategic KPI.

KPI	KPI Minimum Standard	Calculation		
		Frequency	Formula	Source Data
1. Commercialized applications	At least one application developed for commercialization per year beginning as of the second Anniversary	Annually	Not applicable	Commercialized Applications Register

Figure 2.20   Example KPI – commercialized applications

The contribution need not be one that contributes financially, as many organizations have sought non-financial KPI contributions as well (which inevitably contribute to the sustainability of the client). Three examples are shown below:

- A local council that had set up KPIs regarding the percentage of the contract's workforce that resided within the council's boundaries. Employing local residents was deemed important for not only the residents' payment of council rates, but also the community's well-being and family focus. It used these KPIs in evaluating its providers' eligibility and desirability for future council work.

- A bank that encouraged a percentage of profit of its providers' contracts to go to the bank's local community not-for-profit groups as part of a social contribution. The bank would report the provider's contribution as well as its direct contribution as part of the bank's 'positive influence on the community section' of its annual report.

- A telecommunications provider with tens of thousands of owned and leased properties around the country that set up a KPI for its site national maintenance provider to identify at least 20 sites per year that could be disposed of.

ALIGNMENT WITH CORPORATE VALUES/INITIATIVES

Most client organizations want providers to act in accordance with the organization's values and strategic initiatives. These can be in the form of environmental activities, social philanthropy, industry development and employment, and so on. The nature of the KPIs can be quite diverse between organizations and contracts, as the following two examples indicate:

1. A state government legal panel (a panel of different firms that provided legal advice to the government as the need arose) set up a strategic KPI regarding the percentage of women legal professionals used on work given to the panel members. This was part of an overall initiative to get more women into male-dominated professions within the state, including not only the legal profession but also engineering, construction and technology.

2. A global consulting firm wanted to demonstrate that it was actively reducing its carbon footprint. Accordingly, the firm required its new global technology provider to reduce its technology-based carbon footprint. This was done by firstly requiring the provider to conduct a baseline footprint assessment to determine the current baseline and then agreeing on a reduction level per year (and the techniques that would be used to reduce the footprint). The KPI was merely that a reduction had occurred ever year as opposed to a set percentage reduction.

The way the KPI is set up can be diverse. In the example below, a state government contracted out the operations of its five recreational camps. It wanted to ensure that the socioeconomic and other demographic groups that represented the state's demographics also utilized the camps in a proportion roughly equally to their demographics percentage. Accordingly, the alignment of each camp to the achievement of state's community service objectives was measured through the nature of each camp's client groups. Specifically, the nature of the Client Groups was required to fall within the range outlined in Figure 2.21. Each Client Group was required to be recorded only once as a single classification. It was be at the provider's discretion as to which category to classify the camp client, and it could not be changed once classified.

Client Group (as defined in the Contract)	Camp 1 (per cent)	Camp 2 (per cent)	Camp 3 (per cent)	Camp 4 (per cent)	Camp 5 (per cent)
Primary	10–50	10–40	< 30	10–40	10–40
Secondary	10–40	10–40	10–40	10–40	10–40
Tertiary	< 15	< 15	< 30	< 15	< 15
Cultural	5–20	5–20	5–20	5–30	5–20
Sport/Rec	> 10	> 10	> 10	> 10	> 10
Community	10–50	10–50	10–50	10–50	10–50
Corporate	< 10	< 20	< 20	< 10	< 10
Family	< 20	< 20	10–50	< 30	< 20

Figure 2.21   Example KPI – demographic utilization

UNDERLYING BUSINESS PROCESSES

You may want to ensure that the underlying business practices of your providers are sound before getting contractually committed, and not waiting until things go wrong to find out that they are not. Merely having outcome-based KPIs, such as the quality measurements discussed earlier in this chapter, provide nothing in the way of ensuring that the way the work is performed is in accordance with your expectations – they merely ensure that the outcomes were achieved. Organizations have learnt (and some the hard way) that not only is achieving the outcomes important, but also that the means used to achieve them can be just as, if not more, important. The following case demonstrates this.

GETTING OUTCOMES ANY WAY POSSIBLE

A power plant maintenance provider supplemented its dedicated workforce with hired labour from a labour-hire company. Although the contract stated that only certified personnel were to work on certain items of equipment, the temporary labour had no such certifications. Due to the cost and time it would take to get the temporary workers certified, combined with the financial recourse available to the client if the provider fell behind schedule, the provider sought legal advice as to whether it would be in breach of the contract. The lawyer provided an opinion whereby the provider would not be in breach because the contract stated only that the provider's employees needed to be certified and these were not employees as defined in the contract. That was all the provider needed to hear, and they proceeded to use the labour-hire resources whenever and wherever needed to get the work done.

In this case, the client did not contemplate that the provider would top up its labour using outside parties, nor did it restrict the provider in any way. The key here was the provider's labour sourcing and management practices, for which it was allowed total discretion.

Below are two examples of the underlying work practices KPI from different contracts. The first example (Figure 2.22) concerns the safety practices of the provider. As the provider was supplying potentially dangerous maintenance work at an industrial site, safety was of the utmost importance to the client.

The second example (Figure 2.23) concerns staff continuity practices. In this case, the provider operated a telephone-answering switchboard for the client organization, and the client believed it was very important that the same

KPI	KPI Minimum Standard	Calculation		
		Frequency	Formula	Source Data
1. Lost time injuries	No incidents	Monthly	Incident = lost time accidents	Site Medical Log
2. Number of safety inducted personnel	At least 90% of personnel inducted prior to beginning work		Personnel inducted within the KPI Minimum Standard/ Personnel on-site during the month	Site Induction Register
	No more than 10% inducted within three days of beginning work			

Figure 2.22   Example KPI – safety

KPI	KPI Minimum Standard	Calculation		
		Frequency	Formula	Source Data
1. Staff turnover	No staff turnover	Monthly	Not applicable	Contractor's employee records
2. Unfulfilled Positions	No more than four (4) hours per Position unfilled		Not applicable	Attendance Register

Figure 22.3   Example KPI – staff continuity

staff were used day-to-day as their structure, business units and personnel titles were complex. In the event that a staff member did leave the provider, a replacement had to be on the switchboard within half a day or the poor response rates would cause the client's contract managers to receive too many complaints which would consume too much of their time.

The Steps in Developing KPIs

'In the long run, men hit only what they aim at.'

Henry David Thoreau

About this Chapter

It is a difficult challenge to develop KPIs that work well in practice and are not subject to dispute between the parties. Unless you design KPIs carefully, they will be inaccurate, incomplete or implemented in a way that 'gets the numbers' but does not drive the behaviour that you envisioned when you set it up.

Not only will you inevitably lose confidence in KPIs as a performance management tool, but you will also lose confidence in the provider (because they did what was written in the contract, which was not what you meant – and they were supposed to do what you meant). Instead of blaming the provider when it is too late, focus on designing KPIs that will work and are not open to various interpretations.

This chapter shows you how to develop KPIs that will work in seven steps. You need to make sure that whatever KPI measures you want to use are:

- **Relevant** – to the scope of the provider's control (Step 1, Table 3.1 below) and the stakeholders' needs (Step 2, Table 3.1).

- **Holistic** – representative of the collective flexibility and tolerance range of your organization (Step 3, Table 3.1).

- **Clear** as to what is being measured and actionable – goals versus minimum expectations (Step 4, Table 3.1).

- **Readily available**, reliable, and complete – from systematically collected data (Step 5, Table 3.1).

- **Simple and understandable** – to all of the stakeholders in both parties (Step 6, Table 3.1).

- **Will work** – cannot be circumvented (Step 7, Table 3.1).

The seven major steps for developing the detailed KPI measurements are described in Table 3.1 and this chapter takes you through each step. It also provides you with a few additional things to think about.

Table 3.1   Seven steps for developing KPIs

Step	Actions
1. Allocate party responsibilities	• List all work that needs to be done at a high level • Assign accountability for each major activity to a party
2. Conduct stakeholder assessment	• Identify who cares about the contract • Identify what each stakeholder cares about in each quadrant of the Contract Scorecard
3. List scorecard KPIs	• Prepare a list of all KPIs that will be used in the Contract Scorecard
4. Set KPI thresholds	• Set target goals to be strived for (the 'top line') • Set minimum performance required (the 'expectation') • Set the absolute threshold required (the 'bottom line')
5. Generate calculation method	• Identify how, and from where, performance data will be sourced • Ensure the formula is simple and understandable to the stakeholders • Ensure the measurement source data is readily available and reliable
6. Prototype reports	• Prototype the Contract Scorecard 'dashboard' • Design the detailed performance reports for each quadrant including stratifications, trends and desired accompanying analysis
7. Conduct testing	• Obtain current measurements, if available, to determine the degree to which the KPIs are being achieved to set a baseline • Predict desired (expected) behaviours from the KPIs to ensure the KPI portfolio will motivate the right balance of outcomes • Predict potentially undesired behaviours that may result and put in risk mitigation actions

Step 1: Allocate Party Responsibilities – Identify Who is Acountable for What

Many organizations end up with meaningless KPIs because the measurements involve variables outside the provider's control. Thus, the provider is able to invoke the common 'uncontrollable events', or 'force majeure', provisions in a contract when performance is assessed. These provisions release the provider from its obligations if events occurred outside its control.

As an example of this in action, assume you had set up an IT systems availability measurement with your IT infrastructure provider. However, your provider is dependent upon an independent telecommunications provider. If the system goes offline due to the fault of the telecommunications company, and there is a force majeure provision in the contract, your IT infrastructure provider will ignore that outage for the calculation of their availability KPI since it was not their fault. Alternatively, let us say the outage was due to an action your organization was responsible for – say, your applications developers brought down the system while they were making minor changes in code and did not test it properly. Again, this outage would be ignored for the KPI calculation.

All this is fine if that is what both parties had anticipated and agreed to. If not, you might believe the provider is playing around with the calculations when, in fact, they are merely trying to measure only their component of the measurement. To ensure there are no surprises, the areas of control of the parties (as well as any other third parties) need to be carefully specified.

To articulate all of this, the most efficient technique is to prepare a responsibility matrix. This matrix sets out all the major activities under the contract and allocates accountability between the parties (and other third parties, if appropriate). Figure 3.1 provides a partial example of a responsibility matrix for a labour contract.

Under no circumstances should you propose or accept a situation where more than one party (either your organization or a provider) is responsible for a particular service. The reason for this is simple: if both parties share accountability, the likelihood of individuals denying or shifting responsibility (sometimes referred to as blame displacement) increases dramatically. Therefore, if both parties need to work together to provide a service, one party must be nominated as having primary responsibility for it (the lead role); any other parties involved should be considered to have a contributory role. This may seem to be an obvious point, but it is one that is often overlooked or ignored by organizations. There have been many long, drawn-out struggles over service performance, simply because no one clearly defined everyone's responsibilities at an early stage.

Function	Services	Contractor	Client
Overall Management (Section 2.1)	1 Conduct management planning	✓	
	2 Adhere to the quality systems	✓	
	3 Communicate and liaise with stakeholders	✓	
	4 Ensure customer satisfaction	✓	
	5 Conduct audits	✓	
	6 Provision of labour, materials, equipment, and so on.	✓	
Service Delivery Management (Section 2.2)	7 Interface with client activities	✓	
	8 Manage and report multiple visits	✓	
	9 Provide route cause analysis	✓	
	10 Use of client-owned assets	✓	
	11 Manage decommissioned assets (graveyard stock)	✓	
	12 Dispatch work		
	12.1 Normal hours	✓	
	12.2 Outside normal hours		✓
	13 Close out jobs	✓	
	14 Calibrate equipment	✓	
Workforce Management (Section 2.3)	15 Ensure workforce availability	✓	
	16 Competencies and qualifications		
	16.1 Determine minimum standards		✓
	16.2 Ongoing assessment and training	✓	
	17 Provide workforce locations	✓	

Figure 3.1   Partial example responsibility matrix

Once this is complete, you have an end-to-end process picture of what you can hold each party responsible for and, accordingly, their respective KPIs. This matrix becomes part of the contract as well, in the Service Level Agreement (see Chapter 6, 'The Quality Specification – The Service Level Agreement (SLA)').

The next step is to determine what is most important to stakeholders regarding the work under the contract.

Step 2: Conduct Stakeholder Assessment – Distinguish Who Cares about What

Importantly, KPIs should reflect what good service is in the eyes of your organization as represented by its key stakeholders. Many organizations make the mistake of simply collecting figures that are easy to capture. These do not always reflect what the stakeholders really care about, nor do they reflect how the stakeholders perceive good results.

Identifying stakeholder needs is necessary as it ensures that both parties focus on what is truly important and not on the minutia of every possible aspect of the deal that could be measured, as seen in the case below – a classic example of not seeing the wood for the trees.

A TELECOMMUNICATIONS CARRIER GETS CARRIED AWAY WITH KPIs

A major telecommunications company was outsourcing for the first time and had few existing KPIs. A working group was formed from technical in-house engineers, who had been overseeing the services in the past, to determine what the KPIs should be.

After months of work, 70 KPIs were created. The volume of KPIs was due to the discomfort the team felt regarding outsourcing and the potential lack of control over the provider. Both organizations spent enormous effort in putting in place the KPI measurement and reporting systems. Even so, neither party could quickly determine whether the contract was successful at any point without extensive analysis of the 70 KPIs, due to the sheer volume of indicators.

Neither party initiated a KPI refresh during the life of the agreement, so these were kept in place for 5 years. However, the next-generation contract resulted in 12 KPIs and 20 supplementary performance indicators (that were merely tracked, but were not part of the performance incentive scheme).

The process of determining what measurements should be employed continues from the understanding of each party's area of control from Step 1, to identifying the key stakeholders and then determining their primary expectations/needs regarding each dimension of the scorecard. Table 3.2 provides an example of client stakeholders and their expectations about a property management contract (managing maintenance and tenants). Note, however, that not every stakeholder will have an expectation in each quadrant, and nor should they. The stakeholder analysis is designed to uncover what stakeholders really care about and, in totality, to represent the entire organization.

Finding the right stakeholders can be difficult – sometimes everyone cares and sometimes no one does. For example, I was working on two contracts for a bank. One was for facilities management of the bank's offices and the other for new uniforms. Nearly everyone wanted to have a say in the uniforms, and no one cared at all about the facilities management, including the property group, because many would lose their jobs as a result.

Table 3.2   Example stakeholders and their expectations

| Stakeholder | Contract Scorecard Quadrants | | | |
	Quality	Financial	Relationship	Strategic
Executive Management	• Assurance of service quality	• Market prices at all times	• Assurance client interests are represented	• Best practice
Finance Dept	• Accurate and timely data		• Continuous improvement	
IT Dept	• Data compatibility • Accurate and timely data updates • Security			
Occupants/ Tenants	• Timely response to and resolution of issues		• Proactive • Reactive	
Projects Group	• Appropriate recommendations		• Thoughtful • Thorough	• Competitive scanning
Property Management	• Assurance policy is complied with • Satisfied tenants	• Lower than in-house cost • Vacancy reduction	• Notification where Contractor is having difficulties	• New IT systems

Some things to consider in finding the right stakeholders are:

• Do they care enough to invest time in developing the KPIs and getting the right underlying detail in the contract documents?

• Do they care enough to want to see a report that what has been set up has been accomplished?

• Will they complain if they do not get what they want?

• In the case of too many stakeholders, can a representative be elected to represent a stakeholder group?

Sometimes you will believe that a stakeholder should care about something but does not. This could be due to a number of unrelated factors such as not having enough time, having other pressing matters or wanting to avoid accountability. For example, perhaps the finance department is currently working overtime preparing the end-of-year accounts and has no time to even contemplate the financial KPIs of your contract. In these situations, you may have to do it by yourself, or wait until they can focus on it or perhaps get some outside help.

Alternatively, it could be that, for example, the stakeholder really only wants the work delivered on time, and is genuinely not too concerned about much else. You want to only focus on what is important, and thus do not want to make up KPIs that no one really cares about. This assumes, of course, that the lack of caring about other KPIs can be logically justified by the business needs, and is not merely one person's narrow view.

Once you have identified how stakeholders will perceive success, then you can set about ensuring that their expectations will be delivered. Do not expect stakeholders to be able to come up with the specific KPIs; they will merely provide you with their key expectations. Steps 3 to 5 are about determining the exact KPIs. But be warned, it is not an easy process. Some organizations have spent many hundreds of hours going back and forth with the business to get the right measures, but with no one knowing how to set up KPIs that work. Others merely put in whatever the business tells them, never making sure that it will get the expected results.

Step 3: List KPIs – Get the Big Picture

Now you can set out the KPIs in each quadrant as per the stakeholder requirements. This is merely a list of all the items you intend to measure. An example from a recent information technology arrangement is shown in Table 3.3. The next step is to determine what the minimum standards are, as well as the targets, as it is both of these that give you the holistic picture.

Table 3.3   Example Contract Scorecard metrics

Quality		Relationship	
1.	Help Desk and Support Services	1.	Communication
	a. Call queue time	2.	Meet needs
	b. Call answering time	3.	Creative solutions
	c. Call response time	4.	Conflict
	d. Call resolution rate (1st level)	5.	Fairness
	e. Call resolution rate (overall)	6.	External relations
	f. User satisfaction	7.	Industry model
2.	Desktop Supply and Support	8.	Enjoyment
	a. Device relocation	9.	Added value
	b. Device installation	10.	Works seamlessly
3.	Data Networks	11.	Technology leadership
	a. Infrastructure availability		
	b. Reliability		
4.	Computer Room Operations		
	a. Availability		
	b. Reliability		
5.	Applications		
	a. Availability (critical)		
	b. Availability (all other)		
	c. Change turnaround time		
	d. Implementation performance		
	e. Reliability		
Financial		**Strategic**	
1.	Competitiveness against market	1.	Focus on strategic issues
2.	Continuous reduction	2.	Technology baseline improvement
		3.	Technology investments
		4.	Contribution to the Client's businesses

Step 4: Set KPI Thresholds – Pinpoint the 'Care' Points

KPI thresholds represent the performance levels that will cause an action to be taken in the form of cash recourse or reward, non-cash recourse or reward, or some rectification process.

There are three threshold types that you might use in contractual agreements:

1. **Target KPI** – this is a goal for which the provider is typically rewarded if it is achieved, but is not penalized if it is not. It is used when the client would be delighted if the target is achieved, and is willing to reward the provider to do so. Rarely do organizations

have targets for all KPIs – only for the few work areas in which superior results matter.

2.   **Minimum standard KPI** – this type of KPI sets the base level standard of service to be achieved, which may have recourse for failure. It is, in effect, the expected level of service that, if not achieved, may cause the client to believe it is not getting the value that it signed up for and has paid for. Most organizations start here, setting their basic expectations for what they want for their money. It is rare that a KPI would not have a minimum standard because it represents your expectation 'floor' – without which can occur a downwards freefall.

3.   **Absolute KPI** – anything at or below this level will be deemed a complete failure. In many cases, it is defined as a material breach of the contract that invokes the client's right to terminate the contract, in addition to other recourse. This may only apply in a few areas, as with targets. A material breach typically allows termination for breach. However, because it is often expensive and time-consuming to find a new provider, make sure that this threshold is a 'no brainer' with regard to the need to get a new provider.

Figure 3.2 provides an overview of these three types of KPIs as well as the performance management scheme that might be employed when they are met or not met (possible recourse and reward options are discussed in the next

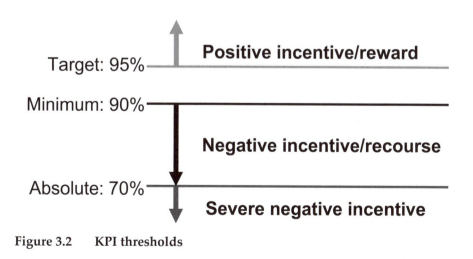

Figure 3.2   KPI thresholds

chapter). Each KPI listed from the previous Step 3 requires the setting out of the thresholds that will apply.

The case below shows why it is important to choose your words rather carefully when setting these thresholds.

WHAT IS A SERVICE LEVEL?

A manufacturing organization was new to contracting out its operations. It knew that performance-based contracts needed KPIs and so established a few, of which the table below is an example.

Service Area	KPI	Service Level
On-Site Support Services	Availability of On-site Support Contact – Critical	• Available to provide support within 30 minutes for 100% of Critical Requests
	Availability of On-site Support Contact – all Other Requests	• Available to provide support within 1 hour for 80% of all Other Requests
	Device Relocation	• >95% within 48 hours
	Installation of SOE Device	• >95% within 48 hours

Unfortunately, the client didn't bother to define what it meant by 'Service Level' in the contract and didn't set up any sort of performance management actions required in the event that the Service Levels were met, not met or exceeded. Most bidders assumed the client meant Service Levels to be a minimum performance standard; however, some didn't. The cheaper bids used the least-cost assumption; that Service Levels were merely 'nice to meet targets' to be achieved when convenient. The more expensive bids used the more expensive assumption, that Service Levels must be met.

Also unfortunately, the client chose a cheaper bid that didn't resource the contract to meet the KPIs, since it assumed the KPIs were possible goals as opposed to a requirement. In order to get the KPIs, the client was forced to pay more (and more than the most expensive bid).

Step 5: Generate Calculation Method – Specify the Maths

The process of developing the detailed performance measurements is an intensive one. The method itself is not especially complex, but depending upon the complexity of the work under contract, the development can take many iterations until the measurements are bulletproof (that is, unable to be interpreted in any other way except that which you intend) as well as drive the right outcomes. Having established the thresholds in the previous step, the agreed calculation now takes place using the formulas and the source data. This process is exemplified in Figure 3.3.

As shown in Figure 3.3, most contracts stop at only specifying the KPIs. However, it is equally important to specify how the KPIs will be calculated and identify what source data (the source of information that must be used in the calculation) to be used is. Most disputes regarding KPIs centre on these last two items. It is not the number that is most argued about, it is how the party doing the calculation determines it. Leaving such calculations to the discretion of the other party can produce questionable, if not unreliable, results. So the dispute is rarely around whether the provider has achieved the KPIs, just the maths used. The case below highlights just this situation.

KPIs THAT DIDN'T FEEL RIGHT

The provider of a fault desk consistently reported the response times as meeting the minimum standard, yet the client's contract manager was being sent an increasing amount of technician complaints about poor response times. There were just too many complaints for the service to be reporting such good numbers. He had an analyst obtain the provider's data for the most recent month and calculate the response times. It added up.

Still suspicious however, he had an analyst go through his emails and attempt to diagnose what the problem was. The analyst was able to determine that the complaints tended to come from two of the fourteen regions. Further investigation of the source data showed that these regions had not been included in the calculation. When the provider was questioned, it was discovered that these two regions had not been coded into the response tracking system due to an 'oversight'.

KPI	Minimum Standard	Target	Formula	Source Data
Response time	>95% within 1 hr Residual within 3 hrs	100% in 1 hr	$\dfrac{\text{Responses w/in 1 hr}}{\text{\# calls}}$ $\dfrac{\text{Responses > 3 hr}}{\text{\# calls}}$	- Response log - Call log

The only KPI specification most contracts have   *The area under most dispute, if left unspecified*

Figure 3.3   KPI development worksheet

If the maths underpinning the KPI and the source data for the calculations are not specified, then a provider that self-reports its performance (which is the norm) is allowed discretion as to how to calculate performance. Not only can the provider make up the maths, they also get to make up which sources of data they want to use. Unsurprisingly, the reported KPI will show that the KPIs have been met. No provider left with total discretion as to how to report its performance would do otherwise.

For this reason, experienced organizations define not only the KPI, but also the detail behind it. They also detail the way in which the KPIs will be reported to ensure that the resultant performance trends and issues can be easily ascertained. Hence, the next step, that of prototyping reports.

Step 6: Prototype Reports – Design the Publication

When your organization wants to use the Contract Scorecard, you must first consider the design of the results on a very high-level dashboard, or summary page, for general distribution. An example of such a high-level dashboard is given in Figure 3.4.

Quality
  ➢ 2/20 KPIs exceeded
  ➢ 12/20 KPIs met
  ➢ 6/20 KPIs failed

Relationship
  ➢ Average score (out of 5)
    • Client = 3.2
    • Supplier = 2.7
  ➢ 4/10 behaviours poor for both parties

Finance
  ➢ 5% increase from prior period
  ➢ 20% decrease against baseline
  ➢ 5% under budget
  ➢ 15% over benchmark
  ➢ 50% contribution to TCO and rising
  ➢ 11/12 invoices on time

Strategy
  ➢ 9/14 outsourcing objectives achieved
  ➢ One co-developed product available for sale
  ➢ 5/20 proposed SMEs (local companies) in use

Figure 3.4   Example of a high-level scorecard dashboard

This dashboard is then supported with a comprehensive performance report, organized by quadrant, that covers, at a minimum, the detailed measurements, root cause and actions to be taken for each KPI within the quadrant. The detailed reporting is for those stakeholders requiring in-depth analysis, trend patterns and explanations of the results of a particular quadrant – for example, those stakeholders interested in only the financial results.

Of course, your organization is likely to have many contracts and may need to report on the success of its entire contract portfolio. This creates a pyramid of reporting as shown in Figure 3.5, which illustrates the increasing detail required to measure and report the Contract Scorecard for a contract portfolio. As shown in Figure 3.5, the portfolio can have any number of contracts (in the figure only two are depicted for simplicity), using any number of the four quadrants, which will comprise any number of KPIs, which will consist of some targets and, typically, always minimum standards.

In addition to reporting by each contract, your organization may need to report the entire portfolio of contracts by quadrant depending upon the needs of your organization's stakeholders. For example, your CFO may only be interested in the financial aspects of the contract portfolio, the general managers in quality, your CEO in the relationship and the board in the strategic aspects – or any combination therein.

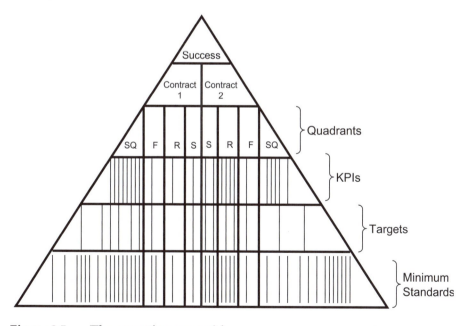

Figure 3.5   The reporting pyramid

Because reporting to stakeholders is a critical aspect of a well-designed Contract Scorecard system, prototyping what reports each stakeholder requires forms a crucial part of the design work. Having KPIs that cannot be rolled up and communicated to stakeholders will inevitably result in reduced stakeholder support for the concept.

Step 7: Conduct Testing – Make Sure it will Work

It is always worth testing a newly designed KPI system rather than assuming it will operate as intended. The best way to do this is to use current performance statistics against the KPIs. This not only provides a baseline with which your organization can gauge the performance of a provider, but also enables your organization to test the KPIs to see if there is any way they can be circumvented.

The case below illustrates the kind of thing that can happen if the provider turns out to be careless, or less than honest, as well as why proper testing is a good idea.

STAFF GET CREATIVE ON RECORDING KPIS

The outsourcing of the helpdesk had led to remarkable improvements in resolution times. As a result, outsourcing of other IT services was deemed the preferred option and many services were put out to tender. However, unbeknown to the customer agency as well as the supplier's management, operators were not logging the calls into the system until the calls had been resolved. Rather, each operator was manually recording and tracking calls. When the call was resolved, it was then entered into the database – thus resulting in the extraordinary resolution times. This came about due to two factors: 1) to save the client money, an automated system had not been installed, and thus proper recording was the responsibility of the operator; and 2) the supplier gave operators bonuses if they exceeded KPIs, primarily that of call resolution times. The operators quickly determined that these call resolution KPIs could be easily exceeded by waiting to log the call, solving the problem, then recording the log date and resolution date. This was discovered a year after the contract was awarded when an astute auditor queried why the operators were so busy manually scribbling things down rather than keying data into a system, an unusual behaviour in most helpdesks.

There is no correct length of time that should be spent on testing KPIs. It depends heavily on the complexity of the work under the contract. However, if for whatever reason, there is little time for actual testing, it is suggested that, at the very least, a brainstorming workshop be held with relevant personnel. Here, even if only for half a day, the KPIs are put through their paces in a theoretical sense, and any loopholes or inconsistencies are attempted to be pried out. If someone in your organization can think of a way to get around a KPI, it is likely that someone in the provider's organization will too.

Other Issues to Consider

If KPIs are not complex enough thus far, there are still a few other issues to consider before you begin to develop them. These include:

- making sure the KPIs add to the totality of the work – so that all work under the KPI has a minimum standard;

- separating PIs (Performance Indicators) from KPIs – creating a second tier of measurements that are not punished or rewarded, merely tracked;

- KPI stratification – creating different standards for different times (for example business hours versus non-business hours), different locations or different business units/personnel;

- careful use of averages – so that large standard deviations do not occur.

All of these are discussed below.

ENSURING KPIS ADD TO THE TOTALITY OF THE WORK

Table 3.4 gives a partial example of real-life KPIs, in this case for on-site support services that we discussed earlier in the case study on page 56. Look at the last KPI in the table where it states '>95 per cent within 48 hours'. This presents a number of problems that might not be immediately obvious. The first is that only 95 per cent has to be completed, but the other 5 per cent apparently does not, as nothing had been specified. This is an issue of making sure KPIs add to 100 per cent.

There were more problems with the clarity of the KPIs in this example as well. First of all, 95 per cent of what? Is it 95 per cent of each device? Is it 95 per cent of all devices? Then, within 48 hours of what? When the provider decides to do it? After the provider is on-site? It is not clear from the example, yet the example represents a very common way in which organizations specify KPIs. In this particular case, the parties did revise the KPIs after the client agreed to pay more money. Table 3.5 shows the revised version. As mentioned in the case, the provider misinterpreted what 'service level' meant; accordingly, the title was changed as well.

Table 3.4   Example KPIs (partial) – original

Service Area	KPI	Service Level
On-Site Support Services	Availability of On-site Support Contact – Critical	• Available to provide support within thirty (30) minutes for 100% of Critical Requests
	Availability of On-site Support Contact – all Other Requests	• Available to provide support within one (1) hour for 80% of all Other Requests
	Device Relocation	• >95% within forty-eight (48) hours
	Installation of SOE Device	• >95% within forty-eight (48) hours

Table 3.5   Example KPIs (partial) – revised

Service Area	KPI	Service Level Minimum Standard
On-Site Support Services	Availability of On-site Support Contact – Critical	• Available to provide Support On-site within thirty (30) minutes of notification for 100% of Critical Requests
	Availability of On-site Support Contact – all Other Requests	• Available to provide Support On-site within one (1) hour of notification for at least 80% of all Other Requests • Support is On-site within four (4) hours of notification for no more than 20% of all Other Requests
	Device Relocation	• At least 95% of Devices are relocated within forty-eight (48) hours of receipt of Relocation Request • 100% of Devices relocated within seventy-two (72) hours of receipt of Relocation Request
	Installation of SOE Device	• At least 95% of SOE Devices are installed within forty-eight (48) hours of receipt of Installation Request • 100% of SOE Devices installed within seventy-two (72) hours of receipt of Installation Request

SEPARATING KPIs FROM PIs

More will be said about penalties and incentives for KPIs later in Chapter 4, but as you design your KPIs, you may decide that some are not as key as to warrant either a reward for excellent performance or recourse for poor performance. If you find yourself in this position, you should immediately question the importance of that KPI. In these cases, you may well decide to create a second tier of Performance Indicators (PIs) that sit beneath the KPIs. These concern themselves with non-critical issues – what might be called the 'nice-to-know' aspects of the deal that typically interest only a small number of stakeholders, or are not mission-critical. This measurements of interest to certain stakeholders, or second-tier measurements, can be obtained systematically, without overloading the process.

KPI STRATIFICATION

Stratification of KPIs is necessary when there are different KPI measurements used for different categories of:

- time (for example, a more stringent requirement during standard hours and more relaxed KPIs for non-standard hours);

- location (for example, turnaround times of 1 hour in metropolitan areas, 4 hours in rural areas and 8 hours in remote areas); or

- business units/personnel (for example, response rate of 1 hour for executives and 4 hours for other personnel).

Table 3.6 gives an example of stratification for standard hours and outside of standard hours.

USE OF AVERAGES

Averages are commonly employed but can give surprising results if the standard deviations are not managed as well. Take, for example, the case where the average response time for a KPI has been set at an average of 24 hours, starting from the time the response request is logged. A response time of 1 hour, and another of 47 hours, will both yield the same average as that specified in the KPI (24 hours on average). If having extremes of fast and slow are acceptable to you, then this average is fine. However, in most cases, you will

Table 3.6   **Example KPI stratification – standard versus non-standard hours**

Call Category	KPI Minimum Standard (measured monthly)	
	Standard Hours Response	**Outside of Standard Hours Response**
Severity 1	>95% within one (1) hour Residual within three (3) hours	>95% within ninety (90) minutes Residual within four (4) hours
Severity 2	>95% within three (3) hours Residual within five (5) hours	>95% within three (3) hours Residual within five (5) hours
Severity 3	>95% within one (1) Business Day Residual within two (2) Business Days	Call actioned at start of the next Business Day and measured at Severity three (3) Standard Hours KPI
Severity 4	>95% within three (3) Business Days Residual within five (5) Business Days	Call actioned at start of the next Business Day and measured at Severity four (4) Standard Hours KPI

want the standard deviations (a measure of the spread or dispersion of a set of data) minimal, and most organizations will want to set a maximum allowed time too. Consequently, it is imperative that the laggards (statistical outliers) be capped and unacceptable timeframes specified. Therefore, in this case, it would be better to have two KPIs for the response time: 1) average time of 24 hours and 2) no single response of greater than, say, 30 hours.

Another issue arises with how the average is to be taken if there are multiple sites and/or items. For example, let us say that a KPI has been specified for the average availability of equipment to be 98 per cent during working hours. There are 100 pieces of this equipment located at 100 sites. If we do not specify that the average be measured per piece of equipment, the provider could very well just average the equipment pool. Subsequently, two locations could have zero availability and if the rest of the equipment pool is operating at 100 per cent availability during working hours, the provider has met its KPI. If that is not your intent, then the average availability of each item of equipment must be the KPI specification. If not, the provider is certainly not in breach of the KPI, even if the perceived intent of the KPI differs between the parties.

4

Schemes for the Consequences of KPI Performance

'Accountability requires consequences. You can't have one without the other.'

Don Schmincke

About this Chapter

KPI consequence schemes encourage providers to deliver to expectation and, where desired, to deliver outstanding work. Schemes can come in the form of positive 'incentives' (rewards) for good performance, or negative 'disincentives' (recourse) for poor performance. While it is commonly assumed that the KPI consequence schemes are monetary, that does not necessarily have to be the case, as we will discuss shortly.

This chapter takes you through your 'carrot' and 'stick' options, which can be reward-based or recourse-based, or both, which can be monetary or not, or some combination.

Exploring the Basis for KPI Schemes – Recourse versus Rewards

Recourse has long been an accepted consequence of not meeting the KPIs that have been set up as minimum expectations, and thus is a very common feature of most contracts. However, in recent years, there is an increasing use of rewards as well. Unsurprisingly, you will find that providers are very keen to have rewards included in their contracts.

Quality KPIs in the Contract Scorecard typically have financial incentives which are either incentive-based (for example, bonuses and/or extensions) or disincentive-based (for example, rebates, invoice credits or liquidated damages) or any combination thereof. Financial KPI measurements may also have such a scheme depending on how much control the provider has over the costs.

However, the relationship measurements and the strategic measurements rarely have such schemes. In the former, the relationship is the responsibility of both parties, not just the provider. If you want to penalize the provider, you must also be willing to penalize your organization too. For this reason, the score for the relationship attributes tends to be used to identify what needs improvement, and bi-party initiatives are created to raise the results.

The strategic goals often have a great deal of noise, or external influences, on their achievement – they may not be fully in the provider's control. If they are, then by all means use a recourse/reward environment; but if not, the strategic quadrant should operate much like the relationship quadrant in that the evaluation is used to identify deficiencies and formulate necessary initiatives.

Penalties against contract fees have long been an accepted practice for failure to meet KPI minimum standards. However, using the word *'penalties'* to refer to financial recourse in your contracts is not recommended. This is because the word 'penalty' has a special meaning in the laws of most countries – typically defined as a genuine pre-estimate of loss by a party due to the performance failure of the other. Most financial recourses used with KPIs do not involve such an estimate of what the client has suffered by way of damages or consequential loss, but rather reflects amounts derived that are intended to motivate the provider not to fail. If you call the financial recourse in a contract a penalty, it might be unenforceable if it does not meet the laws of the country in which the contract was signed (called 'governing law' in the majority of contracts). Consider substitute terms such as *fee adjustment*, *performance rebates* and *invoice credits* with the intent of making it a pricing adjustment, equating the lesser value received with a lesser, but fair, price owed, as opposed to a penalty.

At a minimum, you want KPIs that set the base level standard of performance to be achieved, which may have recourse for failure. Not all KPIs will necessary attract a disincentive. However, if failing a KPI has no consequence, you may need to consider the importance of that KPI since there is no explicit motivation for the provider to do well, or not fail it. This

KPI should be dropped, or relegated to a Performance Indicator (see page 63 for the discussion in Chapter 3).

Unfortunately, many organizations have lost sight of the central purpose of financial disincentives, which is to motivate the behaviour of the provider so that the KPI is met. The goal of any financial disincentive scheme should never be to actually obtain the penalties, but rather to ensure that your minimum expectations are met. The sometimes strange relationship between recourse systems and client contract management behaviour is illustrated by the following case.

A REGIONAL BANK 'EXTRACTS VALUE' FROM ITS CONTRACTS

The management responsibilities for the outsourcing of IT services had been delegated to the finance department of a small regional bank. As IT was now outsourced, it was considered to be primarily a procurement issue rather than a service issue.

The finance department had little IT experience, but knew how to 'extract value' from procurement contracts. Accordingly, it set a budget for the achievement of financial recourse for poor performance. In this manner, the department believed it would demonstrate prudent financial management by continually reducing costs.

The development of processes and resolution of service issues giving rise to performance issues were never considered. In fact, the contract manager had a personal goal to achieve penalties at least equal to his salary. Over time, the bank eventually brought all the services back in-house as outsourcing was deemed to result in inadequate control over quality.

In the spirit of focusing on getting good performance (as opposed to monetary compensation), some organizations elect to allow the provider to claw back financial recourse owed to them, if subsequent performance is above the minimum standard for a specified period of time.

If you have had to apply negative incentives for more than 3 months, your scheme is not working because the provider's performance is not improving. Something could be wrong with the KPIs (they were never realistic in the first place, there is a problem getting objective measurements or the provider is not in full control of the variables). Alternatively, something could be wrong at the provider and diagnosis and treatment of the root cause of performance failure is required.

To help with the latter, another form of disincentive you may want to consider involves an increasing level of performance intervention by the client organization for those KPIs that are not being achieved. Increasingly interventionist actions become useful in contracts where getting money back is not the answer in the long term, and replacing a non-performing provider is economically or politically impractical until all other avenues have been exhausted. In the event of any KPI failures, the pyramid in Figure 4.1 outlines the progressive interventions most commonly made available to the client.

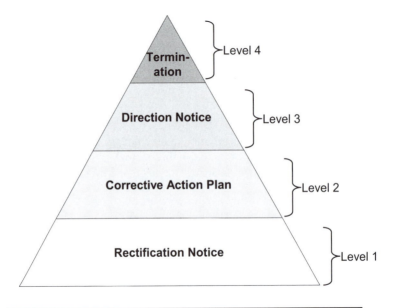

Number of KPI failures	Number of Occurrences of the same KPI failure in a Rolling 3-Month Period			
	1	2	3	More
1	Level 1	Level 2	Level 3	Level 4
2	Level 1	Level 2	Level 3	Level 4
3	Level 2	Level 3	Level 4	Level 4
More	Level 3	Level 4	Level 4	Level 4

Figure 4.1   Progressive intervention pyramid

Your organization's actions might escalate as each KPI failure continues, as follows:

1. **Rectification Notice** – the provider rectifies defective work at no cost by the deadline instructed by your organization.

2. **Corrective Action Plan** – the provider assesses the underlying cause of failure and prepares a plan, approved by your organization, to prevent its reoccurrence.

3. **Direction Notice** – your organization makes its own assessment of the underlying cause of failure, with full cooperation from the provider, and gives instructions on how to raise services to the required KPI levels.

4. **Termination** – if the earlier remedial actions still have not yielded results, termination must be considered. You may want only partial termination of the underperforming services and not the entirety of the agreement. You will want to retain the right, however, to full termination, if partial termination is not practical or economically sound. This right can be powerful without being executed as it provides your organization with strong negotiation power to put in other solutions such as a reduced price.

An example of the write-up of these progressive actions is provided in Table 4.1 and example notice forms of each of these four (rectification, correction action plan, direction and termination) have been provided in the appendix to this chapter.

In recent years there has been an increasing use of rewards as well. Unsurprisingly, providers are very keen to have these included in their contracts.

Rewards are rarely applied carte blanche across all KPIs. With these, the increased performance delivered should bring about a business benefit, but it is often difficult to measure the benefit gained without a direct link to the actions of the providers. In practice, rewards have worked best when KPI target thresholds have been set for only the few services for which exceeding the minimum standard has value to the organization and are thus worth paying

Table 4.1   Example write-up of the progressive actions

Level	Description	Actions
1	Rectification Notice	1. Provider rectifies defective work at no cost to the Client by the Client-instructed due date. 2. Provider determines cause of failure and discusses remedial measures with the Client to the Client's satisfaction. 3. Remedial measures undertaken by the Provider by agreed due date.
2	Corrective Action Plan	1. Provider assesses the underlying cause/s of failure and prepares a Corrective Action Plan to prevent such failures occurring in the future. 2. Client approves the Corrective Action Plan. 3. Supplier implements the actions by the agreed due date.
3	Direction Notice	1. Client makes its own assessment of the underlying cause/s of failure with full cooperation from the Provider. 2. Client issues a Direction to the Provider. 3. The Provider complies with the Direction by the agreed due date.

4	Termination	1. Client determines, in its absolute discretion, as to whether the Contract will be terminated in full or in part.
		2. Should termination result, the Provider must pay for the cost incurred by the Client for the handover of the Contract to a new provider.
		3. Should a determination be made that the relationship continue:
		  a. the cost of continued service will be at a significant cost reduction; and
		  b. the Client will appoint an independent party to evaluate the causes of failure and develop a corrective action plan which the Supplier must implement by the date specified by the Client. This will be at the cost of the Provider.

extra for. Examples include the reduction of fault calls, clearance of backlogs, improved installation times and higher customer satisfaction ratings.

Timing

There are two primary ways in which KPI consequence programmes operate: either on an ongoing regular basis (typically monthly) or on an intermittent basis (annually or less frequently). Regular schemes are nearly always a monetary determination adjusting the value-for-money equation. However, intermittent schemes cover a wide range of possible actions. We will discuss the regular options first, then the intermittent options.

REGULAR REBATE/BONUS SCHEMES

The general premise of a regular monetary scheme is that the price of the work will require adjustments, up or down, based on the quality received. The minimum standard KPI thresholds set the base performance to be achieved for the price paid – a lesser degree of service, then, results in a lower price for that period. Similarly, a higher degree of KPI achievement attracts a higher price for the period. The application of these incentives can occur via three possible means:

- fixed amount per event – each instance of an event accrues fixed recourse/reward amount;

- weighted percentage – the KPIs are weighted against an at-risk amount (in the case of disincentive) or available amount (in the case of incentive); or

- points – good and poor KPI performance accrues positive and negative points.

Fixed amount per event   This is the simplest form of monetary scheme to administer as it tends to be a very straightforward calculation. The client either receives a fixed rebate for each instance of poor performance or pays an additional amount for each instance of superior performance. For example, for each day equipment delivery is late, the client obtains a rebate of $1000 and for each day early, the client pays an additional $1000.

Weighted percentage   Under this method, the provider is penalized/rewarded a percentage of an agreed at-risk amount for each KPI. The different percentage amounts that each has is typically weighted against the commensurate business impact. Table 4.2 provides an example of a percentage-based rebate approach. Here, failure to achieve the monthly KPIs results in a rebate commensurate with the percentages listed in the 'Overall Weight'. In this case there was $200 000 at risk, so if the provider did not achieve, say, the first KPI of call answering time it would need to deduct from its fees 4 per cent of $200 000 ($8000).

Some organizations choose to escalate the rebate scheme if substandard performance continuously reoccurs either in consecutive periods or, for example, 3 months out of 6. An example of this is provided in Table 4.3.

Table 4.2   Example rebate scheme – percentage method

SLA Ref	Service Area KPI	Service Area KPI Weight	Overall Weight
4.2.1	**Helpdesk and support services**		
1	Call answering time	20%	4%
2	Call resolution rate for first-level support	20%	4%
3	User satisfaction survey rating	10%	2%
4	Call response time	20%	4%
5	Call resolution time	20%	4%
6	Call update frequency	10%	2%
		100%	20%
4.2.2	**Desktop supply and support**		
1	Device relocation	50%	5%
2	Install ESOE device	50%	5%
		100%	10%
4.2.3	**Data networks**		
1	Network infrastructure availability	70%	14%
2	Reliability	30%	6%
		100%	20%
4.2.4	**Computer room operations**		
1	Availability	70%	17%
2	Reliability	30%	8%
		100%	25%
4.2.5	**Applications**		
1	Application availability – critical	30%	8%
2	Application availability – other	15%	4%
3	Application change performance (delivery)	10%	3%
4	Application implementation performance	25%	5%
5	Reliability	20%	5%
		100%	25%
		Total	100%

Table 4.3   Example rebate escalation scheme

Service Area	KPI	Service Level	Service Fee Adjustment (Consecutive Months)		
Specified On-site Support Services	Availability of On-site Support – Critical	Available to provide support < 30 minutes for 100% of Critical Requests	20%	30%	40%
	Availability of On-site Support – All Others	Available to provide support < one (1) hour for 80% of All Other Requests	5%	10%	15%
		Available < four (4) hours for remaining 20% of All Other Requests	5%	10%	15%

You might note that in the example in Table 4.3 there is still no guarantee that KPIs will improve, only that the client will obtain more recourse the longer the KPIs fail. For this reason, other organizations combine an escalation provision along with the progressive intervention technique discussed earlier. An example of this is shown in Figure 4.2.

Points   An approach becoming more widespread throughout many industries is the use of a 'Performance Points' Model. This is popular due to its ease

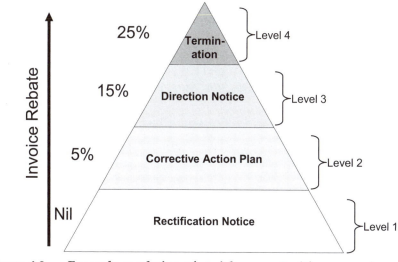

Figure 4.2   Example escalation of at-risk amount with progressive intervention

of calculation, as well as to its being less complex to administer than many traditional schemes. As you may have experienced, the calculation of the KPIs and corresponding amounts owed can get complicated.

The provider is given points for performance against KPIs, and each point is assigned a monetary value. Outstanding service receives positive points, and poor service receives negative points. In this method, different service levels have different point amounts, weighted against the commensurate business impact. Table 4.4 provides an example of the points system for a quality and a financial measurement.

Table 4.4   Points example, telecommunications carrier

Monthly KPI		Performance Points	
Minimum Standard	Target	Failure to meet the Minimum Standard	Target Met
95% of Authorized Services connected within one (1) Business Day 100% of Authorized Services connected within two (2) Business Days	100% of Authorized Services connected within one (1) Business Day	-2 points for every 1% below the min std	+10 points

At the day specified in the agreement, the points are tallied, and the amount owing is calculated. The balance day need not be every month; rather, it is more commonly every 3, 6 or 12 months. In this spirit, some organizations elect to allow the provider to 'claw back' negative points if subsequent performance is above the minimum standard threshold or meets the target threshold for a specified period of time, keeping in mind that it is consistent contract outcomes that the rational organization wants, not the cash back.

An example of the provision written for a points scheme is shown in Figure 4.3.

The points scheme avoids the paper war often associated with monthly recourse schemes. In a traditional arrangement, the provider invoices for the work in a particular month, but the KPI performance report for that month comes in after the invoice has been raised. After receiving the KPI report, the client then typically raises an invoice credit based in its determination of the amounts owing due to failure to meet KPIs. More often than not, the provider does not agree with the calculation and raises a credit adjustment. This little game can go on every month, month after month!

1. Application of the Performance Points

1.1   (**Calculation**) The Client will calculate Performance Points:

      a.   no less than thirty (30) days after receiving the KPI report from the Contractor basis;

      b.   using the formulas specified in the KPI Tables; and

      c.   report the positive, negative and net Performance Points calculated to the Contractor.

1.2   (**Point value**) A value of $1 000 USD for each Performance Point has been set by the parties.

1.3   (**Annual tally**) Prior to 1 February each year, the Client will present the net Performance Points for the previous year to the Contractor. At that time, the amounts payable by the party owing will be agreed.

1.4   (**Caps**) The Rebates and Bonuses shall be capped per year as follows:

      a.   the Bonus payable by the Client is capped at $200 000 USD; and

      b.   the Rebate payable by the Contractor is capped at $400 000 USD.

1.5   (**Payment**) Payment shall occur as follows:

      a.   for a Bonus, the Contractor will raise a special February invoice; or

      b.   for a Rebate, the Client will raise a February credit to be offset against monies owed the Contractor in accordance with the offset rights in the Contract.

1.6   (**No limitation on other rights**) The Rebate does not in any way limit the Client's rights in relation to any additional remedial actions and remedy in the Contract.

Figure 4.3   **Example points scheme provision**

By its very nature, a recourse scheme that allows this to occur sets the scene for disputes. Once the provider raises an invoice, the revenue is booked in its accounts – and it wants that money. Once your organization raises an invoice credit claiming back KPI rebates, costs have been reduced in its accounts – and your organization wants that money back. To avoid costly disputes, consider keeping the KPI incentive scheme off the accounting books with only a periodic tallying up.

In more partnering-orientated deals, the client organization may also operate under a set of KPIs. The client KPIs tend to reflect their responsibility to the provider in such areas as approval turnaround times, delivery of information to deadlines and even attendance at meetings. Like the points attributed to the provider, both positive and negative points can occur depending on whether the client has meet the KPI minimum standards and/ or targets.

In my experience, those organizations that have used a performance points system to determine the effect of KPI achievement have not gone back to any other. The calculation simplicity, straightforward logic and administrative ease means that the parties can focus on getting the results, not on disputing the arcane mathematics found in more traditional approaches.

INTERMITTENT SCHEMES

Intermittent schemes are not calculated and applied every month; rather, the recourse/reward is applied on an annual basis (or less frequently, such as near the end of the contract) or after prolonged periods of poor/good KPI results.

These schemes offer a high-impact, low-cost incentive programme. The high impact comes from having a large carrot or stick, and the low cost comes from the minimal administrative overheads incurred in operating the scheme. Intermittent schemes can act as the sole incentive programme, or can operate in conjunction with a regular monetary scheme. For example, failure to meet KPI minimum standard thresholds may result in a rebate in each month of occurrence, and three continuous months of failure may lead to your organization having the right to terminate the contract.

Intermittent inducements to perform well focus on creating revenue-generating opportunities for the provider. It focuses on revenue because the top line is the most primal driver for all providers – one cannot make profit if one does not have revenue first. These tend to be quite attractive to providers and provide substantial motivation to do well.

The rewards typically offered under a non-monetary scheme include:

- **Contract extension** – typically, a smaller length of the original term is awarded for a specified period of good KPI results. For example, a 3-year contract may have performance-based extensions of 12 months. A simple example of this is provided in Figure 4.4.

- **Active promotion as a reference site** – you may open your site to the potential clients of the provider to tour the provider at work, and/or get

---

4.3   The Client will extend the term of this Agreement for a period of 6 months for each 12-month period, beginning 6 months from the Anniversary Date, under the following conditions:

a.   an extension shall accrue for each 6-month period in which there are no KPI failures; and

b.   all accrued extension/s shall be null and void if there are any KPI failures in the last 6-month period of the Term, unless the Client directs otherwise.

Figure 4.4   **Example extension provision**

even more active and perform periodic roadshows with the provider visiting potential clients or speaking with the provider at conferences.

- **Issue a performance certificate or reference letter** – where you may issue a certificate of good performance, a letter of commendation or write a reference letter for the provider to use in marketing materials or in bids with other potential clients, frame and put in their office, and/or put in the company newsletter.

- **Automatically shortlist for further work** – where the provider gains automatic entry into the final competitive process and bypasses any prequalification stage of a tendering process, thus typically being able to save considerable tendering costs. Note, however, winning the tender is far from guaranteed; the provider merely gets to skip through a few hoops in the tendering process, not all of them.

The deterrents typically offered under an intermittent scheme include:

- **Warning notice** – this operates in a very similar way to a staff warning policy that you may have, in that after a certain number of warnings, then you have the right to terminate the contract.

- **Withhold payment** – whereby you withhold the part of the payment related to the defective work until the performance has improved.

- **Withdraw as a reference site** – make it an explicit obligation that the provider cannot use your organization's name as a reference site in any marketing materials or represent the contract as successful to any individual or organization.

- **Remove from preferred provider list** – this has the effect of blacklisting the provider from future work until performance has improved. This only works if there is a centralized source of information of the preferred and unpreferred providers. However, also note that some governments do not allow this practice – no matter how poorly a provider has performed in a contract, they are always entitled to bid for more work in the interest of transparency or fairness to all.

- **Step-in** – whereby your organization steps in to perform the work in which the KPIs are failing. If your organization does not have the capacity or capability, you can hire another provider as the step-in and the original provider is required to pay the costs of obtaining the provider as well as cover any additional fees/higher charges than that in the contract. An example of this is provided in Figure 4.5.

---

1   Ability of the Client to Step-In

1.1   (**Step-in rights**) Without prejudice to any other remedy the Client may have, if the Contractor fails to meet the KPIs, the Client may, at its discretion, take control of so much of the Services as is necessary for that function to be performed.

1.2   (**Appointment of third party**) The Client may obtain services similar to the Services elsewhere or may make any other arrangements considered necessary by the Client to maintain the Services, appointing any third party to provide the Services.

1.3   (**Good faith**) The Client must act in good faith in exercising its rights under this clause and manage any contract with the third party in good faith.

1.4   (**Notice**) The Client will give notice to the Contractor as soon as practicable of its intention to exercise its rights under this clause. This notice must include:

    a.   the reason for exercising these rights;

    b.   details of the third party; and

    c.   description of the intended contract with any third party.

1.5   (**Duty to assist**) The Contractor must assist the Client and the third party in the exercise of its step-in rights including:

    a.   facilitating access to the Contractor's relevant files and systems;

    b.   providing access to its Confidential Information, information, data, Contract Material and records; and

    c.   making the Workforce available to provide information and assistance;

as required by the Client or nominee.

1.6   (**No remuneration**) The Contractor is not entitled to receive fees, charges or any remuneration whatsoever that relate to the services performed by the Client or an third party under this Clause.

1.7   (**Liability**) Neither the Client nor third party is liable to the Contractor for any act or omission caused during the period of step-in unless the act or omission is caused by gross negligence.

1.8   (**Recovery of amounts**) The Client will be entitled to recover from the Contractor the difference between any amounts paid to a third party and the amount by which the payment of fees or charges has been reduced. The Client must act reasonably, insofar as the circumstances permit, in appointing any third party to provide the Services and in agreeing a fee for those services.

1.9   (**Cease of step-in**) The appointment of the third party will cease when:

    a.   the Client determines, in its absolute discretion, the Contractor has demonstrated its ability to meet the KPIs;

    b.   the Contract is terminated by the Client; or

    c.   the Term expires by the passing of time.

1.10   (**No termination waiver**) Nothing in this clause prevents the Client from being entitled to give notice for termination for cause.

Figure 4.5   Example step-in provision

- **Termination (full or partial)** – at some stage, as a last resort, you may want the right to terminate for poor performance. This can be the right to terminate the entirety of the contract (full termination) or the services for which the KPIs are failing (partial termination). Figure 4.6 provides you with a simple example. It is worth noting that, in the event of partial termination, you should always retain the right to escalate to full termination at your absolute discretion, if you determine that partial termination is not practical.

9.2 In addition to any other rights it has to terminate this Agreement, the Client may, in its absolute discretion, terminate this Agreement in whole or in part with respect to any one or more Services if the provider:

(a) fails to meet at least 3 (three) KPIs, without justification acceptable to the Client, in any 1 (one) measurement period;

(b) fails to meet at least 10 (ten) KPIs, without justification.

Figure 4.6   Example termination provision

These disincentive rights of your organization can be powerful without having to be actually executed. These deterrents can provide your organization with strong negotiation power over the provider to put in other resolutions, or to improve the arrangement.

Chapter Appendices

EXAMPLE RECTIFICATION NOTICE

Instructions: To be completed by Client in entirety

Rectification Notice		
Rectification ID #: _____ Rectification title: _____	Notified by: Client Representative name _____ Signature_____	Date of Rectification Notice: ___/____/___ Date rectification is to be completed:___/____/___ Date rectification was completed:___/____/___
Description of required rectification work (attach specification, if applicable):		
Process by which the Provider shall inform the Client that work has been completed:		
Description of actual rectification work performed:		
Rectification resolution: ❑ Rejected ❑ Deferred – until ___/___/___ ❑ Approved	Rectification approval signature: Client Representative name _____ Signature _____ Date ___/____/___	

This form shall be governed by the terms and conditions of the Agreement.
Nothing in this form varies the rights and obligations of the parties unless specifically identified.

EXAMPLE CORRECTIVE ACTION REQUEST

Instructions: Shaded areas to be completed by the Client

Corrective Action Request (CAR)		
CAR ID #: _____ CAR title: _____ _____	Notified by: Client Representative name _____ Signature _____	Date issued: ___/____/___ Implementation target date: ___/____/___ Implementation actual date: ___/____/___
Recital of events leading to this CAR:		
To be completed by the Provider *(attachments to be provided as appropriate)*	Root cause analysis of problem: Proposed rectification/fix: Proposed prevention plan over reoccurrence (including detailed implementation plan):	
Actual rectification and prevention work undertaken:		
CAR resolution: ☐ Rejected ☐ Deferred – until ___/___/___ ☐ Approved	CAR resolution approval signature: Client Representative name_____ Signature _____ Date ___/____/___	

This form shall be governed by the terms and conditions of the Agreement.
Nothing in this form varies the rights and obligations of the parties unless specifically identified

EXAMPLE DIRECTION NOTICE

Instructions: To be completed by Client in entirety

Direction Notice		
Direction ID #: _____ Direction title: _____	Directed by: Client Representative name _____ Signature _____	Date of Direction Notice: ___/___/___ Date direction is to be completed: ___/___/___ Date direction was completed: ___/___/___
Brief recital of events leading to this direction:		
Brief description of Client's approach to determining the direction:		
The direction to the Provider:		
Implications on the Contract or other work (if applicable):		
Direction resolution: ❑ Rejected ❑ Deferred – until ___/___/___ ❑ Approved	Direction resolution approval signature: Client Representative name _____ Signature_____ Date ___/___/___	

This form shall be governed by the terms and conditions of the Agreement.
Nothing in this form varies the rights and obligations of the parties unless specifically identified.

EXAMPLE TERMINATION NOTICE

Instructions: To be completed by Client in entirety

Termination Notice		
Termination ID #: _____ Termination title: _____	Notified by: Client Representative name _____ Signature _____	Date of Termination Notice: ___ / ___ / ___ Date termination is to take effect: ___ / ___ / ___

Scope of Termination: ☐ Full ☐ Partial (if partial, complete the partial termination section below)

To be completed for partial	Scope terminated:	Variation Request ID #_____ *(form to be submitted with this Termination Notice)*	Resultant Price reduction: $

Description of required disengagement work (attach specification, if applicable):

Deliverables and due date for the disengagement work:

Residual work (list work that may be required to be performed subsequent to the Termination Date). Note: the Contract may contain additional post-termination obligations.

This form shall be governed by the terms and conditions of the Agreement.
Nothing in this form varies the rights and obligations of the parties unless specifically identified.

5

Planning the Contract Scorecard

'When spiders unite they can tie down a lion.'

Ethiopian proverb

About this Chapter

We have spent a fair amount of time discussing each quadrant of the Contract Scorecard, how to develop KPIs and the various schemes by which to motivate your provider to perform well. Now that you are familiar with these quadrants, and the types of KPIs that can underpin each, we can now examine how to determine which of the Contract Scorecard quadrants you choose to employ in any particular contract, and how to specify each of the quadrants in them.

Adoption of all four quadrants may not be applicable for every contract. Hence, the first part of this chapter is devoted to a discussion on adoption and various perspectives that may help guide you as to which quadrants you may want in a particular contract.

Merely setting KPIs will not ensure that the Contract Scorecard is achieved; the contract documents must also ensure that the successful outcomes have been designed to occur. The Scorecard Blueprint, the subject of the middle of this chapter, will help you with this endeavour. Furthermore, the next four chapters discuss each specification required for each quadrant of the Contract Scorecard.

Because of the importance of designing a successful deal at the right time, the Scorecard Blueprint, and the resultant specifications within the contract documents, are best prepared before any competitive tendering or negotiation process is undertaken, hence the discussion of the Contract Lifecycle in the final portion of this chapter.

Adoption – Choosing the Quadrants Appropriate for Each Deal

Now that you have a fair idea of what you might include in each of the quadrants from the previous chapters, it is useful to discuss whether you need all quadrants in all contracts. The answer is that you may not.

The choice of quadrants employed in any organization's Contract Scorecard will be unique to each organization and each deal that organization has. The choice is strictly up to you; you can use as many or as few as you like. However, your choice should always be made according to the nature of your deal and, in particular, what the key stakeholders of the deal want to know on a regular basis and how actively you intend to ensure the myriad of desired outcomes are achieved.

To determine which of the quadrants will be of most use to any particular contract, it may be useful to consider the different perspectives that stakeholders might have. There are possible four stakeholder perspectives that your organization may adopt when assessing success using a Contract Scorecard (Figure 5.1):

1.   Value-for money perspective – what your organization gets for its money.

2.   Context perspective – the setting surrounding how the contract is delivered.

3.   Operations perspective – how the contract is conducted in practice.

4.   Agenda perspective – how the contract fits in the bigger picture.

Value-for-money		Context		
Quality		Relationship		**Operations**
Financial		Strategy		**Agenda**

Figure 5.1   Scorecard perspectives

VALUE-FOR-MONEY PERSPECTIVE

The value-for-money perspective represents what your organization gets for its money. It comprises the quality plus financial KPIs as shown in Figure 5.1. This is the most fundamental perspective of the majority of contracts.

Ideally, your organization is getting the minimum quality measurements that were agreed to in the contract, at a price that meets its financial expectations. This is the base expectation for most of the stakeholders but particularly for the business groups that are on the receiving end of the service and end up paying for it through cost allocations.

Accordingly, if this is a perspective chosen, the most useful people to get involved in the design and management of the scorecard will be those with operational and financial expertise.

CONTEXT PERSPECTIVE

The context perspective represents the setting surrounding how the contract is delivered. It comprises the relationship plus strategic KPIs as shown in Figure 5.1.

Ideally, the contract outcomes are conducted in such a way that the parties work together very well, and, by virtue of having the particular provider supplying contracted services, your organization is in a better position than had it not contracted. This is of particular interest to senior management.

Accordingly, if this is a perspective chosen, the most useful people to get involved in the design and management of the scorecard will be those operating at a strategic level within your organization regarding all contracts and those that have some form of interaction with providers.

OPERATIONS PERSPECTIVE

The operations perspective represents how the contract is conducted in practice. It comprises the quality plus relationship KPIs as shown in Figure 5.1.

Ideally, the contract is conducted in such a way that the outcomes strengthen the commercial relationship and interpersonal interaction, so that the environment is not adversarial or hostile. This is of particular interest to stakeholders directly involved with the provider, either as recipients of the work or items under contract (for example, users or customers) or those that form part of your organization's contract management activities (for example, general managers, project managers, contract administrators, accounts payable, and so on).

Accordingly, if this is a perspective chosen, the most useful people to get involved in the design and management of the scorecard will be those with operational expertise and those who will interface with the provider in some way.

AGENDA PERSPECTIVE

The agenda perspective represents how the contract fits in the bigger picture. It comprises the financial plus strategic KPIs as shown in Figure 5.1.

Ideally, the contract is not only financially effective, but also achieves wider corporate goals. These wider goals are often of most interest to senior management who, at a minimum, do not want the actions of your organization's providers to have an adverse effect on public relations and, preferably, want the entire supply chain of your organization to operate with the same key values.

Accordingly, if this is a perspective chosen, the most useful people to get involved in the design and management of the scorecard will be those operating at a strategic level within your organization regarding all contracts and the financial aspects of contracts.

ADOPTION BASED ON THE PERSPECTIVES

The only success criterion for infrequent transactions such as bulk equipment purchasing may be price. However, as a deal becomes strategically more important and longer in duration, then one should consider using more of the scorecard incorporating speed and accuracy of equipment delivery (value for money perspective). The expectations for a 10-year whole-of-IT deal, for example, will typically be more than purely financial, and success will be based on at least the value-for-money criterion, if not the entire scorecard. If the nature of the deal is to provide equipment over 10 years and work with the client to specify the ongoing equipment needs of the organization, the strength of the relationship and the provider's ability to contribute to strategic goals (all the perspectives and quadrants) will become increasingly important.

Figure 5.2 shows how you may choose to incrementally adopt the various perspectives depending on the two axes:

- Strategic importance of the deal – the deal's potential effect (both risk and benefit) on business as well as the number/importance of stakeholders concerned or affected.

- Duration – the degree to which the deal is a single isolated transaction or is an ongoing requirement in nature

Preparing the Scorecard Blueprint

Once you have decided which of the Contract Scorecard quadrants you will be adopting for a particular deal, you can then being to plan the contract that underpins the Contract Scorecard.

A key lesson that organizations repeatedly learn is that the desired benefits do not inherently occur with the act of signing a contract. The goals need to be articulated and the means by which they will be achieved worked through. This is illustrated in the following case where change management was deemed unnecessary because the act of outsourcing alone was believed to be all that was necessary to get the expected result.

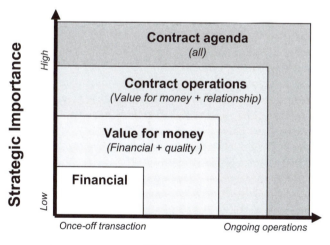

Figure 5.2   **Incremental adoption of the Contract Scorecard**

NO PLAN, NO RESULTS

A law enforcement agency outsourced its IT helpdesk. One of the key reasons for outsourcing was to demonstrate, by example, a new mentality towards working within the force. In other words, to instil a business work ethic. The organization specified the type of people the supplier was to provide, ranging from education, dress, attitude and job dedication. Management believed that if the organization's staff witnessed the professionalism displayed by the provider's workforce (such as wearing suits and staying late at work) the staff would adopt it as a matter of course. No programme for the expected culture change was designed to go along with the desired behaviours – the existence of the supplier's staff alone was to provide the impetus to change. What actually occurred was an entrenching of the existing culture further, as staff quickly asserted an 'us and them' mentality and, in fact, ignored the supplier's staff altogether. In this case, the expectation was very ideologically driven, with little planning into how the goal would actually be achieved.

Compare this with an educational institution that looked at outsourcing as a strategy to get organizational change and planned that strategy with care.

PLANNING HOW THE SOLUTION WOULD WORK MADE IT WORK

The team planning an outsourcing contract in a state-wide educational institution did not assume cultural innovation was a guaranteed benefit naturally occurring from outsourcing. Management was preparing a whole-of-IT outsourcing contract but wanted more that just an operations contract. It believed the supplier would be well placed to introduce sorely needed innovation and re-engineering into a business that had not had the return on investment from IT. Accordingly, it knew it needed more than the standard agreement for this to occur – akin to an operational alliance. It evaluated different re-engineering approaches to determine the one best suited. It designed detailed evaluation criteria and real-life scenarios that the bidders were to respond to. It tested various models within the industry (different payment and risk/reward schemes) until it had a model that it believed would work. The model chosen recognized that the supplier should be paid to generate ideas and business cases first. If the business cases were accepted, the provider was then remunerated for their implementation role. Within the first year, it had received more innovation ideas than it had ever generated internally. The actual number of innovations implemented remained less than had been hoped for, however, as the client had very entrenched ways of operating and was change-resistant. Nonetheless, management believed the introduction of the ideas and supporting business cases alone provided substantial benefits in unfreezing current mindsets on how and why technology was underemployed to move the organization from a change-resistant mentality to a change-embracing one. Thus, the desired relationship, that of the supplier delivering operational services as well as being a vital change agent, was successful.

The Scorecard Blueprint maps out how the deal will be put together to achieve the Contract Scorecard and specifies what contractual documents will specify which aspect of the Contract Scorecard.

Various elements of the contract documents will need to be designed to define the detail that underpins the scorecard to specify, drive, measure and report the elements of your Contract Scorecard such as that proposed in the Scorecard Blueprint example in Figure 5.3.

The quality measurements are most commonly captured in the Service Level Agreement schedule to the contract (explained in Chapter 6), the financial measurements are captured in the contract's Financial Schedule (explained in Chapter 7) and the relationship measurements are in the relationship charter/ code of conduct within the Governance Charter (explained in Chapter 8). The strategic measurements rarely have a single schedule; rather, this is dependent upon the nature of the measurements chosen (explained in Chapter 9). For example, safety measurements can be defined in an occupational health and safety schedule, environmental measurements in an environmental management plan, research and development commercialization in a commercialization investment and royalty schedule, and so on.

The contract documents set out the legal and commercial details of the deal as shown in Figure 5.4.

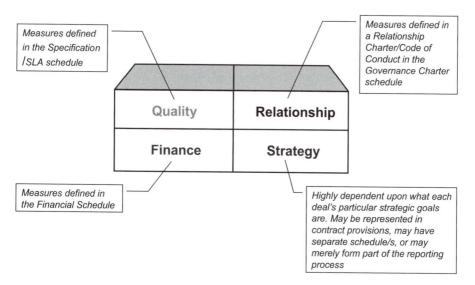

Figure 5.3   Blueprint example

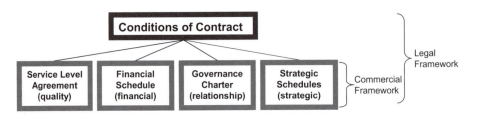

Figure 5.4   The contract documents

The key contract documents discussed in Figure 5.4 are:

- the **Service Level Agreement** (SLA) – the definition of successful work including work/product and reporting specifications, and quality KPIs and so on. This document is discussed in Chapter 6.

- the **Financial Schedule** – the manner in which the work will be billed and payments made. This document is discussed in Chapter 7.

- the **Governance Charter** – how the parties will manage the contract. This document is discussed in Chapter 8.

- the schedules that specify the strategic parts of the Contract Scorecard – of which there can be any number covering the particular strategic goals. Options are discussed in Chapter 9.

The *Conditions of Contract* forms the body of the contract and the *SLA, Financial Schedule, Governance Charter* and *Strategic Schedules* are schedules to the body of the contract. Complex deals may have many SLAs, typically under a Master SLA with service level schedules underneath, representing each major work stream. A complex agreement may also have many Financial Schedules which can involve a transition price schedule, schedule of rates (labour), schedule of fees (work activity prices), schedule of equipment prices (if providing assets for purchase by your organization) and a disengagement price schedule (for unwinding the deal) – just to name a few. There will be as many strategic-related schedules as there are strategic goals set up in the Contract Scorecard, typically a schedule for each goal (for example, an innovation schedule, workforce management arrangements, and so on),

Of course, there are typically more schedules than just these, such as in the example shown in Figure 5.5, but we will only focus on those necessary to realize the type of goals that a Contract Scorecard is designed to achieve.

	Page
Form of Agreement	1
Schedule 1: Interpretation and Definitions	4
Schedule 2: General Conditions	10
Schedule 3: Service Level Agreement	33
Schedule 4: Financial Arrangement	59
Schedule 5: Governance Charter	64
Schedule 6: Mobilization	76
Schedule 7: Disengagement	78
Schedule 8: Contractor's Key Personnel	80
Schedule 9: Contractor's Key Subcontractors	83
Schedule 10: Parent Company Performance Guarantee	86
Schedule 11: Financial Security	90

Figure 5.5   Example outline of a contract

It is worth considering which of these contract documents actually get used the most in practice. As shown in Figure 5.6, the Contract Conditions are used at the start and end of a deal, but only during the term of the deal if the parties get into trouble. In contrast, the commercial schedules are used from the first day to the last day of the deal.

The greatest return on the investment of scarce resources may be in the preparation of the commercial schedules that drive the success of the deal. This is contrary to the large investment that most organizations make in the preparation of the Contract Conditions. The Contract Conditions are primarily designed to protect the parties in the event of problems. However, many of the problems that the Contract Conditions were designed to protect you against could have been prevented by greater investment in the other governing documents.

The next part of the blueprint, after specifying where in the contract documents the underlying details will reside, details the reporting information you will need.

Much of the perceived successes of contracts are merely the initial 'honeymoon' reports (the initial announcement of a deal) published in the media. These are focused on celebrating a deal that has been signed and its anticipated

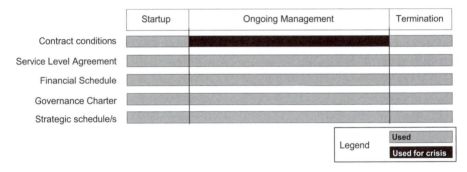

Figure 5.6   Frequency of use

benefits. Rarely does the public get any follow-up report regarding whether any of the desired outcomes were actually achieved. The Contract Scorecard report is your follow-up report, in which an account is given regularly.

When you use the Contract Scorecard, first consider publishing the results on a very high-level dashboard, or summary page, for general distribution. An example of such a high-level dashboard is given in Figure 5.7: this comes from an IT outsourcing contract between two global entities.

This dashboard is supported by a comprehensive performance report that covers, at a minimum, the detailed measurements, root cause and actions to be taken. The detailed report is for those requiring in-depth analysis and explanations

Quality	Relationship

➢ 2/20 KPIs exceeded
➢ 12/20 KPIs met
➢ 6/20 KPIs failed
	➢ Average score (out of 5)
	   • Client = 3.2
	   • Supplier = 2.7
	➢ 4/10 behaviours poor for both parties

Finance	**Strategy**
➢ 5% increase from prior period ➢ 20% decrease against baseline ➢ 5% under budget ➢ 15% over benchmark ➢ 50% contribution to TCO and rising ➢ 11/12 invoices on time	➢ 9/14 outsourcing objectives achieved ➢ One co-developed product available for sale ➢ 5/20 proposed SMEs (local companies) in use

Figure 5.7   Example of a high-level dashboard

of the results of a particular quadrant – for example, those interested in only the financial results, or for those seeking such analysis for all the quadrants.

Always make sure the reporting cycle is short enough so that significant underperformance issues can be identified on a timely basis. Getting a report only once a year can mean there were 11 months full of issues that could have been prevented!

Furthermore, by having an 'issues to be brought to the attention of management' or similar section in the regular reporting cycle, complete with the provider's recommendations, you can identify issues and start work on improvements.

Of course, you may have more than one contract, and may need to report on the success of your entire contract portfolio. This creates a pyramid of reporting as shown in Figure 5.8, which illustrates the increasing detail required to measure and report the Contract Scorecard. You will have the four quadrants, which will comprise any number of KPIs. These KPIs may have target performance levels as well as minimum standards, or combinations thereof.

In addition to reporting by contract, you may need to report the entire portfolio of contracts by quadrant as well, depending upon the needs of your

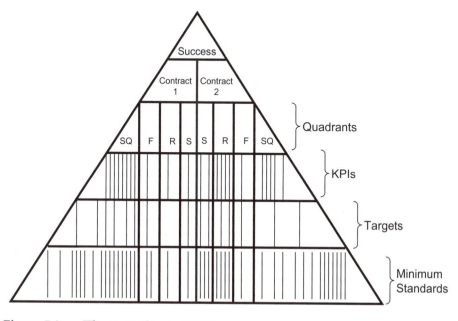

Figure 5.8   The reporting pyramid

stakeholders. For example, your Chief Financial Officer may only be interested in the financial aspects, the Chief Operating Officer in quality, the Chief Executive Officer on the relationship and the Board on the strategic aspects – or any combination therein.

Timing in the Contract Lifecycle

The Contract Lifecycle consists of four phases and nine building blocks (see Figure 5.9). A contracting deal is not just a piece of paper. A deal is more appropriately thought of as a business journey for which the contract is merely one step of that journey.

The Contract Lifecycle was developed and based on the processes that were attributed to achieving success in the 107 researched deals and organizations mentioned in Chapter 1 as well as those processes attributed to the root cause of failed aspects of the deals (see Cullen et al., 2005 for the academic paper on the lifecycle).

Figure 5.10 shows the most opportune timing for the development of the Contract Scorecard in the Contract Lifecycle. You will see that it is the first

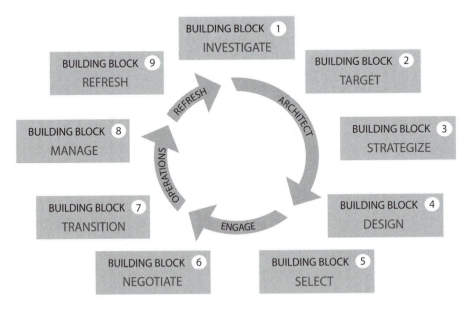

Figure 5.9   The Contract Lifecycle

The Contract Lifecycle

ARCHITECT PHASE

Building Block 1
INVESTIGATE

GOAL
- Acumen, not ideology

KEY OUTPUTS
- Gather insight
- Confirm expectations
- Collect market intelligence

Building Block 2
TARGET

GOAL
- Appropriate services identified

KEY OUTPUTS
- Contracting model
- Target services identification
- Profiles

Building Block 3
STRATEGIZE

GOAL
- Informed strategies

KEY OUTPUTS
- Configuration
- Feasibility & impact analysis
- Strategic roadmap
- Programme
- Skills
- Communications strategy

Building Block 4
DESIGN

GOAL
- Detailed future state

KEY OUTPUTS
- Contract Scorecard
- SLA
- Financial arrangement
- Governance Charter
- Strategic schedules
- All other schedules
- Contract conditions
- Contract management

You are here

ENGAGE PHASE

Building Block 5
SELECT

GOAL
- Best value for money

KEY OUTPUTS
- Detailed tender stages
- Evaluation team
- Selection strategy & criteria
- Bid package
- Bid facilitation
- Evaluation
- Due diligence

Building Block 6
NEGOTIATE

GOAL
- Complete, effective contract

KEY OUTPUTS
- Negotiation strategy
- Negotiation team
- Effective negotiations

OPERATE PHASE

Building Block 7
TRANSITION

GOAL
- Fast set-up, no disruption

KEY OUTPUTS
- Managed staff
- Final plans
- Transition team
- Transfer assets, staff & knowledge
- Governance structures setup
- Engineering
- Acceptance

Building Block 8
MANAGE

GOAL
- Results

KEY OUTPUTS
- Relationship
- Final framework
- Reporting
- Meetings
- Admin & records
- Risk mgmt
- Continuous improvement
- Issues, variations & disputes
- Evaluations

REGENERATE PHASE

Building Block 9
REFRESH

GOAL
- Next generation strategies

KEY OUTPUTS
- Refit current contract
- Outcomes & lessons
- Knowledge refresh
- Requirements refresh
- Options analysis & business case
- Next-generation options

Figure 5.10   Timing in the lifecycle

thing done when designing a deal – even before work starts on the contract documents. This is because it is the contract outcomes, first and foremost, that need to be addressed in the contract, to ensure that the appropriate underlying requirements, KPI measurements and effects of poor/good KPI performance are articulated. Otherwise the contract usually loses its focus and the Contract Scorecard, and the goals it represents, become just a 'nice if it happens' initiative – and not the driver for the deal.

Nevertheless, no matter where you are in the lifecycle, it is never too soon, or too late, to implement the Contract Scorecard, the lifecycle merely depicts the best time in terms of ensuring the deal will be successful in accordance with intent of the Contract Scorecard.

The remainder of this section will examine each of the four phases shown.

ARCHITECT PHASE

The architect phase is where the foundation for contracting is laid; it consists of the first four building blocks: *Investigate, Target, Strategize* and *Design*. The first building block alone, that of conducting investigations that result in your organization learning all it can about a potential contracting initiative from others (clients and providers), will yield important lessons that you will take on when designing you own deal, as the organization discussed in the case below discovered.

A STATE AGENCY GAINS ACUMEN, CHANGES ITS PLANS

A state government agency beginning a Business Process Outsourcing (BPO) initiative had formed some preliminary ideas and expectations, but believed it was prudent to investigate further. It investigated two state government agencies like itself, a federal agency and two private sector companies, studying in particular the service structure and strategy in each case, the sourcing decisions and lessons, and implications for itself, The organization studied public records and contacted key personnel at the firms and supplier.

This investigation helped form, as well as adjust, its previous thinking.

The management of the agency learned, for example, that market offerings didn't have IT systems up to their expectations. So they required the bidders to use the agency's IT system and propose a development process to move to a new system. This approach caused little disruption to operations during transition, and allowed the organization to fully retain all its information during the term of the contract.

Management also found the outsourcing market to be immature and disparate. So it opted for a staged open tender rather than a direct closed tender (invitation only), which had been the original plan. The winning bid ended up being from an organization it would not initially have invited.

In its investigation, management also observed the importance of having both a dedicated transition team and a dedicated contract management team representing the client's need and performing the client's obligations. When these teams were missing, or were not dedicated (had to make time in their normal day for the additional responsibilities), they observed significant problems. So management identified these team members right away and formed the core lifecycle project team quickly. They also gave all other employees significant professional and personal assistance in making the transition. As a result, this state agency didn't suffer the typical staff morale plunge and loss of key personnel that many others experienced.

Most importantly, the investigation taught management the value of the SLA schedule in the contract and the need to develop KPIs, which it had not known about. Management invested 2 months in getting the SLAs and KPIs right for the organization. Both parties credit that work with making the deal work smoothly over the entire term of the contract.

It is during this phase that you should develop the Contract Scorecard and related blueprint. This maps out how the deal will be put together to achieve your desired scorecard. As discussed throughout this chapter, various elements of the contract documents between the parties will need to be designed to ensure the detail underpins the scorecard. Otherwise, the scorecard becomes an afterthought to the deal and, more than likely, a nonessential overhead, which loses its effect.

As those organizations experienced with contracts know, there are a huge number of details to be handled in any contract deal. Most importantly, they know that planning and articulating the details really does matter. It is during the *Architect Phase* that you should pinpoint the required details and long-term solutions most likely to deliver the results wanted in the Contract Scorecard. Providers, too, recognize the eventual pain that ill-thought-out deals cause. As one provider stated, 'The customer from hell is the naive buyer.'

To avoid such naivety, organizations need to walk through the lifecycle before embarking on it, to decide what they need to know and what events or actions need to take place for the deal to succeed throughout its life and as a multigenerational programme (the next contract). For this reason, in the Architect Phase, organizations essentially need to work backwards from the last building block to the first to understand the entire lifecycle. They then need to execute from the first building block onward.

ENGAGE PHASE

The Engage Phase is where one or more providers are selected and the deal is negotiated. It consists of the fifth and sixth building blocks: *Select* and *Negotiate*.

Unfortunately, many organizations start designing their contracts here at the Engage Phase. But skipping the Architect Phase is equivalent to starting to build a house before it is designed, hoping everything will turn out right in the end. The Engage Phase is where all organizations should focus on increasing their bargaining power by leveraging the competitive tension that naturally occurs in this phase.

Competitive bidding is the most common selection technique, with most organizations using a tender (a request for proposal) to see how the marketplace will respond to its needs. This approach pressures providers to deliver their best value for money against their peers under competitive tension. To some this may seem obvious, but there are many clients who do not use a competitive tender. They tend to negotiate with a friendly provider (one that may be already be on-site, one that someone else knows about or one that they have already been approached by) in order to save time and money. The time and money savings are often illusionary however; it is merely a delay of the required investment into a less opportune time when the client has lost its bargaining power after the contract has been signed. We will be discussing more on bargaining power later.

The Contract Scorecard is very useful at this stage to help form part of the evaluation criteria and selection process, enabling your organization to select the provider/s that best demonstrate capability and experience in delivering the outcomes sought in the scorecard. The provider's compliance (or proposed alternatives) regarding the KPIs submitted in the client's draft agreement is a key component of an evaluation. In addition, the specified behaviours in the relationship charter/code of conduct are effective, particularly when used in conducting customer reference checks to ascertain whether the behaviours your organization wants are actually exhibited by that provider to other clients.

Likewise, the strategic goal achievement assessed in reference checks also forms part of the required vendor response.

Not having clear evaluation criteria prior to requesting bids from providers (let alone criteria which ensure that the possible providers have demonstrated experience in delivering the outcomes you are seeking in your Contract Scorecard!) severely curtails your ability to choose a provider wisely. This is clearly demonstrated in the following case.

A BANK APPROACHES THE MARKET WITHOUT UNDERSTANDING ITS NEEDS

A bank issued a voluminous Expression of Interest (EOI) in an open tender process before determining its evaluation criteria. After receiving 14 widely varying bids, the evaluation team realized it needed a structured evaluation methodology to select a supplier.

The 11-member team therefore convened a methodology workshop to develop the evaluation criteria. By its close, the team realized the voluminous EOI had elicited only 30 per cent of the information it needed to select a supplier.

To maintain the bank's credibility in the market, rather than shortlist to fewer suppliers, the team issued its Request for Tender (RFT) to all 14 suppliers.

Evaluating all RFTs added 2 months to evaluation and cost an extra $200 000, (not to mention the cost to the 14 suppliers). It took only 1 day to develop the criteria and the evaluation methodology, which would have prevented this excessive cost.

So much emphasis has been placed on negotiation in contracts that an inexperienced person could believe it is the pinnacle of the lifecycle – involving the greatest amount of work and the greatest risk of signing a bad contract. If it does become the pinnacle, then something, somewhere, has gone seriously wrong earlier. Either your organization:

- based its business case for the deal on ideological and optimistic beliefs rather than real evidence, and rushed naively through the lifecycle;

- had no idea as to the goals it wanted the deal to achieve, how the goals would be accomplished and how success would be measured (the Contract Scorecard), hoping perhaps that the provider would come up with something, or merely expecting success to appear out of thin air;

- did not draft a fair and practical contract that incorporated the long-term solutions required to make the deal successful prior to a tendering process – just grabbed a template, or worse yet, nothing at all, hoping that the provider's version of a contract would somehow represent exactly what your organization needs;

- did not develop a feasible BATNA (Best Alternative To a Negotiated Agreement), so it had no well-thought-out alternative if a provider changed its offer once at the negotiation table. This does happen – usually because it is the first time the parties have really tried to figure out what the client wants, in detail, and what it is willing to pay for those wants, also in detail;

- made itself vulnerable, perhaps by being on a short deadline, thereby giving the provider the leverage to act opportunistically. Again, this is caused by not understanding and following the lifecycle.

When the lifecycle model is followed, negotiation simply involves refining the exact wording of various documents. It should not involve give-and-take negotiations over the intent of the deal because that is when parties win or lose, depending upon the particular individuals involved and the degree of power each party has.

Within the 107 cases, contracts worth over USD $10–25 million a year were negotiated in less than 2 weeks using this approach, whereas other cases worth only a fraction of these took months, and in some cases years, to negotiate.

OPERATE PHASE

In essence, all previous phases prepare for this one. The real action is actually played out in the Operate Phase. This is where the benefits (and problems) of the deal appear.

The Operate Phase, where the deal is put in place, operationalized and managed through its term, comprises the seventh and eighth building blocks: *Transition* and *Manage*. It is in this phase that the benefits of the previous work done, and the failures of the work not done, come home to roost. The Operate Phase either proceeds smoothly as a result of the strategies, processes, documents and relationship management designed in the earlier building blocks or the phase suffers due to misinterpretations, ambiguities, disagreements and disputes.

As contracting becomes a core competency, wise organizations invest more in its management. Regular Contract Scorecard assessments are a key feature of this phase, tracking progress and making refinements to the arrangement based on the results. If they are not, surprising results are likely to occur, as in the case below.

A GOVERNMENT ORGANIZATION LEARNS HOW NOT TO MANAGE A PROVIDER

A government organization assumed that compliance with the contract was a foregone conclusion. It believed a signature on the contract meant that the entirety of the contract would now be delivered. As a result, it believed no oversight of the contract was required and handed over the contract to a low-level junior staff member given the title of Contract Administrator to manage it. The administrator didn't read the contract, as he believed 'it was the lawyers' job.' He also didn't undertake any performance or compliance reviews – merely filed reports, paid invoices and otherwise 'handled the administrative tasks' in accordance to what he believed his job was.

In preparation for the end of the contract, 4 years into the 5-year contract, the government hired an independent audit firm to evaluate the provider's compliance with the contract. This was done more as a formality, rather than in anticipation of any substantial findings.

After an extensive process, the auditors determined that the supplier was only 40 per cent compliant with the contract. Work totalling $200 000 a year had not been performed, most KPIs were not being reported upon let alone being met, many reports were not being generated, and the list went on.

The supplier noted that it had not done the work because the contract required its client to request the work, which they had not done (the administrator didn't know about the work or the requirement to request it). Furthermore, they didn't follow up on KPIs or request missing reports, didn't ask for performance reviews or planning forums, and so on. Sole accountability within the client organization for the contract had rested with the administrator, who was completely unaware of what the government's obligations were.

> The key finding of the audit report was that the client didn't install any governance over the contract, so the supplier was allowed almost complete discretion in what it did.
>
> As a result of this audit, and to better manage its next-generation deal, the government put in place a seven-person contract management team, led by a senior contract manager. This contract management function cost $360 000 a year, but it was required to obtain savings of $830 000 a year through specific contract-management activities, experienced personnel and proactive management.

REGENERATE PHASE

All contracts end, either through early termination or by reaching the natural end of their terms. During a contract's life, organizations and markets change, perhaps in ways that render past decisions inappropriate in the current context. For example, the degree of uncertainty may have diminished, market growth may have created more competition, provider capabilities may have changed and information disparities between the parties may have decreased. Thus, you should reassess the initial sourcing decision before coming to the end of a contract.

The Regenerate Phase, where next-generation options are assessed, consists of one building block: *Refresh*. Following this phase, the lifecycle begins anew, returning to the Architect Phase, where your organization prepares for its next-generation deal(s). Again, the Contract Scorecard is particularly valuable in assessing the deal's overall performance, as well as in determining its overall SWOTs (strengths, weaknesses, opportunities and threats). But without a Contract Scorecard to begin with, a retrospective analysis on success is a very difficult exercise, as the organization involved in the case below discovered.

> ### A UNIVERSITY FINDS NO BASELINE FOR ASSESSING BENEFITS
>
> Toward the end of a 5-year contract, the Vice-Chancellor of a university directed the contract manager to assess whether or not the benefits sought through the contract were actually being achieved. The results of this analysis were critical to the steering committee's planning on future contracting within the organization.
>
> No documentation, other than the original contract, had been maintained and none of the people involved in the original negotiations remained with the university. Furthermore, the current stakeholders all had differing opinions

about the original objectives. Some believed it was designed to save cost. Others believed it was to permit the university to focus on its core activities by contracting out non-core functions. Yet others believed it was strategic in that it was support to allow the university to broaden its educational product offerings.

The contract manager made a valiant effort, but he couldn't determine the intended benefits let alone whether or not they had been achieved. As a substitute, he enumerated actual achievements. What had worked well? First, conducting reference checks and using known approaches to supplier integration led to the supplier working well with other suppliers. Within the contract, locking in explicit accountabilities in the contract reduced finger-pointing between the parties. Then, giving the supplier a greater span of control (that is, responsibility for a process or a function, not just a task) improved the supplier's performance because the work could be measured by business outcomes via KPIs. He also found that using rewards as well as recourse motivated the supplier's behaviours in terms of working towards the KPIs.

All good news of course, but no one could actually establish what the organization's original goal or goals had been, or whether the contract had been successful – only in that the work was delivered, disputes didn't occur and the parties continuously improved it.

Critical Timing to Manage Bargaining Power and the Total Cost of Contract

You are in the greatest position of influence over the shape of the deal in the Architect Phase. Once you notify the preferred provider and begin negotiations, the power curve begins its downward tilt in favour of the provider (see Figure 5.11). For this reason, you do not want to be designing any key parts of a deal, including the Contract Scorecard, after you have chosen the provider.

This shift in bargaining power happens because the other competitors have been eliminated and you are now entering a monopolistic situation regarding the scope of the deal. This is the case, even if the other bidders are on call should the negotiation fall through, since you are rarely able to throw out the preferred provider and start negotiating with the second-place bidder – even if you have retained the right to do so. By this time, your organization is usually under time and cost constraints to execute the contract, further reducing its bargaining power.

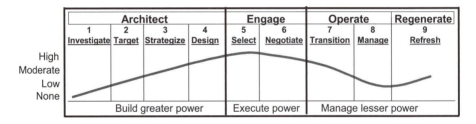

Figure 5.11   Bargaining power and the Contract Lifecycle

As a side note, there are many who think that negotiating with two or more providers at the same time (known as parallel negotiations) increases bargaining power, which you may do – but do so only sparingly. The losing provider would have financially suffered much more than the normal cost of bidding and may be reluctant to play that game with your organization again for a long time, if at all. So, if you want the losing provider to bid for your organization's contracts again some day, and especially if you think you might want them to bid against the chosen provider in the next generation of the deal, take this into consideration or risk having your future bargaining power in the market suffer. There are many organizations for which leading providers will not bid – the cost of winning, and more so losing, is just too high. Some organizations have chosen to pay bidders to prepare a bid in order to get high-quality responses to a deal. You want to make sure your organization does not get that kind of reputation!

After the provider has got the arrangement up and running – setting up facilities, people and process – you are even less likely to switch providers. Once firmly entrenched, the economic and political cost to your organization of switching mid-contract almost always prevents switching providers or backsourcing (bringing work back in-house).

A slight upswing in your bargaining power occurs near the end of a contract. This is the start of the 'second honeymoon' period, where most providers will attempt to woo the client again to gain an extension or further work. At that point, your bargaining power increases slightly and you may be able to get improvements into the deal. However, this is a long time to wait.

Because of the power swing of most arrangements towards the provider after the deal has been announced, you do not want to be designing any part of the arrangement after you have chosen the provider. This is why you design the Contract Scorecard and the deal you want to put to market, and then release it with the market package. Remember, the Contract Scorecard reflects your organization's goals – something you do not wait to develop under a situation where you have lost influence and control.

During the bidding process, the provider can suggest modifications to your contract documents, which you can choose to accept or not. Remember, your contract represents the conditions under which your organization desires to spend its money. This is a very different contract to the provider's version. That version represents the conditions under which the provider desires to provide the work for the price quoted. Most of the obligations will be on your organization in that version, whereas your version will put most of the obligations on the provider.

Basically, using the approach advocated in the lifecycle, you are telling the market, 'If you want my money, here are the conditions under which I want to spend it.' But, if you let providers drive the deal, you are allowing them to say, 'If you want my products/services, here's what you have to do.' The two different perspectives yield very different contracts if one compares the client's version of a contract to the provider's version.

The following case shows what can happen if you attempt to design the deal after choosing the preferred provider.

A STATE GOVERNMENT TAKES 2 YEARS TO DESIGN THE SLA AFTER AWARDING A CONTRACT

A state government was seeking to improve its reputation as a technology leader. It requested offers for an outsourcing contract covering its technology infrastructure in return for the provider building education and research facilities in the state, in addition to other industry development initiatives. Once the winning offer was awarded, it took nearly 2 years to negotiate the outsourcing contract and put in place SLAs. This was because the provider had begun taking over the state's infrastructure upon signing the letter of intent (the intent being that the parties would agree a detailed contract in due course). Once it had begun performing and getting paid for the work there was little motivation to agree to the state's desired onerous conditions. Moreover, in the course of providing the work, the provider discovered many situations where it believed the client had misrepresented itself in the client's tender documents, and thus would also not agree to the desired KPIs without obtaining significantly more money.

Besides the decrease in bargaining power after choosing the preferred provider, there is another factor critical to understand regarding the importance of designing the Contract Scorecard, and the contract that underpins it, during the Architect Phase. This concept is the *total cost of contract*.

The total cost of contract represents the amounts your organization pays out to the provider plus its cost of contract management. Costs can get way out of control if the Contract Lifecycle is not well planned and managed. There is a recommended path and a flawed path in Figure 5.12. The difference is proactive management.

Unfortunately, many organizations start their lifecycle at the Engage Phase where the provider is chosen (where the dashed line turns sharply upwards in Figure 5.12). But skipping the Architect Phase is highly counterproductive when looking at a deal from the lifecycle perspective. In order to save money in the long term, organizations need to invest resources during the Architect Phase.

For example, a study of organizations seeking cost savings (Willcocks and Fitzgerald, 1994) found that management made a 40 per cent difference in cost savings achieved. The risk of self-interest and conflict between client and provider always exists, which is why planning, implementing and operationalizing the details matters. As the CIO of a major bank that had outsourced its IT in 1997 in a 10-year deal commented, 'The major lesson? Getting sufficient *granularity*, in plans, processes and actions, to give us transparency, then control.'[1] Similarly, the account executive of the supplier summed it up in saying, 'Contracts are agreed in concept but delivered in detail. That's why they can break down; the devil is in the detail.'

Organizations that underinvest in the first half of the lifecycle typically end up with a much higher total cost of contract, as shown by the dashed line in Figure 5.12. As all too many deals have shown, without the initial architecting work, high costs inevitably show up later – typically, as loss of control, inadequate quality, extensive out-of-scope charges and excessive management time and effort, and so on. As a result, there tends to be growing belief during the Regenerate Phase that the organization either needs to backsource the contract (bring the work back in-house) or switch to another provider (get a 'white knight' to rescue them).

---

1   This quote is from Bob McKinnon, CIO of Commonwealth Bank, in August 2004. It is from an unpublished research project by Leslie Willcocks and David Feeny into implementing core IS capabilities.

Lifecycle Cost Escalation

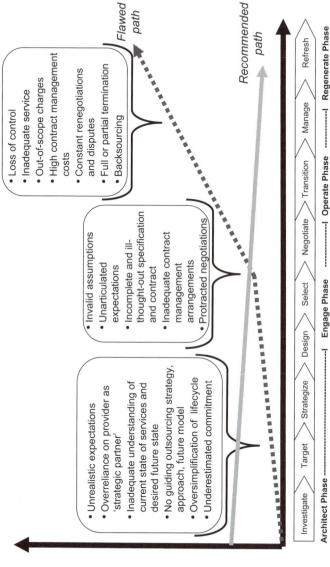

- Unrealistic expectations
- Overreliance on provider as 'strategic partner'
- Inadequate understanding of current state of services and desired future state
- No guiding outsourcing strategy, approach, future model
- Oversimplification of lifecycle
- Underestimated commitment

- Invalid assumptions
- Unarticulated expectations
- Incomplete and ill-thought-out specification and contract
- Inadequate contract management arrangements
- Protracted negotiations

- Loss of control
- Inadequate service
- Out-of-scope charges
- High contract management costs
- Constant renegotiations and disputes
- Full or partial termination
- Backsourcing

Flawed path

Recommended path

Effort/Cost

| Investigate | Target | Strategize | Design | Select | Negotiate | Transition | Manage | Refresh |

Architect Phase ——————————————————| Engage Phase ——————————| Operate Phase ——————————| Regenerate Phase

Building Blocks

Figure 5.12   Total cost of contract curves

Moreover, the contract management function becomes focused on variation management, firefighting and constant renegotiations – rather than any form of results-orientated contract management that a successful Contract Scorecard requires.

This situation is caused by inadequate preparation prior to negotiations with the provider, typically due to shortcuts taken during the Architect Phase. It is not until negotiations commence that you may begin to realize you made false assumptions about what the provider would actually be doing for the price it quoted. You may find that you have expectations you never clearly articulated, and certainly that the specifications and contract are only high-level. You may also begin to realize that your organization has not made adequate (if any) arrangements for managing the contract.

In short, contracting will be most successful if it is viewed as a strategy with a lifecycle rather than as a one-off transaction. You will have more successful outcomes, and your deals will operate in a cost-effective manner, when the entire lifecycle is proactively managed.

When you invest upfront, unpleasant surprises are minimized and the contract is more likely to work as expected. This allows the contract management function to focus on more strategic activities such as benchmarking price/ performance of the contract, relationship building and innovation – items common in Contract Scorecards.

The next four chapters provide detailed advice on the key commercial documents needed to make the contract and the Contract Scorecard happen in a successful manner. The commercial documents are presented in order of quadrant, starting with the quality quadrant that requires a robust specification called the Service Level Agreement.

6

The Quality Specification – The Service Level Agreement (SLA)

'What is conceived well is expressed clearly.'

Nicholas Boileau

About this Chapter and SLAs in General

The Service Level Agreement (SLA) defines what you want for your money. Good ones (ones that lead to outcomes that are more successful) specify:

- each party's accountabilities;

- the work to be performed by *both* parties (not just the provider);

- the reporting requirements of each party to the other;

- the metrics that will be used to differentiate good work from poor work (the quality quadrant of the Contract Scorecard);

- the incentives/disincentives that motivate good performance and mitigate poor performance.

As discussed in the previous chapter, an SLA is a schedule to the contract, and hence part of the legal framework as an obligation. However, it is crucial for it to be written in the language of the work rather than 'legalese' so that everyone can understand and work with it. It is also crucial for it to be prepared prior to going to market to help ensure your organization's needs are met (refer to the previous chapter on the Contract Lifecycle, for *what* to do *when*). The SLA forms your organization's formal 'product specification' and it must be detailed at some point. Leaving it until after you have picked the provider, at which point the power curve begins its tilt to the provider, means they – and not you – will drive the process. To say this may not be in your best interests is an enormous understatement, as the case below highlights so well.

NEGOTIATING THE SLA AFTER LOSING BARGAINING POWER

In this case involving outsourcing in an electrical utility, the SLA was negotiated after the fixed lump-sum contract was signed. No true negotiation ever took place. The SLA ended up being only what the supplier was prepared to deliver for that fixed price, irrespective of client needs or what the client had previously been performing. Furthermore, once in place, the supplier only provided the letter of the SLA and escalated client issues to its lawyers first, who then 'educated' the client organization on the agreement.

In practice, the term Service Level Agreement has had many meanings for different organizations. Sometimes the entire contract and schedules have been referred to as a Service Level Agreement; sometimes it only reflects the KPIs. In other instances, there have been no KPIs and the SLA was simply a traditional statement of work, scope of work or specification. In some cases, organizations have used the term to mean only internal agreements (between business units or departments) to attempt to develop more commercial internal behaviours.

Because of these different meanings, it is vital that all parties to your SLA have a common definition of *exactly what* the SLA *is*, and *what its components are*. To aid this understanding, the key components of a basic SLA are shown below and the discussion of each of these key components is given in the remainder of this chapter. A relatively general and basic example SLA is included in this chapter's appendix as well.

The key elements, or sections, that you might want to consider putting in your SLA include:

1. **About this SLA** – important information to understand, it sets the scene for any reader/user of the SLA.

2. **Scope overview** – summary of responsibilities, potential changes to scope and value-added services.

3. **Work specification** – comprehensive description of the work activities to be performed, products to be delivered and so on by both parties,

4. **Report specification** – comprehensive description of the reporting to be provided by both parties.

5. **KPIs** – the metrics by which the provider's work quality will be gauged (the quality quadrant of the Contract Scorecard).

6. **Recourse/reward regime** – the effect of good/poor KPI performance regarding quality.

A more detailed outline of an SLA is shown in Figure 6.1. Note that it is not vital that your organization uses this SLA outline word for word. If you wanted to have a separate schedule for the work specification, a separate one for reporting and a separate one for KPIs, then that is entirely up to you. What really matters is that that you have specified your requirements in a manner that is easily understood by all individuals in both parties that might be reading the document, that all readers can find the information they want quickly and that you have addressed all your expectations in a non-ambiguous manner. However, keep in mind that the contents of the SLA represent what you want for your money, and having it all in one spot may be the most convenient solution for the stakeholders in both parties.

Section 1: About this SLA

The first section of the SLA sets the scene for your audience by giving useful background and navigational information. It can provide any of the following details as succinctly and clearly as possible. (Note: not all of the following bullet points may be applicable to your organization's needs.)

- **Purpose/background** – explains how the deal came about and what the SLA has been designed to accomplish. Both of these areas help all readers of the SLA understand more about the deal and how this SLA fits in.

- **Stakeholders (optional)** – explains who cares about this deal, both within your organization and external to it and what they most care

---

1   About this SLA
    1.1   Background
    1.2   Format of this SLA
    1.3   Customers and stakeholders (optional)
    1.4   Service interdependencies and related responsibilities (optional)

2   Scope overview
    2.1   Responsibility matrix
    2.2   Potential variations (optional)
    2.3   Value-added services (optional)

3   Work specification
    3.1   Item #1 from responsibility matrix
        3.1.1   Goals/objectives of the work item
        3.1.2   Description and requirements of each activity comprising the item
    3.2   Item #2 from responsibility matrix
        3.2.1   Goals/objectives of the work item
        3.2.2   Description and basic requirements of each activity comprising the item
    3.3   Item #N from responsibility matrix
        3.3.1   Goals/objectives of the work item
        3.3.2   Description and basic requirements of each activity comprising the item

4   Reporting specification
    4.1   Strategic reports
    4.2   Performance (KPI) reports
    4.3   Operating reports (volumes, usage, capacity, etc)
    4.4   Progress/status reports (projects, changes, improvements, etc)
    4.5   Incident/exception reports

5   Key Performance Indicators (KPIs)
    5.1   Overview
    5.2   KPI #1
    5.3   KPI #2
    5.4   KPI #N

6   Effect of KPI performance
    6.1   Substandard performance
    6.2   Superior performance

Attachments (as required)

Figure 6.1   SLA outline

about. This helps the management of both parties know who they may be dealing with throughout the term of the agreement. Finding out the hard way is never efficient.

- **Format** – explains the various sections of the SLA and, in a complex deal, explains the SLA schedule and the other schedules. This helps any reader know where they can find the information they are seeking.

- **Service interdependencies (optional)** – explains how the SLA and the scope of work fit into the entire supply chain in a complex multi-vendor environment. This helps readers understand the bigger picture of the end-to-end service delivery and where the handoff points from one party to another occur in terms of the work.

Section 2: Scope Overview

As the name suggests, the Scope Overview provides a brief summary of the work areas covered by the SLA. Most importantly, this section includes a summary table of which party is responsible for what – called the *Responsibility Matrix*. This matrix is designed to prevent any confusion as to who is supposed to do what. It is also vital to understand this when developing KPIs since the KPIs can only be within a party's span of control to be effective. That is why it is the first step in developing KPIs (see Chapter 3).

To articulate the span of control of each party, the most efficient technique is to prepare the responsibility matrix. This sets out, in a very high-level table, all the major activities under the SLA and the allocated accountability between the parties (and other third parties, if appropriate). Figure 6.2 provides a partial example of a responsibility matrix for a printing contract (see also the previous example in Figure 3.1, page 50).

When using this matrix, the parties are better served when they adopt the principle that one or the other party is in charge of each work activity (no 'double ticking'). Those that try to share responsibility most often end up with no one accountable.

Another useful rule besides the 'no double ticking' rule is that each item with a tick must have at least one verb. This way you know what the party is supposed to be doing. For example, using Figure 6.2, item 3.3, if the matrix stated only 'Stock records' it is not clear what the responsible party is to do. Are they to stock records, as in store them somewhere? Are they to record stock? Are they to manage the records pertaining to stock? Any of these are possible interpretations, which means that the matrix has failed its objective to avoid doubt as to who is doing what. For this reason, a better description might be 'Ensure accurate stock records' if the responsibility was to maintain accuracy as was the case in Figure 6.2, item 3.3.

Activity	Responsibility	
	Contractor	Client
1. Order Management (section 3.1)		
1.1 Provide online ordering system	✓	
1.2 Provide customer service support	✓	
1.3 Order stock as required		✓
2. Printing (section 3.2)		
2.1 Artwork		
2.1.1 Deliver artwork		✓
2.1.2 Code and file artwork	✓	
2.1.3 Make changes to artwork as instructed	✓	
2.1.4 Maintain offsite backup	✓	
2.2 Print new stock	✓	
2.3 Conduct emergency print runs	✓	
2.4 Replace unsatisfactory stock	✓	
3. Inventory Management (section 3.3)		
3.1 Maintain form register	✓	
3.2 Stock levels		
3.2.1 Set minimum stock levels and reorder points		✓
3.2.2 Print reorder	✓	
3.3 Ensure accurate stock records	✓	
3.4 Obsolete stock		
3.4.1 Declare obsolete stock and provide destroy instructions		✓
3.4.2 Quarantine and destroy obsolete stock	✓	

Figure 6.2   Partial example responsibility matrix

Lastly, it is important to understand that this matrix is *not* the specification; this is dealt with later in the SLA. This matrix is just the scope at a glance, so that everyone can get across the key responsibilities quickly. So, if the line has more than a few words, you are probably starting to specify and run the danger of saying one thing in the matrix and another in the specification (section 3 of the SLA). Most organizations reference the specification in the matrix, though it is even better to create hyperlinks[1] so that users of electronic documents can quickly click and go to the actual specification.

This Scope Overview section of the SLA may also include useful information for readers such as:

- **Potential variations** – which describe foreseen events that may occur over the life of the agreement and possibly affect changes to the scope or KPIs. The longer the duration of the contract, or the more changes that your organization is going through, the more likely the SLA will need to be varied and it is useful to indicate the degree of possible future variability. In addition, because the SLA is provided along with all the other contract documents to potential bidders (see the previous chapter's discussion of the Contract Lifecycle, page 96) it helps bidders form their solutions.

- **Value-added services** – which were offered by the provider and accepted by the client organization, but are not part of the required scope. In other words, it is the 'free stuff' given by the provider. Having a value-added section helps both parties – your organization in making sure gratis items are actually delivered, and the provider in having a record so your organization does not forget that these are goodwill gestures.

Section 3: Work Specification

This section of any SLA tends to be the biggest part of it because it provides the detailed description of the work that all parties are to perform. To make the whole SLA easy to follow, this section follows the exact order of the responsibility matrix from Section 2. I should add at this point that there are *no* points awarded for creativity in writing SLAs; in fact, it is quite the reverse.

---

1   A hyperlink on Microsoft Word is a clickable link in text or graphics on a page that takes you to another place in the document.

If the SLA appears to be a random jotting of obligations, everyone will have a hard time working with it, and might even just throw it out.

But it is not just logic that makes SLAs successful. It must give the right amount of description necessary to avoid any misunderstandings as to the nature of the work to be performed by each party – not just today, but for anyone that might refer to it throughout the entire life of the deal.

Of course, misunderstandings are inevitable due to the always-present expectation gap between the parties. This is caused by different assumptions regarding the required work. Client organizations assume the SLA represents the minimum work that will be conducted and that the provider will do all other things that are 'necessary' with no extra charge. Providers generally assume the SLA is the maximum, and price the work accordingly. The better written your SLA is, the smaller the expectation gap and degree of resulting variations or disputes.

Generally speaking, work specifications should not detail *how* tasks are to be done. They should simply and clearly describe *what* is to be performed. In other words, work specifications should not look like a procedure manual. However, there may be instances where you must specify the exact process, but use caution whenever you do. In these instances, it is vital that your procedural specifications are as complete and comprehensive as possible. If your procedural specifications are missing a few steps, ambiguous or confusing, you are setting your organization up for trouble. If you add procedures later, most providers would levy additional charges if it results in additional work. And why not, if your lack of preparation puts them out of pocket?

For this reason, work descriptions tend to use wording that does not explicitly limit the work, and use language such as 'including, but not limited to,' 'for example,' and 'activities such as.' It also helps to avoid misunderstandings by having explicit exclusions phrased like 'for the avoidance of doubt, it does not include such things as ...'

Anything not reasonably defined (and by reasonably, I mean that an independent arbitrator or non-involved reader would interpret the meaning in the same way) has the greatest likelihood of attracting additional charges. The provider made its interpretation of the loose language when it quoted on the work, typically the cheapest interpretation possible in order to win. If you want to change that interpretation because what you wanted was not exactly what you said in the SLA, very few providers would let you do so freely. When it comes to the work specification, always remember it is *not what you meant* that will get done, *only what you actually specified.*

Shown next are two examples of a work specification. Both of these are for the same work, for call logging. See which you prefer.

The first one (Figure 6.3) cannot quickly or easily be referenced, either by people on the telephone or within the document, since it uses arrows and bullets which should be avoided in all commercial documents. The second one (Figure 6.4) has each specification numbered with an alphanumeric system.

Services
The Contractor will provide a system to log incidents. The Contractor shall receive and log all calls raised by the Client's and the Contractor's staff. The general scope shall include the following: ➤ Log the incident in a central database allocating a unique reference. ➤ Record the following information: • unique incident number; • name of user, user category, business unit and location; • incident category, description of the incident; • area/person currently assigned to resolve the incident; • resolution actions performed to date; • status of the incident (for example, open, resolved, closed); • date/time incident: reported, resolved, closed; • any other details as agreed by the Client. ➤ Assign a priority. The priority will be agreed between the Client and the Contractor at the time of problem logging. ➤ Notify the caller of the following details: • unique incident number; • priority; • next steps; • approximate timings of response/resolution. ➤ Notify other users if the Incident may affect other users – communicating the issue, the likely cause and estimated resolution time to those affected Users. ➤ Notify the Client of all incidents not fixed in specified resolution time.

Figure 6.3   Example work specification – bad practice

Services	Objectives
1. The Contractor shall: a. (**System**) provide a system to log Incidents in accordance with the System Technical Specification (Schedule 5); and b. (**Processes**) log, record, assign a Priority, and conduct notification processes for all calls in accordance with the Operator's Manual.	• Quick response • Complete and accurate records • Timely notifications

Figure 6.4   Example work specification – better practice

You will also notice that the second one is shorter than the first. This is because the first one incorporated procedures into the specification. The second one refers to an Operator's Manual for the procedural specification.

The first one also merely requires the provider to use a 'system'. Since the expected system is not specified, the provider has total discretion as to what it wants to deem a system and it will never be in breach. This could be a PC-based system, a paper-based system or just a system of jotting things down. The second has the system specified in a Systems Technical Specification that is in another schedule.

It is worth noting that this specification section also tends to produce the most entries in the contract's glossary. This is most commonly the first schedule to a contract, providing a list of all the words used in a contract that have been given specific meaning. It is the contract's dictionary. Reserved terminology found in the glossary is depicted within the text of a commercial document by the first letter being capitalized (although capitalizing the entire word, underlining or italics are also all common techniques).

This is important. If the words you use are not defined, each individual in each party are allowed to make up their own definitions. There could be many versions of interpretation with many different people and no one will be right or wrong.

As shown in Figure 6.4, the meanings of four phrases (*Incidents, System Technical Specification, Priority* and *Operator's Manual*) have been defined in the glossary. All readers must then use that definition and not put their own spin on it.

Contrast this to Figure 6.3. In the first sentence alone, all readers get to make up whatever they wish with regard to what a system is, as discussed earlier. They also get to make up what an incident is. If the provider decides not to log something, they can do so by claiming it was not an incident. Because the term is not defined, they are not wrong, no matter what the client had meant by the word.

Writing a specification that will be interpreted the same way by different people, not only within a single organization, but also between parties, is a skill that takes years to acquire. Most specification writers believe they do a good job and certainly their intentions may be good, but what they mean is not always what they say. Unfortunately, in a dispute, it does not matter what they meant, only what was written in the contract. A typical independent review of a specification will find material ambiguities in nearly every sentence! Unfortunately, most organizations do not conduct such reviews and consequently find out later, after the contract has been put into operation, that the specification should have been much clearer.

The key to a good specification review is having it reviewed by someone who thinks differently to the person who wrote it. For example, if an engineer wrote the specification, have it reviewed by an accountant. If anything requires an explanation, it needs a better specification. If the reviewer can offer multiple interpretations of a particular item, it needs a better specification. If the reviewer has to make any assumptions to understand it, it needs a better specification.

Section 4: Reporting Specification

This section of the SLA specifies what reports are due to whom and when. It is also important to at least outline the contents of each report. Most organizations have either far too much data or not enough, and nearly all of them are missing 'intelligence' – that is, insightful analysis of what the report is indicating. However, very few actually specify what analysis they want to see. You want to make sure that the receiving party is happy with the sort of information that will be presented.

An example of a reporting specification from a fault rectification contract is shown in Figure 6.5. The Title column provides the name of the report, the Key Fields column lists the information required, the Trend Analysis column gives the analysis required, the Distribution List column lists the individuals who are to receive the report and the Timing column shows how often the report is to be produced.

For most contracts, a specification similar to Figure 6.5 will suffice. However, some organizations prototype the exact report they want to see and include it in the SLA to make sure they are going to get what they want.

Section 5: Key Performance Indicators (KPIs)

The KPIs specified in the SLA are designed to drive the quality performance behaviour of the provider. This is where you put all the quality measurements

Title	Description	Key Fields	Trend Analysis	Distribution List	Timing	Report Category
1. Master Ticket Turnaround Time	Closed Master Tickets and turnaround time performance and trends	• Minimum, Target and actual KPI per Category • Number of Master Tickets raised per Category • Number of Master Tickets closed per Category • For each Master Ticket that did not meet the minimum KPI by Category – an explanation, rectification and prevention	Every month since Commencement by National and Regional: • Actual KPI, in total and by Category • Number of Master Tickets raised and Master Tickets closed every month • Closed Tickets carried over from previous month	National and Regional Managers	Monthly	KPI
2. Client Satisfaction	Rating results of Closed Tickets by segment	• Minimum, Target and actual KPI per segment • Number of '1' ratings • Number of and list of Tickets with a '5' rating and explanation, rectification and prevention	Every month since Commencement by National and Regional: • Actual KPI, in total and by segment • Number of tickets with a '5' rating	National and Regional Managers	Monthly	KPI
3. Open Master Tickets	Open Master Tickets at the time of report	• Number of Open Master Tickets per Queue Type • List of Expired Ticket numbers per queue	Every month since Commencement by National and Regional: • Number of Tickets per que at time of report • Number of Tickets with Expired KPIs per queue at time of report	National and Regional Managers	Monthly	Operating
4 Request Analysis	Analysis of the pattern of requested services	• Number of Requests per Request Code	Every month since Commencement by National and Regional: • Number of Requests per Request Code	National Manager	Quarterly	Operating

Figure 6.5   Example reporting table (partial)

discussed in Chapter 2. See the appendix at the end of this chapter for an example.

Section 6: Effect of KPI Performance

The effect that the SLA's KPIs will have on the provider is specified in this section. This is where you put all the recourse/reward programmes for the quality KPIs discussed in Chapter 4. See the appendix for an example.

Appendix: Example SLA

SCHEDULE 3 – SERVICE LEVEL AGREEMENT
Provision of Labour

Contents

1 ABOUT THIS SLA

1.1 Purpose, background and format

1.1.1 (**Purpose**) The purpose of this Service Level Agreement is to define the obligations of the Service Provider in performing the Services. This SLA does not detail how the Services are to be provided, such detail shall be provided through the procedures and operations documentation and manuals provided in part by the Client (CPPs) and in part by the Service Provider.

1.1.2 (**Background to this SLA**) This SLA is a schedule to the Contract. The Contract was awarded to the Service Provider under a competitive tender. An initial version of the Contract, SLA and other schedules were provided to the Service Provider for bidding purposes and this SLA represents the final agreed SLA.

1.1.3 (**Format**) This SLA has, as its key components, the following:

    a.   **Section 1: Context** – this section provides an overview of the SLA and the stakeholders.

    b.   **Section 2: Scope Overview** – this section provides an overview of the SLA and the parties' operational responsibilities.

    c.   **Section 3: Work Specifications** – this section describes the obligations of the Service Provider with regard to the delivery of the Services.

    d.   **Section 4: Reporting Specification** – this section lists the reports to be provided by the Service Provider and when due.

    e.   **Section 5: KPIs** – this section describes the metrics that will be used to evaluate the Service Provider's performance.

    f.   **Section 6: Effect of KPI Performance** – this section describes the impact of the (Service Provider's performance.

    g.   **Attachments** – this section includes the attachments to this SLA.

1.1.4 (**Definitions**) In this Schedule, except where the context otherwise requires, all reserved words, phrases and terms are:

    a.   denoted with the first letter of each word being capitalized; and

    b.   specified in Schedule 1 – Definitions to the Contract.

1.2 Stakeholders

1.2.1 (**Tables**) The tables below provide an overview of the key stakeholders to this SLA and their primary requirements. This allows the parties to understand who, both internal, and external to, the Client has a stake in the SLA, and what they care most about regarding the overall Services.

1.2.2 Client stakeholder table

Client Stakeholder	Primary requirements
1. Executive management	a. Value for money b. Assurance of good practice, quality service and legislative compliance c. Assurance Client's best interests are represented
2. Finance department	a. Accurate, timely and compatible financial data
3. IT department	a. Data compatibility b. Accurate and timely data updates c. Secure environment
4. Customers	a. Timely response to and resolution of issues
5. Projects group	a. Appropriate recommendations and input into future projects
6. Policy group	a. Assurance that policy has been complied with b. Knowledge of areas in which the Service Provider is having difficulties or encountering obstacles c. Recommendations for policy changes

1.2.3 External stakeholder table

Stakeholder	Primary requirements
1. Client customers	Availability and accuracy of the Services
2. Other suppliers and providers	Seamless integration of the entire supply chain
3. Media	KPI Failures and total costs of contract may attract media attention

2 SCOPE OVERVIEW

2.1 Responsibility matrix

2.1.1 (**Purpose**) The responsibility matrix is a summary table highlighting which party is responsible for what at a high level. The detailed description of the responsibilities is in Section 3 Work Specification. Cross-references to Section 3 have been provided in the matrix.

2.1.2 Responsibility matrix

Service	Responsibility	
	Service Provider	Client
1. Policy and Procedures (section 3.1)		
1.1. Prepare and maintain CPPs		✓
1.2. Prepare and maintain Service Provider policy and procedures	✓	
1.3. Comply with all policy and procedures	✓	
1.4. Provide ongoing recommendations	✓	
2. Quality Management (section 3.2)		
2.1. Operate a quality management system	✓	
2.2. Prepare annual QMP	✓	
2.3. Conduct reviews and implement improvement strategies	✓	
3. Workforce management (section 3.3)		
3.1. Operate a Workforce management framework	✓	
3.2. Prepare annual WMP	✓	
3.3. Ensure competent Workforce	✓	
3.4. Conduct training, assessments and manage knowledge	✓	
3.5. Maintain Attendance Register	✓	
4. Security management (section 3.4)		
4.1. Provide definition and indicative list of Category 1 and 2 events and findings		✓
4.2. Operate a security management framework	✓	
4.3. Participant in the Client's security initiatives	✓	
4.4. Conduct self-assessments	✓	
4.5. Report security breaches	✓	
4.6. Assist the Client in audits	✓	
5. Complaints management (section 3.5)		
5.1. Operate a complaints management framework	✓	
5.2. Manage complaints	✓	
5.3. Conduct monthly reviews	✓	
6. CFE (section 3.6)		
6.1. Provide and maintain CFE		✓
6.2. Use and control CFE	✓	
7. Provide reports (section 4)	✓	

2.2 Potential variations

2.2.1 (**Purpose**) This section provides an indication of what may occur during the Term that could affect the SLA. All variations must comply with the variation provisions in the Contract to be valid.

2.2.2 (**Rationalization**) During the Term, the Client will be undergoing a site rationalization programme. The results of this programme may affect this SLA in that Workforce numbers may be reduced once sites are divested.

2.2.3 (**Contact centre**) During the Term, the Client will be implementing a new contact centre. The contact centre may take up the some of the complaint management obligations currently the responsibility of the Service Provider.

2.3 Value-added services

2.3.1 (**Purpose**) This section provides the services that the Service Provider shall provide above and beyond the scope as outline in the responsibility matrix (Section 2.1).

2.3.2 (**Seminars**) The Service Provider shall provide two half-day seminars regarding evolving and leading practices relevant to the Client. Topics and attendees shall be approved by the Client prior to issuing invitations.

2.3.3 (**Facilitation**) The Service Provider shall facilitate introductions requested by the Client to other customers of the Service Provider in which to share ideas and management techniques.

3 WORK SPECIFICATIONS

3.1 Policies and procedures

3.1.1 (**Objectives**) The key objectives for the Service Provider's provision of policies and procedures are to have high quality and consistent Services delivery.

3.1.2 (**Approved policies and procedures**) The Service Provider shall establish, implement and maintain policies and procedures, which at a minimum, comply with all CPPs, with regard to the Services that meet the approval of the Client.

3.1.3 (**Compliance**) The Service Provider shall ensure compliance, at all times, with all approved Service Provider policies and procedures and CPPs.

3.1.4 (**CPPs**) The Service Provider shall make recommended improvements to CPPs for the Client's consideration on quarterly basis.

3.2 Quality management

3.2.1 (**Objectives**) The key objectives for the Service Provider's provision of quality management are the controlled development, implementation and improvement of procedures that contribute to the Services and achievement of KPIs.

3.2.2 (**System**) The Service Provider shall:

    a.   design and operate an ISO 9001:2000 certified quality management system covering the scope of this SLA;

    b.   ensure regular monitoring, measurement and analysis of the effectiveness of the SLA quality management system is performed; and

    c.   implement processes needed to continually improve the effectiveness of the SLA quality management system.

3.2.3 (**QMP**) The Service Provider shall prepare an annual Quality Management Plan amending as appropriate in accordance with the variation provisions.

3.2.4 (**Reviews**) The Service Provider shall conduct periodic systematic reviews that:

    a.   assess compliance with the Service Provider's defined processes, the quality management framework and identify gaps in the Service delivery requiring improvement;

    b.   include input and feedback from Customers on the Service Provider's service delivery; and

    c.   analyze complaints and disputes to determine causation to ensure Service Provider's defined processes achieve desired outcomes.

3.2.5   (**Implement improvement strategies**) The Service Provider shall:

a.   develop and implement improvement strategies, where reviews reveal poor performance, non-compliance, or Customers' satisfaction issues; and

b.   record and retain the history of strategy recommendations, and shall all track the implementation regarding progress and achievement.

3.3   Workforce management

3.3.1   (**Objectives**) The key objectives for the Service Provider's provision of Workforce management are to deliver the adequate numbers (as per the Workforce Management Plan) of appropriately trained and skilled Workforce to provide the Services.

3.3.2   (**Framework**) The Service Provider shall provide frameworks (strategies and plans) to ensure appropriate Workforce are employed, including but not limited to:

a.   recruit and retain Workforce with appropriate competencies; and

b.   develop and implement succession, backfill, and the like to ensure the appropriate competencies are available at all times to fill identified positions, leave (in all forms) and vacancies (whether temporary or otherwise).

3.3.3   (**WMP**) The Service Provider shall prepare, no later than eight (8) weeks prior to each Anniversary Date, and once approved by the Client, comply with the Workforce Management Plan, amending as appropriate in accordance with the variation provisions within the Contract.

3.3.4   (**Competent Workforce**) All Workforce shall:

a.   be professional and knowledgeable about Client structures and all locations;

b.   demonstrate a detailed understanding of the Services; and

c.   ensure care at all times to avoid injury or illness and comply with OHS Standards.

3.3.5   (**Training and Competency**) The Service Provider shall:

a.   ensure that the Workforce are appropriately trained, and assessed as competent, in all requirements within this SLA including, but not limited to:
i.   quality management;
ii.   client service practices;
iii. recording accurate and necessary data stipulated in this SLA;
iv.   CPPs and site-specific SOPs;
v.   CFE;
vi.   OHS requirements and compliance; and
vii. other training as directed by the Client.

b.   monitor and assess proficiency of the Workforce on an ongoing basis to measure the effectiveness of training programmes and amend where ineffectiveness is identified.

3.3.6 **(Training by the Client)** The Service Provider is required to send all Workforce to Client-provided training as directed by Client. The costs of sending the Workforce, and backfilling positions, shall be borne by the Service Provider.

3.3.7 **(Knowledge management)** The Service Provider shall ensure that:

a. all the SLA and Client-specific knowledge is coded into the 'what-if' scenarios with the directories;

b. the Client knowledge database, if implemented, is current and accurate regarding the scope of this SLA; and

c. the Workforce has immediate access to such knowledge without being dependent on any one individual's knowledge.

3.3.8 **(Attendance Register)** The Service Provider must provide and maintain an Attendance Register at each site, which is accurate and fully reconcilable to time sheets.

3.4 Security management

3.4.1 **(Objectives)** The key objective for the Service Provider's provision of security management is to safeguard all information in which the Service Provider has in regard to the Client, its personnel, Customers or any other Client-related information.

3.4.2 **(Framework)** The Service Provider must provide the following security management activities:

a. establish a management framework to manage information security for the Services; and

b. establish an organization structure to implement security measures.

3.4.3 **(Security initiatives)** The Service Provider shall participate, upon request by the Client, in:

a. security forums;

b. security coordination and cooperation within the Client and with external organizations;

c. vulnerability assessments, audits, and so on, of the Service Provider's environment, for which the Service Provider shall provide all necessary access, personnel and records; and

d. Client-directed security self-assessments of the Services and/or environment in consultation with the Client.

3.4.4 **(Security breaches)** All security breaches and security issues identified by any of the Workforce must be immediately reported to the Client.

3.4.5 **(Client audits)** The Service Provider must:

a. participate fully in any audits conducted by the Client;

b. allow unfettered access to all records, documents and the like (as required by the Client in its absolute discretion); and

c. implement the audit findings as directed by the Client.

3.5 Complaints management

3.5.1 (**Objectives**) The key objectives for the Service Provider's provision of complaints management are the:

    a.   early identification and clarification of complaints; and

    b.   cost-effective resolution of complaints in a timely manner.

3.5.2 (**Framework**) The Service Provider shall design and operate a complaints management framework that:

    a.   addresses, at a minimum ISO 'Complaints handling' or equivalent, as amended from time to time;

    b.   is readily accessible to Customers;

    c.   uniquely identifies every complaint and enables timely retrieval of documentation; and

    d.   ensures that all aspects of the complaint are documented and dated.

3.5.3 (**Manage**) The Service Provider shall ensure all complaints are:

    a.   recorded within 24 hours of receipt;

    b.   immediately notified to the Client;

    c.   acknowledged by the Service Provider to the Customer making the complaint, upon being recorded; and

    d.   given full and unfettered cooperation as required by the Client.

3.5.4 (**Review**) The Service Provider shall conduct monthly reviews of complaints to identify and mitigate system and practice deficiencies.

3.6 CFE

3.6.1 (**Objectives**) The key objectives for the Service Provider's CFE obligations are that CFE is controlled and used solely for the Services.

3.6.2 (**Use**) The Service Provider must only use CFE (for example, consoles, DRN terminals, office equipment, and consumables) provided by the Client in the provision of the Services.

3.6.3 (**Control**) The Service Provider must:

    a.   maintain an accurate inventory of all non-consumable CFE provided by the Client;

    b.   manage CFE in such a manner to avoid misuse, ensure conservative usage and ensure accountability;

    c.   ensure the non-consumable CFE is in good working order at all times;

    d.   notify all CFE deficiencies, losses, damage, and breakages to the Clier and

    e.   reimburse the Client for all CFE that has been lost, stolen, or damaged while under the control of the Service Provider.

4 REPORTING SPECIFICATION

4.1 Provisions

4.1.1 (**Objectives**) The key objectives for the Service Provider's provision of reports are to have timely and accurate information.

4.1.2 (**Reports**) The Service Provider shall provide the suite of reports in the manner, and of the specific content, as specified by the Client. The reports shall include, but not be limited to, the reports listed in the tables below.

4.1.3 (**Due dates**) The Service Provider must deliver reports by the following due dates:

    a.   monthly reports by the 15th of the month following the reporting month;

    b.   quarterly reports by the 20th of the month following the reporting quarter; and

    c.   annual reports no later than 1 March of the year following the reporting year.

4.1.4 (**Recommendations**) The monthly reports shall be accompanied by a letter of recommendations to the Client, the subject matter being at the Service Provider's discretion.

4.2 Monthly reports

Title	Description of Contents
a. KPI performance report	1. KPI Minimum Standard, Target and actual KPI performance 2. Performance points calculated 3. Cause analysis for any KPI Failures 4. Trend analysis of KPI performance compared to previous month 5. Status on any Rectification Notices, Corrective Action Plans, or Direction Notices
b. Workforce report	1. Workforce numbers trained by training programme 2. Comparison of training and numbers against the WMP 3. Trend analysis of Workforce numbers per Business Day
c. Complaints report	1. Number of Valid Complaints and total complaints 2. Review findings

4.3 Quarterly reports

Title	Description of Contents
a. CPP improvement recommendations	1. Policy 2. Issue noted 3. Recommendation
b. Workforce capacity analysis	1. Reconciliation of Workforce numbers by Business Day and week to the WMP capacity plan for the quarter

4.4 Annual reports

Title	Description of Contents
a. KPI performance report	1. KPI Minimum Standard and Target 2. Trend analysis over actual KPIs and performance points for each of the twelve (12) months 3. KPI achievement plans for the forthcoming year, no less than the KPI Minimum Standards
b. Workforce report	1. Workforce numbers trained by training programme 2. Trend analysis of training and numbers against the WMP for each of the twelve (12) months 3. Workforce capacity and training plans for the forthcoming year
c. Complaints report	1. Trend analysis of Valid Complaints and total complaints 2. Review implementation summary
d. Recommendations	1. Summary of recommendations for the year

4.5 Ad hoc reports

4.5.1 (**As directed**) The Service Provider must prepare ad hoc reports as directed by the Client and deliver as per the due date requested. The cost of any ad hoc report outside the standard capability of the Service Provider's information systems will be negotiated on a case-by-case basis.

5   KEY PERFORMANCE INDICATORS

5.1 Provisions

5.1.1   (**Measurement**) The Service Provider must:

  a.   have the systems and procedures necessary to accurately measure its performance against the KPIs; and

  b.   provide access to the Client upon request to verify accuracy.

5.1.2   (**Consequences**) For the consequences of a KPI Failure, refer to the subsequent clauses under Section 6 ('Effect of KPI performance').

5.1.3   (**Tables**) The tables making the remainder of this section define the agreed minimum performance standards for the provision of the Services.

5.2 Workforce management (specification in section 3.3)

KPI		Calculation			Performance Points	
Minimum Standard	Target	Frequency	Determined by	Source Data	Min Std Failure	Target Met
1. None	No Turn-over	Monthly	Service Provider	HR records	none	+ 3 points
2. No more than 4 continuous hours per Position unfilled	No unfilled Position hours	Monthly	Service Provider	Attendance Register	-1 point per hour per Position greater than the Min Std	+ 3 points

5.3 Security management (specification in section 3.4)

KPI		Calculation			Performance Points	
Minimum Standard	Target	Frequency	Determined by	Source Data	Min Std Failure	Target Met
3. No Category 1 security breaches observed by Client[1]	n/a	Monthly	Client	Security breach file	-10 points for each breach	n/a
4. No Category 1 findings	n/a	Ad hoc	Client	Audit report	-10 points for each finding	n/a
5. Three Category 2 findings	n/a	Ad hoc	Client	Audit report	-10 points for each finding greater than the Min Std	n/a
6. Implement Category 1 findings within 1 month of report	n/a	Ad hoc	Client	Audit report	-1 point for every Business Day over the Min Std	n/a
7. Implement Category 2 findings within 2 months of report	n/a	Ad hoc	Client	Audit report	-1 point for every Business Day over the Min Std	n/a

5.4 Complaints management (specification in section 3.5)

KPI		Calculation			Performance Points	
Minimum Standard	Target	Frequency	Determined by	Source Data	Min Std Failure	Target Met
8. No more than 1 Valid Complaint	n/a	Monthly	Client	Complaint register	-5 points for every Valid Complaint greater than the Min Std	n/a

[1] To avoid doubt, please note that security breaches notified by the Service Provider to the Client shall not accrue Performance Points in order to encourage such notifications.

6 EFFECT OF KPI PERFORMANCE

6.1 Provisions

6.1.1 **(Performance Points)** The Performance Points will be applied as follows:

    a.   **(Calculation)** The Client will calculate net Points on a monthly basis.

    b.   **(Non-cumulative)** No points shall be carried forward from previous months.

    c.   **(Value per month)** Each point is worth (+/-) $1000 as the case may be.

    d.   **(Cap per month)** Bonuses for meeting or exceeding KPI Targets are capped at $20 000 per month. Likewise, the rebate for failing to meet KPI Minimum Standards is capped at $20 000 per month.

    e.   **(Payment)** Incentives shall automatically be added to, or deducted from, as the case may be, the invoice following the month in which performance occurred in accordance with the offset rights provision in the Contract.

    f.   **(Plan)** Should the Service Provider be in accrued deficit for two continuous months, the Service Provider shall prepare a performance improvement plan addressing the areas in which inadequate performance of the Services contributed to the deficit. This plan shall be communicated and agreed by the Client.

6.1.2 **(Defect Notices)** In addition to provision 6.1.1, the Client may issue negative Performance Points for any non-compliance with the SLA other than in relation to the KPI Minimum Standards. Such non-compliance shall be recorded in a Defect Notice, and may accrue -0.5 (half) a point per Defect Notice at the absolute discretion of the Client.

6.2 Effect of good KPI performance

6.2.1 **(Extension)** The Client will extend the term of the contract for a period of 6 months for each twelve (12)-month period beginning six(6) months from the Anniversary Date under the following conditions:

    a.   an extension shall accrue for each six (6)-month period in which there are no KPI Failures; and

    b.   all accrued extension/s shall be cancelled if there are any KPI Failures in the last six (6)-month period of the Term, unless the Client notifies the Service Provider in of an extension granted and the conditions under which it has been granted.

6.3 Effect of poor KPI performance

6.3.1 (**Pyramid**) In the event of any KPI Failures, the following pyramid outlines the remedial action available to the Client in addition to Performance Points.

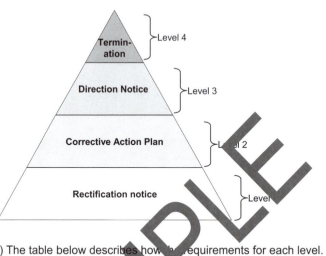

6.3.2 (**Levels**) The table below describes how the requirements for each level.

Level	Description	Actions
1	Rectification Notice	1. The Service Provider rectifies defective work at no cost to the Client, by the Client instructed deadline.
2	Corrective Action Plan	1. The Service Provider assesses the underlying cause/s of failure and prepares a Corrective Action Plan to prevent such failures. 2. The Client approves the Corrective Action Plan. 3. The Service Provider implements the actions by the agreed deadline.
3	Direction Notice	1. The Client makes its own assessment of the underlying cause/s of failure with full cooperation from the Service Provider. 2. The Client issues a Direction Notice to the Service Provider. 3. The Service Provider complies with the Direction Notice by the agreed deadline.
4	Termination	1. The Client determines, in its absolute discretion, as to whether the contract will be terminated in full or in part. 2. Should termination result, the Service Provider must pay for the cost of changeover to a new Service Provider. 3. Should the relationship continue, the cost of continued service must be at a significant cost reduction agreed by the parties, unless the parties agree on alternative action/s. 4. For a continued relationship, the Client will appoint an independent party, at the cost of the Service Provider, to evaluate the causes of failure and develop a corrective action plan that the Service Provider must implement by the date specified by the Client.

6.3.3 (**Application of the Levels**) To determine the consequences of the KPI Failures and corresponding action to be taken by the Client, the table below will be referred to.

Total number of KPI Failures	Number of Occurrences of the same KPI Failure in consecutive months			
	1	2	3	More
1	Level 1	Level 2	Level 3	Level 4
2	Level 1	Level 2	Level 3	Level 4
3	Level 2	Level 3	Level 4	Level 4
More	Level 3	Level 4	Level 4	Level 4

6.3.4 (**Examples**) Two examples of this are shown below:

a. Two KPI Failures in a rolling two (2)-month period will result in a Level 2 action – a Corrective Action plan required.

b. If a KPI Failure occurs four times in a rolling four (4)-month period, it will result in a Level 4 – Termination, noting Levels 1–3 would have been completed.

7   ATTACHMENTS

7.1 Rectification Notice form

Instructions: To be completed by Client in entirety

Rectification Notice		
Rectification ID #: _____ Rectification title: _____	Notified by: Client Representative name _____ Signature_____	Date of Rectification Notice: ___/____/___ Date rectification is to be completed:___/____/___ Date rectification was completed:___/____/___
Description of required rectification work (attach specification, if applicable):		
Process by which the Provider shall inform the Client that work has been completed:		
Description of actual rectification work performed:		
Rectification resolution: ❑ Rejected ❑ Deferred – until ___/___/____ ❑ Approved	Rectification approval signature: Client Representative name _____ Signature _____ Date ___/____/___	

This form shall be governed by the terms and conditions of the Agreement.
Nothing in this form varies the rights and obligations of the parties unless specifically identified.

7.2 Corrective Action Request form

Instructions: Shaded areas to be completed by the Client

<table>
<tr>
<td colspan="3">Corrective Action Request (CAR)</td>
</tr>
<tr>
<td>CAR ID #:

_____
CAR title:

_____
_____</td>
<td>Notified by:
Client Representative name

_____
Signature

_____</td>
<td>Date issued:
___/____/___
Implementation target
date: ___/____/___
Implementation actual
date: ___/____/___</td>
</tr>
<tr>
<td colspan="3">Recital of events leading to this CAR:</td>
</tr>
<tr>
<td rowspan="4">To be completed by the Service Provider
(attachments to be provided as appropriate)</td>
<td colspan="2">Root cause analysis of problem:</td>
</tr>
<tr>
<td colspan="2">Proposed rectification/fix:</td>
</tr>
<tr>
<td colspan="2">Proposed prevention plan over reoccurrence (including detailed implementation plan):</td>
</tr>
<tr>
<td colspan="2">Actual rectification and prevention work undertaken:</td>
</tr>
<tr>
<td colspan="2">CAR resolution:
❑ Rejected
❑ Deferred – until ___/___/___
❑ Approved</td>
<td>CAR resolution approval signature:
Client Representative name

_____
Signature _____
Date ___/____/___</td>
</tr>
</table>

This form shall be governed by the terms and conditions of the Agreement.
Nothing in this form varies the rights and obligations of the parties unless specifically identified.

7.3 Direction Notice form

Instructions: To be completed by Client in entirety

Direction Notice		
Direction ID #: _____ Direction title: _____	Directed by: Client Representative name _____ Signature _____	Date of Direction Notice: ___/____/___ Date direction is to be completed: ___/____/___ Date direction was completed: ___/____/___
Brief recital of events leading to this direction:		
Brief description of Client's approach to determining the direction:		
The direction to the Service Provider:		
Implications on the Contract or other work (if applicable):		

Direction resolution:
  Rejected
  Deferred – until ___/___/___
  Approved
	Direction resolution approval signature:
	Client Representative name
	
	_____
	Signature_____
	Date ___/____/___	

This form shall be governed by the terms and conditions of the Agreement.
Nothing in this form varies the rights and obligations of the parties unless specifically identified.

7.4 Termination Notice form

Instructions: To be completed by Client in entirety

Termination Notice		
Termination ID #: _____ Termination title: _____	Notified by: Client Representative name _____ Signature _____	Date of Termination Notice: ___/____/___ Date termination is to take effect: ___/____/___
Scope of Termination: ☐ Full ☐ Partial (if partial, complete the partial termination section below)		
To be completed for partial termination only	Scope terminated:	Variation Request ID #_____ *(form to be submitted with this Termination Notice)*	Resultant Price reduction: $ _____
Description of required disengagement work (attach specification, if applicable):		
Deliverables and due date for the disengagement work:		
Residual work (list work that may be required to be performed subsequent to the Termination Date). Note: The Contract may contain additional post-termination obligations.		

This form shall be governed by the terms and conditions of the Agreement.
Nothing in this form varies the rights and obligations of the parties unless specifically identified.

GLOSSARY EXCERPT FROM THE CONTRACT

For purposes of this book on the Contract Scorecard and to be able to better understand this example SLA, the following terms have been extracted from the example's contract.

Reserved words

Reserved word/phrase	Definition
Anniversary Date	The day that the Contract commenced for each year subsequent to the Commencement Date.
Attendance Register	The Workforce sign-in/sign-out book at each site that records, at a minimum: 1. date; 2. start time and Workforce signature; and 3. end time and Workforce signature.
Business Day	Monday through Friday excluding public holidays in the state of Delaware.
Category 1	High-risk event or finding requiring urgent remedial action as specified by the Client.
Category 2	Moderate risk event or finding requiring timely remedial action as specified by the Client.
Client	[Client name]
Client Furnished Equipment	All items provided by the Client (for example, consoles, terminals, office equipment and consumables).
Client Policies and Procedures	All policies, procedures, guidelines, manuals, instructions and the like provided to the Service Provider by the Client.
Commencement Date	The date the agreement officially begins: January 1, 2007.
Complaint	Any verbal or written expression of dissatisfaction with a decision, product, behaviour or service provided by the Service Provider under this SLA.
Contract	This Contract that includes this SLA and all other schedules that are incorporated into the Contract, as amended from time to time in accordance with the terms of the Contract.
Corrective Action Plan	Plan prepared by Service Provider for level 2 KPI Failure per provision 6.3.2.
Customer	Any individual that uses the Services.
Defect Notice	Issued by the Client for poor Service Provider performance, other than in relation to the KPIs in accordance with this SLA, which attract negative Performance Points.
Direction Notice	Notice prepared by Client for KPI for level 3 KPI Failure per provision 6.3.2.

Reserved word/phrase	Definition
KPI Failure	Failure by the Service Provider to meet the KPI Minimum Standard.
KPI Minimum Standard	The basic level of performance the Service Provider is required to perform under this SLA.
KPI Target	The superior level of performance the Client is seeking under this SLA, if applicable.
OHS Standards	OHS laws, as well as the Client's policies related to OHS.
Performance Points	Positive and negative points given by the Client for the performance of KPIs as well as in relation to Defect Notices.
Position	The number of personnel and hours agreed in the WMP capacity plan.
Quality Management Plan	The plan prepared in accordance with the Quality Management Plan specifications prepared by the client.
Rectification Notice	Notice prepared by Client for level 1 KPI Failure per provision 6.3.2.
Service Provider	[Service Provider name]
Services	The work performed by the Service Provider under this SLA.
Term	The duration of the Contract from the Commencement Date to the Termination Date.
Termination Date	The date the agreement is due to expire: January 1, 2010, unless otherwise agreed or notified in accordance with the agreement.
Transition Period	The period as defined in the Contract during which the transition will occur.
Turnover	Workforce that have departed from their employer, except if removal has occurred as the result of a direction by the Client.
Valid Complaint	A complaint that has been approved as a genuine complaint by the Client.
Workforce	The group of individuals that perform any of the Services whether they are Service Provider employees, contracted staff or personnel within a subcontractor, irrespective if whether permanent or casual.
Workforce Management Plan	The plan prepared in accordance with the Workforce Management Plan specifications prepared by the client.

Acronyms

Acronym	Definition
CFE	Client Furnished Equipment
CPP	Client Policies and Procedures
KPI	Key Performance Indicator

Acronym	Definition
OHS	Occupational Health and Safety
QMP	Quality Management Plan
SLA	Service Level Agreement
SOP	Standard Operating Procedure
WMP	Workforce Management Plan

7

The Financial Specification – The Financial Schedule

'Round numbers are always false.'

Samuel Johnson

About this Chapter and the Financial Schedule in General

Contracts vary from completely fixed to completely variable price, and anything in between. Successful organizations decide how they want their supplier prices to be charged to meet internal financial needs, to easily compare bids and to manage the payment process. Those that do not run the very high risk of severe cost overruns, just like the organization in the following case.

A PROVIDER GETS, AND USES, COMPLETE DISCRETION IN HOW TO CHARGE

The general manager of an international airline made an agreement with the top executive of a provider because they had worked together before and trusted each other. The deal was simple enough. The provider would take over call centre operations, the provider's core business, so that the airline could focus on its core business. This was to be a strategic partnership, so both parties believed they only needed a brief, high-level Memorandum of Understanding (MOU). The contract and other specifications would be developed over time.

Years later, after both executives had left their companies, an internal audit revealed that there was never a signed contract or a specification and, as a result, the supplier had been over-billing for years. Each business unit was being charged a price per call, and simultaneously the centralized accounts payable section was being charged for full cost recovery (even for such items as toilet paper at the provider's facility). The over-billing resulted from there being no detailed descriptions of the services included in the 'price per call' nor the items to be charged as 'reimbursable costs'.

The airline learned this lesson the hard way, for, as knowledgeable buyers know, you should never give providers complete discretion over what or how to charge you. Your organization must decide all the issues addressed in the Financial Schedule as part of your contract, *before* you seek competitive quotes.

The solutions you want to specify in the Financial Schedule include:

- **Costs** – description of each party's own costs that they must bear themselves;

- **Reimbursables** (optional) – what costs you will refund the provider and how, or alternatively, that no reimbursements of any kind will be permitted;

- **Invoicing** – how invoices are to be submitted and what happens if incorrect;

- **Payment** – how payments are to occur and when payment will be deemed;

- **Charges** – what the provider can charge as its prices to the client;

- **Key Performance Indicators** – the metrics by which the provider's financial outcomes will be gauged (the financial quadrant of the Contract Scorecard); and

- **Benchmarking** (optional) – how benchmarking will occur and what is to be done with the results.

The discussion of each of these key components is given in the remainder of this chapter. A relatively general and basic example Financial Schedule is included in this chapter's appendix as well.

Section 1: About this Financial Schedule

Best practice in contract writing suggests that all contract schedules begin with an introduction so the reader knows the intention and function of the schedule. Accordingly, this section of the contract provides the reader with the purpose of the Financial Schedule and a bit of background, if that would be useful to their understanding. It also can provide some context in the event of a dispute regarding intention.

Section 2: Costs

This clause details *which* party will bear *what* costs. If this is not clear, you may get an invoice that surprises you. For example, invoices from legal firms tend to be quite a surprise. Not only in the labour charged, but in all the extra 'costs' such as stationery, photocopying, secretarial services, telephones and so on.

In this section of the Financial Schedule, you first describe what each party is to bear regarding own costs, such as:

- giving effect to the provisions of, and performance under, the contract;

- complying with law, acts, regulations and the like whether they existed at the time of the commencement date or not;

- stamp duties and other duties, taxes, fees or charges payable to any government body in respect of, arising from, or in connection with the contract;

- the insurances the party is obligated to have and maintain in the contract including deductibles or excesses;

- mediation and/or court proceedings;

- rectification of any audit findings applicable to the party; and

- the exercise or enforcement of its rights under the contract unless otherwise agreed or determined by an expert, arbitrator or the courts.

Then you might specify the individual costs to be specifically borne by a party. An example is shown in Figure 7.1 but your specific circumstances may be quite different. In this example, the provider was given some accommodation but had to fit it out, had to pay for its telephones and tools, could not charge

---

2.2 (**The Contractor**) The Contractor must bear its own costs of all of the:

    a. fit out and telephone expenses in the workspace provided by the Client per Schedule 3 – SLA, clause 3.2.1 ('Workspace and storage');

    b. mobile phones and mobile phone expenses as required in Schedule 3 – SLA, clause 3.6.1 ('24-hour communications');

    c. tools and equipment needed to perform the Services;

    d. costs, losses, expenses, and/or damages howsoever incurred resulting from a Force Majeure Event or any other delay or disruption in the progress of the Services.

Figure 7.1   Example costs borne by the provider

extra for force majeure events (otherwise known as 'uncontrollable events', or in the old days as 'acts of God').

Section 3: Reimbursables (Optional)

Before we get into the actual charges in the next section, the treatment of reimbursables must be addressed. Many contracts have a hidden 'at cost' component often called reimbursables. Do not assume that these are immaterial costs that do not warrant your careful attention. Often, they can add up to large figures if you do not have mitigation controls in the contract and supply your own diligent oversight.

If the provider is able to claim certain out-of-pocket expenditures, the amounts they are allowed to claim must be specified in this section of the Financial Schedule. Such claims may be for airfares, accommodation, meals and similar expenses, but can also include equipment hire, uniforms, printing and any other item not explicitly in the contract charges (Section 6).

This section of the Financial Schedule is only relevant if you will be refunding the provider some of its expenditures. The primary purpose of this provision is to clearly state what will be reimbursed, if anything. If you will not be reimbursing anything, *then this must be clearly stated*. If your contract says nothing, then there are no rules and a provider that charges you for costs has not contravened anything (other than your assumption, of course).

An example provision related to specified reimbursements is provided in Figure 7.2 and comes from a maintenance contract.

7   **Reimbursables**

7.1.1 (**Subcontractor fees**) The Contractor is entitled to be reimbursed for fees paid to Subcontractors, provided that:

a. satisfactory evidence has been provided to the Client; and

b. the Contractor has complied with the Client's Procurement Policy.

7.1.2 (**Spare parts, materials and equipment hire**) The Contractor is entitled to be reimbursed for spare parts, materials, and equipment hire if satisfactory evidence of the cost has been provided to the Client.

7.1.3 (**Off-Site workspace and storage**) Should the Client revoke the provision of on-site workspace and/or storage pursuant to Schedule 3 – SLA, clause 3.2.1 ('Workspace and storage'), the Contractor is entitled to be reimbursed for the additional costs if the Client has approved those additional costs prior to incurrence by the Contractor.

Figure 7.2   Example reimbursables provision

Section 4: Invoicing

This clause gives the rules about invoicing and payment. A very basic provision should at least state:

- when the provider's invoice/bill/payment claim is due, and whom to send it to;

- the particular format required, including whether it is to be paper-based or electronic;

- tax treatment of the invoice;

- a list of anything that needs itemization;

- any ordering information, such as a purchase order number, work order number or contract number; and

- the supporting information or evidence that must be provided, such as subcontractor invoices, materials, equipment hire charges, and so on.

You may also want to consider having a time limitation on invoices so that bills do not come in long after the work has been done. Your accounting department probably hates receiving late invoices as it upsets their ability to manage liabilities, cash flows and budgets. It has been known for some providers to put in invoices years after the work was performed. Most organizations set a limit of 6 months in order for the provider to be eligible for payment. However, the most important thing is that you give them a reasonable time to invoice you, depending on the nature of the contract.

Lastly, consider what you want to do with invoice errors. These do happen and do not need to cause conflict between the parties. It can be as simple as stating that the client will immediately notify the provider when an error is detected (whether the invoice has been paid already or not) and can choose to offset the amounts owing, or issue a credit adjustment separately, at its discretion.

An example provision related to all these issues is shown in Figure 7.3 for the same maintenance contract that was looked at in Figure 7.2 (for continuity).

Section 5: Payment

It is too simplistic to assume that the only provision required here is the payment term (for example, 30 days from receipt of a properly rendered invoice). Of course, that is one of the issues addressed in this section of the Financial Schedule, but there are other issues you must consider as well.

The first one deals with late payment and whether the provider is allowed to charge interest for the days past due. Conversely, a decision needs to be made as to whether your organization will receive a discount for early payment. Either way (or both), the provision needs to state what interest and whether the charge/discount is billed separately or added to the next invoice. To ensure any interest calculation is not disputed, the date of payment also needs to be specified. This is more controversial than you might think. You will need to decide whether payment is deemed when issued by the client or when received by the provider, recognizing there could be many days in between if using postal services. Likewise, for electronic payments – you will need to decide whether it is the date the funds have been transferred out of the client's account or deposited in the provider's account.

Then there is the issue of whether payment will be deemed to constitute acceptance of the work/items. Often defects are not detected until after payment, so you may want to consider explicitly stating that payments are not acceptance, are not evidence of the client's satisfaction and are payments on account only.

3 **Invoicing**

3.1 (**Submission**) Invoices must be submitted:

   a. monthly, in arrears by, the 4th of each month;

   b. as a tax invoice in accordance with the Goods and Service Tax Act;

   c. to the Client's Authorised Representative;

   d. electronically, unless the Client directs otherwise; and

   e. clearly stating each signed off Work Order number being invoiced.

3.2 (**Invoice itemization**) With the exception of an invoice for the bonus possible in Schedule 3 – SLA, clause 5.3 ('Effect of good KPI perfomance – performance certificate and bonus'), each invoice must itemize the following charges separately, with a zero value if no charge was incurred:

   a. the Management Fee;

   b. Reimbursables separated by preventative works, minor works, and reactive works;

   c. spare parts separated by Critical Spare Parts and other spare parts;

   d. materials;

   e. equipment hire

   f. applicable taxes;

   g. Rebates; and

   h. any other charges (itemized individually).

3.3 (**Supporting evidence**) Each invoice must be accompanied by supporting evidence to enable the Client to approve the invoice including:

   a. copies of Subcontractor invoices and evidence of payment to the Subcontractors;

   b. receipts/invoices of all expenditure items; and

   c. additional information requested by the Client to verify the amounts.

3.4 (**Taxes**) The Client must pay to the Contractor the taxes relating to the taxable purchases. In doing so:

   a. the parties shall work cooperatively to calculate and reduce applicable taxes to the minimum required by law;

   b. if the Client asserts in writing, with reasonable support or an exemption certificate, that certain charges are not subject to tax, the Contractor will refrain from collecting and remitting such taxes and provide a refund if such taxes have been collected previously from the Client; and

   c. the Contractor must, upon request by the Client; supply a declaration of tax residence and obtain certification by the relevant tax authorities to enable the Client to utilize applicable double taxation treaties.

3.5 (**Time limitation**) The Contractor is not entitled to payment for any Services, work, materials, or reimbursement of any kind if not invoiced within three (3) months after the Service has been delivered, irrespective of whether or not a Subcontractor has submitted its invoice.

3.6 (**Invoice errors**) If the Client determines that an invoice has an error, whether already paid or not, the Client:

   a. must immediately notify the Contractor; and

   b. can choose to offset the amounts owing, or issue a credit adjustment separately, at its discretion.

Figure 7.3   Example invoicing provision

Lastly, consider whether you want *offset rights*. These allow monies owed by a party to be deducted against monies owning. For example, the right to offset any KPI financial recourse against outstanding invoices.

An example provision related to all these issues is shown in Figure 7.4 that continues the same maintenance contract looked at in Figure 7.2 and Figure 7.3.

Section 6: Charges

Contracts can vary from completely fixed sum, to completely variable, and anything in between. The three basic options for pricing are *Lump-Sum Fixed, Unit and Cost Based.* It is worth noting, however, that pricing model combinations, or hybrids, are more common today than any pure form, particularly with complex deals. The discussion of this section of the Financial Schedule walks you through each one of these, to put you in a good position to determine which option/s will work best for your organization.

The type of pricing arrangement you select will depend, among other things, upon the predictability of the demand/use of the service, predictability of the cost to provide and financial flexibility of the client.

---

4   **Payment**

4.1   (**Due date**) All amounts properly invoiced, and not in dispute, must be paid by the Client within fourteen (14) days of receipt of the properly rendered invoice.

4.2   (**Late payment**) The Contractor is entitled to charge interest for payments made after the due date specified in clause 4.1 ('Due date') above, at an annual interest rate of 7%.

4.3   (**Offset rights**) Without prejudice to any other rights, the Client may deduct from any monies that are otherwise payable to the Contractor:

　　a. monies which are payable, or owed, to the Client whether under this Contract or otherwise; and

　　b. monies expended by the Client to make good any breach or non-compliance by the Contractor of any provision of this Contract.

4.4   (**No waiver**) Nothing in clause 4.3 ('Offset rights') above affects the right of the Client to recover from the Contractor the whole of the debt of any balance that remains owing after any deduction or offset.

4.5   (**Date of payment**) The date of payment will be deemed to be:

　　a. if made by electronic transfer, the date the request was made to the Client's bank; or

　　b. if made by cheque, the date the cheque is received by the Contractor.

4.6   (**Payments are not acceptance**) Any payment by the Client is a payment on account only and is evidence against, or an admission by, the Client:

　　a. that the Services have been completed in accordance with the Contract, or to the Client's satisfaction; or are without defects; and

　　b. that it represents the value of the Services undertaken.

Figure 7.4   Example payment provision

Modelling the desired price framework in the Financial Schedule provides a better understanding of the potential impact of each potential cost to your organization and the potential total cost of the contract.

LUMP-SUM PRICING

The fixed lump-sum option (also known as the firm fixed price option) represents a single sum contract (for example, $2 million per annum. to operate a call centre). The fee is typically presented as a fixed annual cost for which invoicing is done on equal monthly basis, or as a lump sum for specific deliverables or milestones. An example provision is given for you in Figure 7.5. This contract had a series of lump sums for achieving milestones in a software development project.

Lump-sum contracting can be effective where demand levels and the cost to supply are both highly predictable – otherwise, the price will be anything but fixed. The critical success factors surrounding this option are listed below and described in this section:

- definite fixed demand and explicit scope specifications;

- certain cost to supply (or provider has demonstrated the capability to cover losses and has put in place contingent financial arrangements);

- explicit out-of-scope charges/schedule of rates;

5.1 (Milestone charges) – The Contractor is entitled to charge the following progress payments for the milestones below as specified in Schedule S2 – SLA:

Milestone	Description	Charge
Milestone 1	Mobilization	$80 000
Milestone 2	Stage 1 – Detailed design	$370 000
Milestone 3	Stage 2 – Build	$525 000
Milestone 4	Stage 3 – Testing and acceptance	$180 000
Milestone 5	Project closeout	$60 000

Figure 7.5   Example lump sum

- continuous forecasting against fixed price limitations;

- diligent variation management.

The rationale behind choosing a lump sum is primarily to lock in costs, thus obtaining predictable and controllable expenditures. However, some organizations choose it in order to have a single-figure invoice rather than a complex array of charges. The catch is, to obtain this single sum you often have to pay a premium, because a portion of the fixed price relates to the provider's risk in terms of the volatility of the cost to supply. If the provider cannot afford to take on this risk, disaster for both parties can be the result, as the following case highlights.

A MANUFACTURER SETS UP FOR FAILURE

This national diversified manufacturer of packing products has nearly 8000 staff in 242 plants in 40 countries. Manufacturing firms have outsourced subassembly and finished products for a long time. Thus, outsourcing the entire IT shop to one supplier made sense to this manufacturer to enable it to focus on its core business. After a competitive tendering process, a contract was awarded to a provider for which the manufacturer would be its first client in the country. The provider was new to the area and had built into the price an assumption that they would win new clients once they won this contract. The manufacturer sold all of its IT assets to the provider and in return signed a long-term contract on a lump-sum basis.

The provider was never able to attract any other clients and, once the perilous financial situation had gone on for a year, it began to attempt to claw back money from the manufacturer. To do this, it put in a new account manager, a lawyer, who proceeded to reinterpret every line of the contract. Variations, poor-quality work and disputes became the norm. As a result of this poor performance and extensive disputes, the contract was terminated 2 years after it had begun and a new provider brought in. Subsequently, the original provider closed its operations.

Outsourcing on a large scale to a single supplier under a fixed price necessitates a diligent supplier selection and management programme. But the manufacturer didn't understand the risks and how to manage them. It opportunistically picked a new, and inevitably unviable, provider that didn't have the necessary experience or financial strength to underwrite its fixed bid. Making the situation worse, the manufacturer didn't install any requisite governance and safety guards. There were no time limitations on invoicing (that is, preventing claims over 6 months from when work was completed), scope was poorly defined, no minimum KPIs were established and there were no agreed variation or dispute resolution processes.

However, the manufacturer did go with the same pricing option for the second-generation deal and experienced far superior results. This time it knew that it needed to perform careful planning, selection and management. It had two teams of lawyers (each generating an opinion or solution, with the client having them argue then select the best one), used scenario and behaviour testing to select the provider, as well as extensive viability assessment and an experienced management team.

Premiums are not the major drawback to this option, however. The biggest disadvantage is the inevitable misinterpretations (intentional or otherwise) between the parties over what is in and out of scope and the controversial out-of-scope services that attract additional fees.

In most cases, due to a variety of causes all triggering variations, the quoted fixed price was rarely the one actually paid out over time. Common causes are:

- volumes fluctuated over the fixed price cap;

- additional work, that was not in the specification or SLA, needed to be performed;

- the provider's interpretation of the work did not align to the client organization's interpretation and the provider held the balance of power, thus their interpretation triumphed;

- the client organization's needs changed, thus changing the scope of work;

- external price increase triggers occurred (for example, exchange rates, labour rates, cost of materials, and so on).

Consequently, this option is notorious for the need for variations. Since the provider has locked in its remuneration, what you are getting for your money is also locked in. If, for any reason, your provider is able to have a case for work being deemed out-of-scope (not in the fixed price), then it will normally charge you an additional fee.

Therefore, the key to success, when using a lump sum, is first to ensure that there are very explicit scope specifications. Then you must specify how variations are to be determined. Since most contracts tend to be longer than most people's planning horizon, the future can unfold in ways that the people that drafted the agreement did not, or could not, anticipate.

So you will need an explicit specification for charges regarding 'out-of-scope' work, which is typically a schedule of rates. When a schedule of rates for out-of-scope work is included in the Financial Schedule, the option you are then employing has evolved to a hybrid form (a combination of options). It is usual for an experienced client organization using the lump-sum model to adopt a hybrid in this fashion.

Even so, many client organizations often make out-of-scope work non-exclusive so that they can bring in alternative providers if the current provider charges too much, is not the best for that particular work or does not provide what they are looking for. You can even have an alternative provider just to facilitate a bit of competition.

Of course, this only works under the following two conditions: 1) there is an alternative provider readily available; and 2) the current provider does not have the power to unduly influence or reject the work of the other (for example, will not support the piece of added equipment, will only accept work by others with a release of liabilities, will not release KPIs, requires large fees for its own testing and investigation, and so on).

If these two conditions do not exist, the out-of-scope work is, in effect, a mini-monopoly held by the incumbent provider. One must always try to avoid being the client of a monopoly – there is little or no bargaining power available to such a client.

Another issue that commonly arises with lump-sum contracts is your ability to reduce price when your organization's requirements fall short of the volumes in which the price was fixed. For this reason, the fixed prices are most commonly banded. That is, there are fixed price bands for explicit volume ranges. Whatever band the actual volume falls into is the price paid, thereby granting you some flexibility to scale upwards and downwards.

There are likely to be other price limitations besides volumes that will affect whether the price is really fixed or not. These are often found in footnotes within the provider's bid, which can 'unfix' the price. Some of these limitations can include materials availability, labour availability and other capacity restrictions. Other limitations often revolve around pricing assumptions such as the Consumer Price Index (CPI), foreign exchange rates, availability of resources, and so on. Accordingly, an explicit agreement as to what are *all* the limitations becomes a key management focus at the contract drafting stage, and your organization's continuous forecasting against these agreed limitations becomes a key management focus once the contract is in effect.

Lastly, organizations with lump-sum agreements have found it difficult to unbundle lumped prices to assess cost drivers or benchmark individual work activity or asset costs. The need for underlying data then also becomes important in this option. Thus, organizations experienced with lump sums typically require a report regarding the underlying breakout of the invoice's single figure, if not with each invoice, then at least on a regular basis.

In summary, the rationale, risks and management issues of each option are reiterated in an example in Table 7.1.

Table 7.1   Rationale, risk and issues of lump-sum price

Example	Typical Rationale	Inherent Risk	Management Focus
$20M per year for call centre, complaints management and CRM (customer relationship) support	• Potential to lock in cost • Predictable costs within the specified volume bands • Explicit financial goal	• Misinterpretations over what work is 'in scope' and 'out-of-scope' of the price • Can lose track of individual cost drivers, as everything is lumped into one figure • Can be difficult to obtain reduced price if less volume is required • A portion of the fixed sum relates to the risk determined by the provider in terms of the volatility of cost to supply • Provider may lose money and start cutting quality; or worse, it may go broke	• Defining and managing explicit scope specifications • Agreeing charges for out-of-scope work • Monitoring price limitations such as volume constraints • Continuous forecasting against fixed-sum limitations • Maintaining ability to unbundle lumped prices to assess cost drivers or benchmark

UNIT-BASED PRICING

Unit-priced contracts charge a price per specific transaction unit (for example, $3 per call). This is a utility form of contract, whereby you only pay for what you use. An example of this is given in Figure 7.6, where the contract for document storage and destruction services has a different unit rate for type of service and uses different item 'units' as well. Only a small part of the total charges have been included in the example.

Unit pricing is also referred to as a 'time and materials' pricing arrangement if both the 'time' and 'materials' portion each have a stated unit rate. However, if the 'materials' portion is at cost or cost plus (see the following section), it is in fact a hybrid and the 'time' portion is managed differently from the 'materials' portion.

The rationale behind choosing a unit-priced model is primarily ensuring the ability to have fluctuating demand, while also being able to obtain volume discounts. Some organizations, however, choose this option because the work/items are charged back to business division on a usage basis, so they require an invoice from the provider itemizing each business unit's usage and respective charges. In this manner, invoicing is aligned to the business' charge-back needs.

5. Storage transaction charges

Service type	Item	Charge
a. Destruction	Business carton 10 litres	$1.40 per carton destroyed
	Business carton 20 litres	
	Business carton 30 litres	$1.80 per carton destroyed
	Business carton 40 litres	
b. Additions	New business cartons for storage 10, 20, 30, 40 litres	$0.70 per new carton
c. Retrieval	Business carton 10, 20, 30, 40 litres	$2.90 per item retrieved
	Document/voucher	
	File Retrieval	
d. Replacement/ re-filing	Business carton 10, 20, 30, 40 litres	
e. Permanent removal	Business carton 10, 20, 30, 40 litres	$1.10 per carton removed

Figure 7.6   Example unit price (partial)

The critical success factors surrounding this option are listed below and described in this section:

- demand management and warning triggers;

- setting the right volume guarantee or minimum guaranteed payment;

- explicit scope specifications on what work is included in the unit and what mechanisms will be employed to change the scope specification.

The last point on agreeing the work included in the unit is demonstrated in the two cases below. The first case is where the work kept changing and the second case involved an expectation gap of what the client would be getting.

CHANGING THE SCOPE COMPRISING THE 'UNIT'

A telecommunications equipment manufacturer had a unit price contract for the installation and configuration of its Standard Operating Environment (SOE) on all its personal computer equipment (desktops, laptops, notebooks, and so on). However, the manufacturer didn't consider that it might change its SOE over time when it arranged the unit price.

As a result, the impact of adding a product to the SOE wasn't incorporated into the original contract – neither a separate schedule of rates for possible product inclusions nor a process by which product additions (or removals for that matter) would be agreed between the parties had been put in place. Both SOE additions and removals occurred frequently and the manufacturer merely accepted the prices charged as it believed it had no other choice. The manufacturer eventually requested a renegotiation, in effect a re-offer, by the provider to gain some market discipline in an otherwise ad hoc, high-cost scenario. The requote was then subject to an evaluation by an independent consultant who assessed it against current market rates and assisted negotiating a more 'industry standard' deal.

NOT DEFINING WHAT THE 'UNIT' IS TO INCLUDE

A government-owned enterprise of 35 000 staff wanted to rationalize the number of application development providers it used. The CIO made a 'take it or leave it' offer to two of its 28 incumbent application developers. 'Give me as much labour as I need for a fixed hourly rate of 10 per cent more than what it costs me now in-house.' They both grabbed it.

The deal should have worked well. Rationalizing from 28 to two best-of-breed suppliers was anticipated to provide economies of scale and knowledge as well as maintain competition. Limiting the service scope to only applications development limited the risk of failure causing significant harm. The cosourcing approach was designed so that the three parties would become seamless – particularly since the enterprise required both the suppliers to work as one for each development. This being a pure labour contract meant that, in the event of failure, switching costs were not a significant barrier to terminating the agreement. The enterprise had good outcomes across the board according to the CIO. However, other stakeholders had another story.

In this case, the approach didn't lead to the seamless service delivery the enterprise envisioned; rather, it led to accountability confusion. The enterprise's staff believed the provider was to provide project management and development methodologies and leadership. The providers understood they were to provide only 'bodies' to follow the directions of the enterprise. At the time this was written, the vacuum created was still not resolved. To this day, the enterprise is refusing to pay more for methodology and the providers are refusing to give it away for free.

To minimize the overall costs under this option, most organizations guarantee some sort of minimum volume or guarantee a minimum payment to cover the basic permanent resources the provider requires. This base often has a fixed lump-sum price, giving rise to a hybrid price model. Otherwise, providers are forced to charge a high unit price when your organization's demand is too unpredictable or has no underlying minimum requirement in which to cover the provider's underlying fixed costs.

The main risk associated with this option is exceeding budget, as resource supply is effectively unlimited. When a function is insourced (performed internally), the in-house team often has to refuse more work due to resource constraints. Only in unusual circumstances would an external provider say no to more work. This is particularly pertinent if there has been pent-up demand. On the other hand, the provider may be able to generate latent demand (generate increased demand for services that may have been dormant). Therefore, your organization's ability to forecast and manage its demand becomes paramount.

It is still far too common to find, however, that adequate demand tracking and management systems and procedures do not exist within organizations. There have been many cases where organizations assumed the provider would perform demand tracking on their behalf, even though this was not made explicit in the agreement. Such organizations expect the provider to warn them 'if they are using too much' without being asked to do so. Such organizations have suffered frustration when given large, but valid, invoices. They suffer even more frustration when they ask the provider to perform demand management services as part of the contract – and get an even higher invoice adding in the new work. For this reason, unit-priced contracts often have a cap on demand limiting how much work the provider can perform before they need to seek approval from the client. But this is a poor substitute for the client actually performing the demand tracking and management that is required.

Lastly, as with the lump sum, the scope of what is included in the unit must be explicit in the Financial Schedule. For example, under a cost per call contract for a helpdesk, does the cost per call include logging, tracking and follow-up or just logging? The Financial Schedule must also be explicit as to when the counting of the units can start. For example, when can the provider start counting the hours under an hourly rate schedule – when the workers arrive at your office or when they leave their office? If you are not explicit, the provider can start counting at whatever point it chooses.

In summary, the rationale, risks and management issues of each option are reiterated in Table 7.2.

COST-BASED PRICING

Cost-based, or cost-plus, contracts allow the provider to pass on its costs plus a percentage mark-up (for example, cost plus a 3 per cent mark-up) or a fixed management fee (for example, cost plus $1 million per annum). An example is

Table 7.2   Rationale, risk and issues of unit-based pricing

Example	Typical Rationale	Inherent Risk	Management Focus
• 1st level Help desk – $3 call • Consulting – $50/ hour	• Volume discounts • Can reduce costs by reducing demand • Can track unit costs • Assists charge-back systems • Ability to choose the work required, when purchasing is optional	• There can be a premium if provider does not have a base guaranteed workload • Exceeding budget as supply is effectively unlimited, particularly if there has been pent-up demand or latent demand created	• Tracking and managing demand, as price is directed related to usage

shown in Figure 7.7. In this case, the provider was required to invoice a fixed management fee, but all its expenses were to be handled via a separate bank account where the client would deposit the reimbursed expenses after the client had certified that the expenses were valid.

This approach has value when the demand is unpredictable, the scope cannot be explicitly specified, and/or and the underlying costs are volatile.

The critical success factors surrounding this option are listed below and described in this section:

- detailed client knowledge of normal or best cost;

- cost reporting, benchmarking and auditing/validation;

- good accounting systems of the provider;

1	**Management Fee and Pass-through Expenses**
1.1	(**Management Fee**) In consideration of the Contractor performing the Services, the Client must pay the Contractor the Fixed Management Fee within thirty (30) days of receipt of the properly rendered invoice.
1.2	**Pass-through Expenses**
1.2.1	(**Expenses Account**) The Contractor must:
	a) establish a bank account separate from its normal trading accounts into which the Client will pay money for the purpose paying Pass-through Expenses.
	b) advise the Client of the details of the account within ten (10) Business Days of the Commencement Date, and must notify the Client of any change to these details during the Term within ten (10) Business Days of the change occurring.
1.2.2	(**Claiming expenses**) To obtain payment for Pass-through Expenses, the Contractor must:
	a) review, analyse and certify to the Client each month all claims for Pass-through Expenses;
	b) provide all information requested by the Client to enable the Client to analyse the Pass-through Expenses, including the work and services performed for that month against the claims made on a Site by Site basis, including, without limitation, copies of any tax invoices issued for supplies to which the claims relate;
	c) indemnify the Client in respect of:
	(i) any interest or penalties as a result of the Contractor not collecting a tax invoice in respect of a supply or where the Contractor fails to pay the any amounts due and payable by the date for payment; and
	(ii) any false claims made by the Contractor for reimbursement of Pass-through Expenses.
1.2.3	(**Payment into Expenses Account**) The Client will, subject to the requirements of clause 1.2.2 being met, certify the Pass-through Expenses due and payable for that month and deposit the certified funds into the Expenses Account.

Figure 7.7   Example cost-based financial arrangement

- mitigating controls over the provider's buying behaviour and prices it pays for the 'at cost' components.

The rationale behind choosing a cost-based price is primarily to have full knowledge of the provider's cost or because the provider cannot realistically predict what the costs will be (often the case with project work). A further benefit is that your organization is able to retain a better understanding of operations and can do more detailed benchmarking, if desired.

In theory, many organizations believe that this option gives greater control as well, but this can be illusory. Just because the provider can produce evidence that a cost was paid, it does not make it the best cost or even the actual cost. For example, it is well known that one can arrange travel with an agency that will print full retail value of an airfare, and give large volume discounts at the end of the year. Without mitigating controls, such as an assumed discount for travel built into the contract, a provider is not prevented from passing on the full retail value. This is why this option can have a high overhead due to the oversight needed to verify that best cost really is achieved.

To ensure best cost, some client organizations require the provider to obtain three quotes prior to committing to a purchase. Without a mitigating control, such as the requirement for an open tender in the contract (a tender publicly advertised), it is easy to arrange such quotes so that the winner is the lowest of three high prices.

Furthermore, without mitigating controls over the type of supplier that provides the at cost component, many providers arrange to get the goods/services from related companies. This is fine under competitive circumstances, but leads to higher prices where competition has not occurred. The following case highlights what can happen if this is not controlled.

A TELCO DISCOVERS COST IS NOT ALWAYS WHAT IT SEEMS TO BE

A European telecommunications company was advised by its consultants to form a service delivery joint venture (JV) rather than a traditional outsourcing arrangement for all of its IT services, as it 'was the best way to ensure compatible goals'. Therefore, it did. Although the telco had formed other JVs in the past to enter new markets, this was the first in which the JV would be providing services back to the company. Management didn't investigate how equity/service JV relationships work in practice and didn't set up any form of retained competencies, contract management or even JV oversight.

The telco was quite surprised to discover that the provider partner would sell labour and equipment to the JV at inflated 'cost' to make an immediate profit rather than wait to split the profit from the potential distribution of JV dividends. Management later put in a contract management team and an independent JV oversight board, but this was nearly 2 years after the JV had been operating – after significant cost escalation and inadequate service.

The cost-based option can cause you to bear a very high management overhead. It is inherent in this option that the provider does not have a motivation to reduce costs, particularly if it attaches a percentage mark-up over the cost base (for profit and overheads). In fact, the provider is motivated to increase the cost base to increase its earnings. As a result, you typically have to become involved in the provider's business and instruct the provider in lower-cost alternatives.

Continual auditing of the provider's cost is the norm here, because of this lack of inherent motivation for the provider to keep its costs low. The auditing needs to be continual because you can only redirect the provider's purchasing behaviour moving forward, not recoup past outgoings. Thus, if you find that the provider should have been able to provide goods/services at a lower cost, you may not get any money back, just cheaper prices going forward. The frequency of audits, and the audit costs, also tends to increase once an organization discovers a cheaper price. It no longer believes the provider is doing all things necessary to keep costs to a minimum; this leads to further auditing of cost evidence and buying behaviour.

To ensure costs are auditable, you would typically require extensive itemization in the provider's invoice, and also require evidence of the cost (such as copies of the third-party invoices) submitted with each invoice.

The cost-based option works well when the market price for a service or asset, or the hours taken to perform work, are either readily available from an independent source or are well known by both the parties (no information disparity). The client organization is well informed and the provider knows it, so any attempts to charge outside the expected amount without the client organization's previous accord will harm the relationship.

In summary, the rationale, risks and management issues of each option are reiterated in Table 7.3.

Table 7.3   Rationale, risk and issues of cost-based pricing

Example	Typical Rationale	Inherent Risk	Management Focus
• Equipment cost + 3% mark-up or • Equipment cost + $330k per annum	• Full knowledge of cost dynamics • Retain knowledge of operations • Can track unit costs, in particular when calculating Total Cost of Operations (TCO)	• Costs are known, but in the control of the provider • Costs incurred prior to investigations thus can only correct future behaviour, not recoup past 'losses' • Provider is often reliant upon client directions • Provider does not have inherent motivation to reduce cost	• Maintaining a detailed understanding of cost drivers and market prices • Directing provider's efficiency • Auditing and benchmarking of provider's costs and efficiency

CONSIDERATIONS REGARDING THE OPTIONS

There are many factors when considering which of the options, or combinations thereof, will work best for you. One of these considerations is *not* which one will be easiest. Each option has its own critical success factors, inherent risks and different management techniques required. All are very difficult if not chosen well and without appropriate management strategies.

However, there are a few salient factors to take into account, including:

- how certain you are that volumes will not fluctuate and scope will not change over time;

- how confident the provider can be in predicting its cost to supply;

- how skilled your organization is at managing the financial arrangement.

The simple decision flowchart below (Figure 7.8) has been designed to help guide your thinking process. Keep in mind that different scope bundles (logical groups of work) may call for different pricing options; thus you will need to go through the decision process for each of the scope bundles.

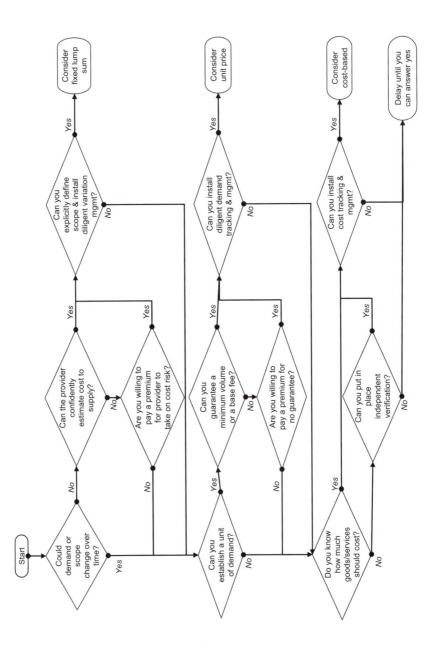

Figure 7.8   Decision flowchart

In all eventualities, it is likely you will need to use all the pricing options in a reasonably complex arrangement – thus your organization will need to be good at designing and managing all of them!

Section 7: Key Performance Indicators (KPIs)

The KPIs specified in the Financial Schedule are designed to drive the obligations of the provider regarding the financial quadrant of the Contract Scorecard performance. This is where you put the financial measurements discussed in Chapter 2.

Section 8: Benchmarking (Optional)

Many contracts are now incorporating some form of benchmarking in their longer-term contracts. It is a highly desired practice by client organizations but is often poorly executed. The discussion within this section of the Financial Schedule provides you with examples of benchmarking clauses and the experiences of those who worked with them. The purpose of this section of the Financial Schedule is to specify how the benchmarking will take place, and when and what is to be done with the results.

The benchmarking provisions within contracts are often quickly agreed to without much consideration. However, once a benchmarking exercise has actually been conducted, what to do with the results can become hotly disputed.

Take the example in Figure 7.9. It appears to be a straightforward contractual provision. Fundamentally the parties were to agree on the consultant, the terms of reference and share the costs of the benchmarking study. If it found that the current market prices were lower than those being levied, the charges were to be reduced to the market price. Simple.

The parties did agree on the consultant, a well-known international benchmarking firm (which many parties with similar provision do not). But that was the last time they agreed on anything to do with the benchmarking.

The consultant found that market prices were 20–35 per cent cheaper, so the client invoked clause 1.6 (Adjustment to Contract Charges) to adjust the

1.   **BENCHMARKING STUDY**

1.1. **Date of Benchmarking Study**

Within 18 months of the Commencement Date, a Benchmarking Study will be undertaken on the terms of this Clause 1.

1.2. **Benchmarking information**

The Supplier must ensure that all information it has which is required for the Benchmarking Study is made available and that it gives all reasonable assistance to ensure the success of the Benchmarking Study.

1.3. **Benchmarking organization**

The Client will initiate the Benchmarking Study by proposing to the Supplier the name of a suitable organization specialising in such studies. The parties must both agree upon the appointment of the organization to undertake the Benchmarking Study.

1.4. **Terms of reference**

The benchmarking organization will be provided with terms of reference agreed between the Client and the Supplier. The terms of reference will include determination of the range of costs associated with the delivery of equivalent services in equivalent technical environments to manufacturing customers in equivalent locations.

1.5. **Cost**

The Client and the Supplier will meet the cost of the Benchmarking Study in equal shares provided that both parties agree that the cost of the Benchmarking Study is reasonable. The cost of the Benchmarking Study is not included in the Contract Charges.

1.6. **Adjustment to Contract Charges**

Upon the completion of the Benchmarking Study, the Contract Charges shown in section will be adjusted as follows:

a) if the then current Contract Charges are outside the lowest price quartile (where the quartile consists of one quarter of the respondents to the Benchmarking Study) then the Supplier shall commit to reducing the Contract Charges so that they fall within that quartile;

b) the adjustment will take effect within three months of the completion of the Benchmarking Study; and

c) any dispute arising as a result of an adjustment under this clause will be referred to the Dispute Resolution Committee.

Figure 7.9   Benchmarking case

contract charges accordingly. The provider then invoked clause 1.7 (Disputes) to dispute the findings, claiming that the data was not in accordance with clause 1.4 (Terms of Reference) – it was not from data regarding '*equivalent* services in an *equivalent* technical environment' nor was it from '*manufacturing* customers' nor in '*equivalent* locations'. The provider's interpretation of 'equivalent' was so narrow that no organization in the consultant's database qualified.

The parties went to alternative dispute resolution with a mediator. After a lengthy process, the mediator determined in favour of the provider and agreed that none of the data used was 'equivalent'. There was eventually a happy conclusion to this case. The client organization continued with the contract until its expiry after 2 years, and then went to retender. It achieved well over 35 per cent cost savings by packaging the work differently and switching providers.

The problem with forcing the provider to immediately meet benchmarks, as in the above case, is that it tends to be quite a heavy-handed approach. It, in essence, assumes that the provider is intentionally overcharging. Once evidence is found regarding the 'overcharging', the provider is forced to comply – regardless of the situation that gave rise to the prices in the first place.

For example, the situation described below occurred regarding a client with an extreme situation of higher charges. The client was found to be paying prices for every service far exceeding the market price 4 years after signing, including:

- desktop and LAN services that were 54 per cent above the market median;

- the highest-ever encountered per call price for helpdesk services, exceeding the median per call by over 250 per cent, and the most expensive rate in the market by 57 per cent;

- data centre services that were 55 per cent above the median when expressed in terms of monthly cost per MIPS (million instructions per second) and 30 per cent above the median when expressed in terms of monthly cost per Gb (gigabyte).

Why were the costs in this situation so high? It is natural to assume that the provider was ripping off the client. But, in reality, some very basic decisions that the client had made affected the prices, so that they ended up paying much more. First, the client organization required that the helpdesk and data centre be on their site and wholly dedicated to them. Second, the client organization made the provider buy the client's IT assets at book value rather than the significantly lower market value. This cost, plus the financing cost, was then amortized into the price over the entire term of the contract. Third, the contract had fixed the future technology acquisitions at the costs that existed at the time the contract was formed. During the 5-year term, the price/performance ratio in the industry dramatically improved – but the client organization was stuck with 5-year-old prices. Fourth, the entire invoice amount was at risk for quality KPIs failure. This had the effect of ensuring that the quality KPIs were far below industry norms, due to the severe risk put upon the provider. For example, the contract only held the helpdesk to a 40 per cent of calls to be resolved on first contact with helpdesk, when the industry norm at that time was 70 per cent.

Merely stating that a provider has to meet a benchmark does not mean that they can. In the above case, significant re-engineering would have been required – moving the helpdesk and data centre off-site would have been just the start. For this reason, better results have been achieved when the benchmarking exercise is conducted in order to formulate an improvement plan, whereby the parties are able to work through why costs are higher, or services are lower than the market, and work together to implement solutions progressively.

An example of such a clause is shown below in Figure 7.10. Note that clause 1.4 requires an improvement plan that is to be implemented by an agreed date. In a worse case scenario, if the plan cannot be agreed, the client organization then has the right to terminate in clause 1.5. Those that have used a clause like that shown below have never had to invoke termination.

Benchmarking can work very well if it is done in the spirit of goodwill, and with the goal of continuous improvement. Give your provider the time to

---

1. **Benchmarking**

1.1. (**Exercises**) The Client may commission, or conduct itself, benchmarking exercises for all or part of the Services throughout the Term.

1.2. (**Terms of reference**) The Client shall provide the Contractor with the terms of reference regarding any benchmarking exercises that shall include the scope of the exercise and the benchmarking sample to be used.

1.3. (**Duty to assist**) The Contractor must comply with any request, and provide full cooperation, including access to relevant records and personnel, to the Client or its nominee in relation to any benchmarking exercised insofar as it pertains to the Services, this Contract, or the Client.

1.4. (**Results**) The results, but not the underlying data, of the benchmarking exercise will be summarized and presented to the Contractor. If the Contract costs are above the benchmark costs, or Contract KPIs lower than the benchmark KPIs, the Contractor shall, if requested by the Client:

   a) prepare an improvement plan to meet, or exceed, the benchmarks that meets the satisfaction of the Client; and

   b) implement the improvement plan by the agreed deadline.

1.5. (**No agreement**) If an improvement plan cannot be agreed, the Client may terminate this Contract.

1.6. (**Costs**) Each party shall bear its own costs with regard to any benchmarking exercises and implementation of the results. External fees in conjunction with benchmarking exercises shall be borne by the Client.

Figure 7.10   Example benchmarking provision

re-engineer to get there, and be prepared to make some concessions yourself. Otherwise, disputes are inevitable.

Appendix: Example Financial Schedule

SCHEDULE 5 – FINANCIAL SCHEDULE
Document Storage & Destruction Services

Contents

1. ABOUT THIS FINANCIAL SCHEDULE

1.1. (**Purpose**) This schedule identifies the charges the Contractor is entitled to and the method of invoicing and charging.

1.2. (**Supplements contract provisions**) This schedule is in addition to the Part F – Financial provisions (charges, invoicing, payment, etc) within the Contract, and all such provisions apply.

1.3. (**Definitions**) In this schedule except where the context otherwise requires, all reserved words, phrases and terms are specified in Schedule 2 – Definitions.

2. COSTS

2.1. (**Each party**) Each party must bear its own costs, fees, and expenses including those incurred:

a.   to give effect to the provisions of, and performance, under this Contract;

b.   in complying with law, acts, regulations and the like whether it existed at the time of the Commencement Date or not;

c.   regarding stamp duties and other duties, taxes, fees, or charges payable to any Government body in respect of, arising from, or in connection with this Contract;

d.   for the insurances the party is obligated to have and maintain in this Contract;

e.   for mediation and/or court proceedings;

f.   for official enquiries as per clause 40 in the General Conditions ('Official enquiries');

g.   for rectification of any audit findings applicable to the party; and

h.   to exercise or enforce its rights under this Contract unless otherwise agreed or determined by an expert, arbitrator, or the courts.

2.2. **(Regarding mobilization and disengagement)** The Contractor shall be responsible for the costs of all the:

a.   mobilization work to the extent it has been specified in the Mobilization Plan and this Contract; and

b.   disengagement and post-termination work to the extent it has been specified in the Disengagement Plan and this Contract.

2.3. **(Regarding Force Majeure)** The Contractor accepts the risk of all costs, losses, expenses, and/or damages (including damages for breach of contract at law) howsoever incurred resulting from a Force Majeure Event or any other delay or disruption in the progress of the Services under this Contract. The Contractor shall not be entitled to any monetary compensation of any kind or to recover any losses, costs, damages and/or expenses (including damages for breach of contract at law) suffered or incurred by the Contractor and/or in respect of a Force Majeure Event.

3. CHARGES IN GENERAL

3.1. **(Currency and taxes)** All prices in this schedule are:

a.   in US dollars;

b.   tax inclusive; and

c.   fixed for the Term.

3.2. **(Further charges)** The Contractor is only entitled to charge the payments specified in this schedule. The Contractor is not entitled to any further charges or reimbursements for any expenditures whatsoever unless approved by the Client prior to incurrence by the Contractor.

3.3. **(Decreases)** In the Contract, the Contractor has a duty to attempt to reduce charges through efficiency gains and shall do so. Notwithstanding that obligation:

a.   the Client may request a charge decrease if any benchmarking exercise shows that the charges are above benchmarked data, which

b.   the Contractor has the right to reject if reasonable cause/evidence has not been shown by the Client.

4. CLIENT'S RIGHT TO OFFSET

4.1. **(Deduct monies)** Without prejudice to any other rights, the Client may deduct from any monies that are otherwise payable to the Contractor:

a.   monies which are payable to the Client whether under this Contract or otherwise; and

b.   monies expended by the Client to make good any breach or non-compliance by the Contractor of any provision of this Contract.

4.2. (**Rebates**) Where there has been a Quality KPI Failure in accordance with Schedule 4 – SLA, the Client is entitled to the rebate so specified. The Client may choose to offset the amounts owing, or invoice separately, at its discretion.

4.3. (**No waiver**) Nothing in this clause 4 shall affect the right of the Client to recover from the Contractor the whole of the debt of any balance that remains owing after any deduction or offset.

5. INVOICING AND PAYMENT

5.1. (**Submission**) Invoices are to be submitted weekly to the Client to:

Name:	Liaison Officer C/- Account Processing
Address:	1 Main Street Somewhere, USA
Direct line:	(612) 830 6694
Facsimile:	(612) 830 6435
Email	John.smith@acme.com

5.2. (**Invoice itemization**) Each invoice must itemize the following charges separately by different Client branches and departments, with a zero value if no charge was incurred:

  a. weekly storage charges itemized by item;

  b. storage transaction charges itemized by service type and item;

  c. courier charges itemized by service type;

  d. other transaction charges itemized by service type and item; and

  e. destruction charges itemized by service type and item.

5.3. (**Supporting information**) Each invoice must be accompanied by any information the Contractor deems appropriate to justify the charges.

5.4. (**Payment**) All amounts property invoiced and not in dispute shall be paid by the Client within thirty (30) days of receipt of the invoice.

6. CHARGES

6.1. Weekly storage charges

Service type	Item	Charge per week per carton
a. Retention	Business carton 10 litres	$0.09
	Business carton 20 litres	
	Business carton 30 litres	$0.28
	Business carton 40 litres	$0.36

6.2. Storage transaction charges

Service Type	Item	Charge
a. Destruction	Business carton 10 litres	$1.37 per carton destroyed
	Business carton 20 litres	
	Business carton 30 litres	$1.76 per carton destroyed
	Business carton 40 litres	
b. Additions	New business cartons for storage 10, 20, 30, 40 litres	$0.66 per new carton
c. Retrieval	Business carton 10, 20, 30, 40 litres	$2.91 per item retrieved
	Document/voucher	
	File Retrieval	
d. Replacement/ re-filing	Business carton 10, 20, 30, 40 litres	
e. Permanent removal	Business carton 10, 20, 30, 40 litres	$1.10 per carton removed

6.3. Courier charges

Service type	Item	Charge per event
a. Delivery	Business carton 10, 20, 30, 40 litres	$0.66
	Document/voucher	
b. Collection	Business carton 10, 20, 30, 40 litres	
c. Routine courier	Business carton 10, 20, 30, 40 litres	$9.90
d. Priority courier	Business carton 10, 20, 30, 40 litres	$10.45
e. Urgent courier	Business carton 10, 20, 30, 40 litres	$18.50
f. Expedite courier	Business carton 10, 20, 30, 40 litres	$20.90

6.4. Other transaction charges

Service type	Item	Charge per event
a. Fax – Routine	Routine document/voucher fax	$2.91 per fax
	Urgent document/voucher fax	$6.89 per fax
b. Stationery	Bar Code Labels	no charge
c. File Insert	Inserting documents, vouchers, slips into current files	$2.91 per insert
d. Box provision	Provision of business cartons	$2.50 per box
e. Labo...	Data entry for cataloguing documents	$8.25 per 15 minutes

6.5. Destruction charges

Service type	Item	Charge
a. Bins	Secure 240 litres bin service	$17.60 per empty
	Loan – Secure 240 litres bin service	$20.9 per empty
	Rental per bin (normal and loan bins)	$1.10 per week per bin
	Cancellation fee	$82.50 per bin
	Missing bin replacement and delivery	$77.00 per bin
	Delivery or removal of non-missing bins	$33.00 per site (total deliveries, removal, and transport)
	Unscheduled transport of bins	
b. Destruction	Bulk paper	$0.49 per lb
	Mixed media	$2.53 per lb
	Secure bag	$13.20 per bag

7. FINANCIAL KEY PERFORMANCE INDICATORS

7.1. Provisions

7.1.1 (**Tables**) The tables below define the agreed KPIs for the provision of the Services.

7.1.2 (**Measurement**) The Contractor will have such tools and procedures as are necessary to accurately measure its performance against the KPIs and will provide the Client upon request with access to and information regarding such tools and procedures to enable them to verify their accuracy.

7.2. Benchmarking

KPI	Minimum Standard	Frequency	Calculation		Source Data
			Formula		
1. Benchmark	Contractor charges not more than 5% above benchmark price.	Annually	Contractor charges = average charge per Service Type over the year		Monthly invoices
			Benchmark price = as determined by Client's benchmarking team		Benchmark report

7.3. Invoicing

KPI	KPI Minimum Standard	Frequency	Calculation	Source Data
			Formula	
2. Invoicing deadline	Invoice received by the 4th day of each month	Annually	Received date = date stamped by Client's accounts payable	Client's accounts payable records
3. Invoicing accuracy	No inaccuracies		As determined by Client's accounts payable function	

7.4. Effect of good KPI Performance

7.4.1 (**Extension**) The Client will extend the term of the contract for a period of 6 months for each 12-month period from the Anniversary Date under the following conditions:

a.   an extension shall accrue for each 12 month period in which there are no Financial KPI Failures; and

b.   a Termination Notice has not been issued by the Client regarding Quality KPI Failures in accordance with Schedule 4 – SLA at any time, including subsequent to the award of the extension.

7.4.2 (**Retraction of extension**) All accrued extension/s shall be cancelled if there are any Financial KPI Failures in the last 6-month period of the Term, unless:

a.   the Client directs otherwise; and

b.   notifies the Contractor in writing of any extension/s granted and the conditions under which the extension/s has been granted.

8

The Relationship Specification – The Governance Charter

'The ultimate test of a relationship is to disagree, but hold hands.'

Alexandria Penney

About this Chapter and the Governance Charter in General

Good governance has been a topic of great interest in business in recent years. Not only because of recent corporate governance failures and corporate scandals, including Enron, Tyco and WorldCom which gave rise to the US Sarbanes Oxley Act of 2002. There have also been numerous contract governance problems, reported all over the world, which have increased costs and resulted in inadequate work quality.[1]

A decade of in-depth studies demonstrates that work cannot be contracted for and then not managed if an organization desires its deals to be successful. For example, an economic study conducted in 2002 found that the quality of services as assessed by the client organization is affected to a greater degree by the nature of the client and its management techniques than by economic factors such as competition (Domberger et al., 2002). Failure to focus upon critical issues or adopt key processes has also been argued to lead to an adverse affect on the client organization realizing its objectives (Nagel and Murphy, 1996). An extreme case of this is shown below, where not only did the client *not* put in any management, but also what little management it did believe was necessary was outsourced to the provider.

---

1   See 'U.S. failing to monitor millions spent on contract labour', 4 Nov. 2005, www.management-issues.com; Review of the Whole of Government Information Technology Outsourcing Initiative' Richard Humphry, Audit of Contract Management Practices in the Common Administrative Services Directorate, May 2004, www.nserc.ca/about/PIR/cmp/cmp_e.pdf; 'Accenture contract review', www.window.state.tx.us/comptrol/letters/accenture.

THE IMPACT OF BELIEF IN NO MANAGEMENT REQUIRED WHEN 'PARTNERING'

An insurance company had entered into a 'strategic partnership' with an IT organization. The board, believing that the supplier was now its official IT department and would act accordingly, saw no need to retain any IT capability. Furthermore, it believed since it 'wasn't in the business of IT anymore' it didn't need skills duplicated within the supplier. Accordingly, it outsourced the entirety of its IT people, processes, technology and strategy to the supplier. The board also put the supplier in the role of contract manager – effectively putting the supplier in charge of its own contract. Five years later, IT strategy was non-existent and IT costs were demonstrably higher than the market. The organization has started to rebuild its IT organization, beginning with the hiring of a CIO.

Contracts do not manage themselves and good management of contracts does not happen by accident. This chapter shows you how to prepare a Governance Charter, a key document in ensuring good governance of a contract by both parties.

There are many perceptions of what the term governance means, and a number of context-specific interpretations. For the purposes of the Contract Scorecard, and the contract relationship in general, governance consists of the rules, processes and behaviour of the parties that facilitate involvement, accountability, effectiveness and consistency between the parties.

Merely having a good working relationship between the individuals within the parties should not be relied upon in lieu of having proper governance in place. This is because relationships are between people, not organizations, and people sometimes are sacked, are promoted or leave to join a new company. If there is no proper governance structure and procedures that exist independently of the personal relationship, far too much reliance can be placed on the unwritten understanding which is difficult to identify and prove, and has a habit of changing over time, when different people become involved with the deal.

Organizations that desire effective relationships to be consistently demonstrated by both parties, at all levels in either party, have adopted a form of agreement, called a 'Governance Charter'. The Governance Charter is a relatively simple tool that facilitates successful management of the deal for both parties because it forces the parties to think about and agree how they will work together. It imposes a commitment on both sides to manage the deal in a diligent and agreed manner thereby ensuring strong controls as well as facilitating an efficient working relationship.

It defines the management roles and responsibilities of each party, the meetings and reviews, and the processes surrounding issue, dispute and variation management – all of which are critical to the success of your deal.

This chapter walks you through each element of the Governance Charter listed below:

1. **Relationship structure and roles** – who in each party is responsible for what;

2. **Relationship Values Charter/Code of Conduct** – how all individuals involved with the contract are to conduct themselves (the relationship quadrant of the Contract Scorecard);

3. **Meetings** – who will get together to discuss what and how often they will do it;

4. **Reviews** – who will assess what and how often;

5. **Issue management** – how problems and ideas for improvements will be raised, tracked and resolved;

6. **Variation management** – how amendments, modifications and corrections will be raised, tracked and accepted or rejected;

7. **Dispute management** – how difference of opinion will be raised, tracked and resolved.

While you may find in your contracts that some of these matters have been addressed in some capacity, rarely will you find them all readily accessible in one spot in an easy to understand format. When good governance needs to be an ongoing process, that process is not assisted by having odd clauses scattered throughout the contract. Rather, the Governance Charter provides the 'one-stop-shop' document providing the agreed governance mechanisms.

The rest of this chapter discusses each section of the Governance Charter, and provides you with tips on preparing and managing it. An example is also provided in the appendix to this chapter.

Section 1: About this Governance Charter

Best practice in contract writing suggests that all contract schedules begin with an introduction so the reader knows the intention and function of the schedule. Accordingly, this section of the Charter provides the reader with the purpose of the Governance Charter and a bit of background, if that will be useful to aid their understanding.

Section 2: Governance Structure

This section provides an organization chart regarding the management of the contract. A table depicting the accountabilities of the roles in the structure follows it.

Without clarity as to the individuals' roles in both parties, understanding who is managing what, who can approve what and who to go to for what becomes a drawn-out exploratory process.

If you think about how many people might have a discussion, some form of correspondence, or even just contact with anyone in other party – there could be quite a few people acting with presumed authority and inadvertently committing your organization or conducting *estoppel* (varying the contract by their conduct). A fair number of disputes arise this way: an internally unauthorized individual says or does something they perhaps should not have, and both of the parties are left with the fallout.

To put in place the desired governance structure, a simple diagram such as that shown in Figure 8.1, can provide much needed clarity in, and control over, relationships. In this case, the diagram was for a complex maintenance contract in a state-based utility. Because it was a centralized client confined to one state, the governance structure was relatively straightforward in terms of hierarchy and inter-party relationships.

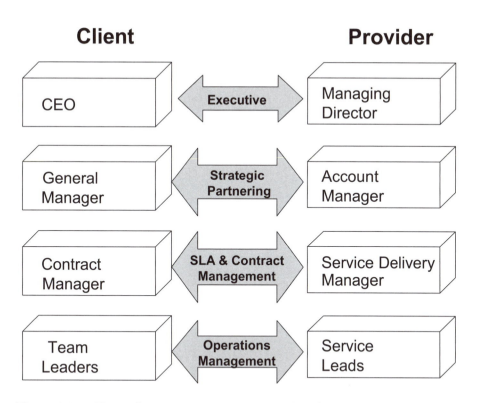

Figure 8.1   Example governance structure – simple

The next diagram, Figure 8.2, was for a global equipment contract in a decentralized client, making the governance structure more complex although the deal itself was relatively straightforward. In this case, relationships between the parties were required at a global level, then at a country-based level for each of the countries in which the client operated.

Once the structure has been planned, you define the responsibilities of each role. Table 8.1 provides an example of this, using the governance organization chart depicted in the simple governance structure from Figure 8.1.

It is important that the accountabilities are mutually exclusive, that is: two people within the same organization should not have the same accountability regarding the contract; if they do, then clarity of responsibilities cannot be achieved.

You may want to consider having accountabilities within the table, including signoff authorities such as monetary amounts and/or document approvals

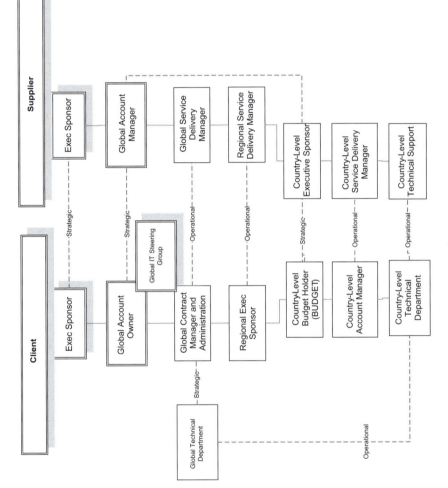

Figure 8.2 **Example governance structure – more complex**

Table 8.1   Example accountabilities

Client	Provider
1. CEO a. Resolve disputes with Managing Director b. Planning and strategic relationship management	1. Managing Director a. Resolve disputes with CEO b. Planning and strategic relationship management
2. General Manager a. Liaise with Account Manager to resolve escalated issues b. Conduct annual strategic reviews	2. Account Manager a. Liaise with General Manager to resolve escalated issues b. Conduct account planning
3. Contract Manager a. Liaise with Service Delivery Manager b. Manage client's day-to-day responsibilities c. Approve invoices, resolutions and variations or escalate d. Conduct performance reviews	3. Service Delivery Manager a. Liaise with Contract Manager b. Manage provider's day-to-day responsibilities c. Prepare reports and meeting information d. Conduct audits
4. Team Leaders a. Liaise with Service Leads to resolve issues b. Attend fortnightly operations meetings	4. Service Leads a. Liaise with Team Leaders to resolve issues b. Supervise workforce c. Lead operations meetings

(that is, invoices, reports, variation requests, and so on), if this kind of detail is important to the deal.

All of this goes a long way to clarify roles, and in doing so provides you with proper control over relationships, as well as saving your organization a great deal of frustration regarding who to contact for what, without which things can easily get out of control.

Section 3: Relationship Values Charter (or Code of Conduct)

The Relationship Values Charter, or Code of Conduct (whichever you prefer), was discussed in Chapter 2 regarding the relationship quadrant of the Contract Scorecard. If you remember, this part of the Governance Charter specifies the behaviours all parties are to exhibit during the course of the contract and details the scoring mechanism that will be used.

In Chapter 2, an example was provided regarding a maintenance contract in the utilities industry (Figure 2.18, on page 36). In Figure 8.3 is another example, that of a communication equipment manufacturer and its major global

---

RELATIONSHIP VALUES CHARTER

1   Overview

1.1   (**Purpose**) This Relationship Values Charter identifies the behaviour that the parties agree to exhibit during the course of the Term of the Contract. The parties have agreed that if the Contract is to operate effectively, both parties must drive towards a 'partnering' style of relati onship. To achieve this, the parties have set out their common goals in this Relationship Values Charter that are to operate during the Contract and shall use this as a process for relationship review and improvement.

1.2   (**No effect on legal relationship**) The parties agree that their legal relationship must always be governed by the Contract. Nevertheless, the parties have identified that this process needs to be implemented to enable both parties to operate effectively without the Contract being relied on in every instance.

2   Conduct to be Demonstrated by the Parties

Conduct	Description
1. Service expectations	We do not desire to apply Service Fee Adjustments. The Services will be of a consistent high standard, comparable to market standards, and the End Users will be delighted.
2. Communication	We will communicate frequently, openly and honestly with each other
3. Meet needs	We will be both proactive and reactive to each other's needs. We will provide each other time and management focus.
4. Creative Solutions	We will constantly search for better ways of doing things
5. Conflict	We recognize conflict as natural and will focus on solving the problem, not apportioning blame. We will resolve conflict at the lowest level appropriate.
6. Fairness	We will be fair to all parties
7. External relations	We will project a united front and will not discuss sensitive issues with individuals outside of the relationship
8. Industry model	We desire our relationship to be seen as an industry model
9. Enjoyment	We enjoy working together and respect one another
10. Added Value	We will both derive more value from our relationship than just the exchange of money for services.
11. Work seamlessly	The IT services value chain will appear seamless to the End User.
12. Technology leadership	We wish to have recognized technology leadership in the provision of the Services.

3   Scoring the Behaviours

3.1   (**Survey**) Each party will conduct a survey of 50% of its staff every six months. The 50% of staff not surveyed in the first survey shall be surveyed in the second survey. Each party shall conduct its survey at its expense.

3.2   (**Scoring**) The parties agree to score their perception of the other party according to the following.

1	2	3	4	5
Unacceptable	Below expectations	Adequate	Above expectations	Delighted

3.3   (**Target score**) The parties seek an average score for each party of at least '4' for each period.

3.4   (**Analysis**) Each party shall provide the other with a justification of each score given, improvements deemed desirable, and proposed solution for incorporation into the Improvement Agenda.

3.5   (**Report**) The Service Provider shall provide the combined trend analysis and report for each survey.

Figure 8.3   Example Relationship Values Charter

information technology infrastructure provider. This charter was designed before the client went to market and was used to draft the relationship-related questions in the request for tender, to guide customer reference checking and to evaluate the relationship on a biannual basis.

Modelling the desired behaviours through the Relationship Values Charter is invaluable before selecting the provider because it enables you to evaluate which providers best demonstrate that they already exhibit these values with other clients.

Evaluations using the Relationship Values Charter can take many forms. It is important to note, however, that the Relationship Values Charter is designed to measure perceptions of behaviours, not the actual behaviour. Yes, the behaviour may be lacking, but equally possible is that the behaviour is fine but the perceptions regarding the other party's behaviour needs managing. Furthermore, in assessing perceptions, you avoid disputes as to whether a party did or did not do something well; it is the other party's perception that is being assessed and that is not open to dispute – everyone is entitled to their opinion.

When assessing the perception of each party, it will be important to determine who will be providing their opinions. Relationships exist at many levels between the parties, of which one level may be functioning well while others may not be as healthy. Some organizations choose only to gather the opinions of the contract managers in each party. However, at a minimum, consider assessing the options over everyone in the governance structure defined in Section 2 of the Governance Charter.

Another decision is how often to assess the relationship. The range tends to be quarterly, biannually or annually depending on the stability of the relationship. A new relationship may require frequent evaluations to establish the desired norms. A relationship in which either party is experiencing high staff/management turnover also requires frequent evaluations to re-establish the desired norms. Well-functioning, established relationships may only need a health check annually.

When the perceptions of behaviour do not score well, you then need to create an improvement initiative to improving the perception, behaviours or both. Financial penalty and reward systems have not generally worked, because the goal of the Relationship Values Charter is to identify and fix behaviour problems for the mutual benefit of both parties. Unfortunately, financial incentives have been known to create an environment that fosters disputes, rather than a spirit of problem solving, and in some cases have led to collusion between staff within the parties.

Section 4: Meetings

Face-to-face contact is critical in any successful commercial relationship, and a partnership-style relationship cannot exist without it. If the parties are not meeting regularly, they may not be talking enough. Meetings are an important part of governance, and these are detailed in this section of the Governance Charter.

There are a variety of meetings that you may want to conduct throughout the life of an arrangement. Strategic meetings such as assessing the overall success of the contract, the Contract Scorecard, the Relationship Values Charter as well as the strategic planning and benchmarking of costs and KPIs tend to occur annually. Technology forums, where new products and technologies are presented and improvement opportunities are identified, also tend to occur annually.

Performance-related meetings such as the review of the KPIs, audit findings, technology refresh and consolidation initiatives, milestone progress and variation patterns should occur more frequently.

Some meetings are not just to solve issues but also to forge a partnering style relationship, such as regular partnering workshops and continuous improvement meetings where shared goals, visions and values are developed, partnering principles are reinforced and business opportunities are thrashed out.

The most frequent type of meetings are those concerning operational matters, covering the current day-to-day operational issues requiring attention of both parties, the raising of variation requests and either approval or rejection, and update of procedures and documentation and staffing moves and changes.

The section of the Governance Charter pertaining to meetings can be as simple as the following table, Table 8.2, which lists 13 meetings ranging from weekly to annually. This type of table works well enough for most contracts.

However, some organizations have found they need to specify meetings in more detail, such as the example in Figure 8.4. This particular client organization wanted to ensure that the meeting accomplishes what the stakeholders expected, that there was no ambiguity about the nature of the meeting and that everyone would have the information required prior to the meeting. As a result, the meetings went off without a hitch.

It is worth noting that the Governance Charter also gives the rules for these meetings. For example, only the specified individuals are permitted at a particular meeting, unless notified in advance to the other party. This avoids

Table 8.2 Example meetings table

Timing	Meeting	Typical Topics
Annual	1. Contract Scorecard	a. Review of Contract Scorecard results b. Future action items
	2. Relationship Values Charter	a. Behaviour perception evaluation (bi-party code of conduct) b. Areas needing improvement c. Future action items
	3. Executive Relationship	a. Future strategies of both parties b. Strategic initiatives regarding this deal c. Review of overall performance
Bi-annual	4. Partnering Workshop	a. Develop shared goals, vision and values b. Develop partnering principles c. Business opportunity development
	5. Agreement Review	a. Review of audit findings b. Review of variations trends c. Review and updating of documentation d. TCO (total cost of ownership) tracking e. Cost and service level benchmarking
	6. IT Strategy	a. IT strategic planning for the forthcoming year b. Technology refresh and consolidation initiatives
Quarterly	7. SLA/Contract Review	a. Review of KPIs, fee adjustments and against baselines b. Milestone progress confirmation c. Identification of improvement opportunities
	8. Technology Forum	a. Presentation of new product releases/new technologies b. Discussions relating to technology trials
	9. Capacity Planning	a. Review capacity planning report and recommendations
Monthly	10. Service Review	a. Present all reports listed in SLA b. Review monthly reports and performance over past month c. Planning for upcoming month d. Staff moves and changes e. Upcoming projects f. Potential future variations
	11. Pre Invoice Meeting	a. Review proposed invoice b. Review service fee adjustments
Weekly	12. Operational	a. Current day-to-day operational issues requiring attention of both parties b. Update of asset registers, documentation and schedules c. Review of variation requests

Purpose	Review performance, provide improvement directions, and approve plans for the upcoming year
Authority	The Annual Review will have authority to * Approve Contractor bonus * Recommend variations and changes in contract operations * Set Contract Outcomes for the following year * Approve the Management Plans
Attendees	Client * Contract Executive * Contract Manager * Finance Manager Contractor * Account Executive * Account Manager * Finance Manger Other personnel as required
Chair	Client Contract Executive - Agenda to be distributed at least 5 days prior to the Annual Review
Minutes	Contractor – Minutes to be distributed within 48 hours of the Annual Review
Key topics	* Quality of performance and delivery against KPIs over the previous 12 months * Achievement of strategic objectives set in previous Management Plans * Performance against Contract Outcomes * Regulatory and contract compliance * Fees and charges * Management Plan approvals * Other issues relevant to the performance of the Services as the Client determines
Timing	Within 60 days of each anniversary of the Commencement Date.
Reports required prior to the Annual Review	Two weeks prior to the Annual Review, the Contractor to distribute the Management Plan results for the year and the updated Management Plans including: * Workforce Management Plan * Strategic Management Plan * Disengagement Plan * Risk Management Plan * Technology Upgrade Plan One week prior to the Annual Review, the Contractor to distribute the updated schedules including: * Key Personnel Register * Subcontractors Register * Other schedules which may have been varied, or require variation One week prior to the Annual Review, the Contractor to distribute the * Issues Register summary report (high priority only) * Variations summary report (major variations only)

Figure 8.4   Example detailed meeting specification

any perceptions of being ambushed by 'surprise guests'. And to ensure that the specified people actually do attend, some organizations have made attendance at meetings a KPI when there is concern that individuals from the parties might be haphazard with their attendance.

The chairing and minuting responsibilities are described as well because, in many cases, merely specifying that meetings are supposed to occur is not to enough to ensure these actually take place. You must also ensure specifications are carried out, as the following case exemplifies.

THE MEETING PLAN STAYS UNIMPLEMENTED

A government agency had put substantial effort into defining the meetings that would take place. It handed over the contract to the contract manager, satisfied that this deal would work well. The contract manager never ended up reading the contract, despite good intentions to do so – it was a voluminous contract and there just wasn't enough time and he had so many other things to do. In addition, he believed contracts were there to use in the case of dispute, so there wasn't any need unless the parties got into an argument they couldn't solve.

As a result, the meetings were not held. It wasn't until an independent government auditor wanted to see the minutes of meetings that the current contract manager for the client, the third in 3 years, found out that meetings were detailed in the contract. Furthermore, neither party was assigned the role of organizing any of the meetings – so both the contract manager at the client and his colleague at the provider refused to accept accountability, both stating that attendance would have occurred if the other had called any of the specified meetings.

While a structured communication and meeting approach will serve any organization well, the degree of communication, the frequency of meetings and particular attendees that are required ultimately depends on:

- the maturity of the arrangement;

- whether KPIs are being met;

- the commercial value of arrangement;

- how close the contract is to renewal;

- the degree of potential changes to either party's business;

- the degree of proposed changes to the services;

- the nature, number and importance of projects in process.

Section 5: Reviews, Evaluations and Audits

Compliance with a contract is never guaranteed by virtue of that contract alone; it merely provides recourse or remedy in the event of failure to comply. Anything you want to make sure is happening you will need to check.

Conducting audits and reviews of contracts is not something every organization focuses on. There are usually so many operational fires to be fought that review and compliance processes can easily be overlooked. However, imagine if you never reviewed your staff. They can become disinterested, unmotivated or (worst of all) you may not know what they are actually doing.

One-sided reviews tend to be counterproductive – it becomes a mudslinging event and both parties have a stockpile of mud. Accordingly, both the provider and the client organization need to be audited, usually separately, and in somewhat different ways. This section of the Governance Charter addresses all three types of audits/reviews beginning with bi-party reviews.

BI-PARTY REVIEWS

Bi-party auditing looks at both parties equally and focuses on: 1) compliance; 2) variations; and 3) behaviour.

With regarding to compliance reviews, in every review of every contract I have performed over the last two decades, I have always found both parties non-compliant, in a material manner, with the contract documents. For this reason, although it is much more common to only audit the provider's compliance, one should recognize that they are not the only party with obligations to fulfil.

Next are variation reviews. Variation reviews focus on two aspects: 1) formal variations and their causes; and 2) variation by conduct (the legal term is *estoppel*). Variation by conduct occurs when the parties behave in a manner contrary to, or not specified in, the contract. Any reasonably complex arrangement, particularly one in which many people from each party can interact, has a high probability of variations, both formal and informal, both of which indicate problems. The latter in particular, as they tend to occur very frequently, often without any particular process, and management is not even typically aware changes have taken place. The purpose of the review is to find out where actual behaviour is different to the contract and fix either the behaviour or the contract. Usually the contract is defective, as the people working with the deal on the ground have developed better ways of doing business than the authors of the contract had foreseen.

Lastly, there is the 'behaviour review' using the Relationship Values Charter from Section 3 of the Governance Charter. This is a 'soft' review whereby you look for functional and dysfunctional behaviours exhibited by the people in both parties who have any form of role regarding the arrangement. It is often people's behaviour that creates ineffective or inefficient arrangements, not the contract itself. The goal of this review is not to identify which parties behaves better, but rather to identify which aspects of the relationship are working, and which are not working, and then to agree on a process for fixing those areas that need improvement.

A RELATIONSHIP SO GOOD, IT CAN'T BE TRUE

An electrical power generation utility evaluated the relationship every quarter, and had an improvement agenda to focus on the key gaps. In fact, the relationship was deemed so unusually superior that an independent consultant was brought in when a new general manager took over at the client. This was to verify that it was, in fact, arms-length (no collusion, and so on) and good governance was in place. Nothing unseemly was found. Only minor tweaking of process transparency (forms and signoffs) was recommended, stating, 'The commercial relationship and behaviours exhibited were what parties everywhere aspire to.'

REVIEWS OF THE PROVIDER

From the client's perspective, the provider is the natural focus when beginning a review programme. The client wants to know that its money is being spent in the way it expects. The following checklist (Table 8.3) covers the most common items in a review programme over the provider.

REVIEWS OF THE CLIENT

Governance involves reviewing not only the provider's performance but also your organization's own management effectiveness. The uneconomic, inefficient and ineffective use of contracted work will inhibit an organization's ability to achieve its objectives. The greatest efficiency and effectiveness gains are often

Table 8.3   Review checklist over the provider

Subject matter	Items to consider checking
Billing	❑ check that the provider is billing in accordance with the terms of the contract (that is, contract was fixed fee, but they are billing time and materials; the quote was tax inclusive but they are billing as if it is tax exclusive; or progress billing has been instituted where there is no agreement); ❑ check that the work under invoices rendered has been completed in full; ❑ check that anything charged as a reimbursable expense is valid, best cost was achieved and that it was not to form part of the fee; ❑ check whether your organization is doing some of the provider's work, or reworking the work, because if the provider does not do it well enough, this should be taken out of previous payments, and potentially permanently removed the provider's scope and the price reduced.
Performance and risk	❑ check that the calculation of KPIs and the source data used for the calculations are correct; ❑ check that the insurances required are current and for the correct amounts; ❑ check that the supplier has adequate business continuity planning and disaster recovery plans; ❑ check that any subcontracting agreements have key obligations similar to the prime contract (the contract with the head provider) such as privacy, confidentiality, insurances, defect liability periods, indemnities and so on.
Value for money	❑ check for out-of-scope charges as these are typically at too high a price, since they tend to be poorly scoped and purchased on an ad hoc basis once the provider has 'gotten in'; ❑ check for automatic Consumer Price Index increases where there is little labour component as many suppliers put that in to increase their margin, even when actual costs are falling; ❑ where assets are involved, check whether the assets have reached the end of their depreciable life and, if so, whether the price should be reduced by the annual amortization amount, or whether the client should get new assets for no change in price.

in how your organization plans for and uses the provider's services, as the case below discovered. In this case, there was nothing wrong with the contract. It was the way it was implemented within the client that caused the trouble.

OUTSOURCING RESULTED IN DUPLICATE SYSTEMS

A stockbroker outsourced all of its IT operations as part of an automation 'paperless office' initiative. It was assumed that once the technology was in place staff would merely disregard the old way of doing things and move right into the new. What happened, however, was that staff just added the new processes to the old rather than create new, more efficient processes, thus ending up with two systems – one paper-based, and one electronic. This was discovered 18 months into the contract when internal audit was performing a review. They discovered that neither system was functioning effectively and the hybrid created was exceedingly time consuming. As a result, a specific 'no paper' policy was implemented.

The client's own processes and people need to be audited as well to ensure its organization is doing its part to control costs and make the arrangement successful. A more diligent client always results in a more diligent provider, whereas a lax client tends to get lax providers. The following checklist (Table 8.4) covers the most common items in a review programme over the provider.

Table 8.4   Review checklist over the provider

Subject matter	Items to consider checking
Buying wisely	❑ check that fixed fee limits have not been exceeded as your organization may be paying too much for the portion of consumption over the limit; ❑ check whether there is a guaranteed minimum capacity or volume – if not, your organization could be paying too much contingency money; ❑ if there is a guaranteed minimum capacity/volume, check whether it has been met on a regular bases as this represents capacity purchased but not used; ❑ check whether your organization can better control demand and reduce cost by buying less, or buying smarter (that is, such as out of peak periods, and so on); ❑ identify contracts where your organization can aggregate demand and increase purchasing power; ❑ assess the degree to which the original business case has been achieved as goals tend to be forgotten in lieu of an operational focus.
Payments	❑ check whether your organization has purchased in advance rather than arrears, whether the work was actually obtained and whether discounts were received; ❑ check whether your organization is paying early where the discount is greater than your organization's cost of borrowing; ❑ check whether your organization is paying late and incurring any avoidable interest charges; ❑ check whether your organization seeks any evidence of charges before approving payment.
Contract Management	❑ check whether your organization is not doing something, or doing something poorly, that is increasing costs (that is, frequent changes to scope); ❑ assess the budgeting process and compare to actual costs of contract (provider charges and contract management resources); ❑ assess whether appropriate contingency plans have been put in place in the event of the provider being unable to continue providing the work (due to force majeure, insolvency or any other factor); ❑ assess whether appropriate plans have been derived to invoke rights and obligations in the contract; ❑ check whether your organization is automatically extending contracts even where there is a competitive market; ❑ check whether your organization has due processes and protocols for approvals (such as variations, performance assessments, work orders, and so on).

Each review, the scope of the review, which party is to conduct it, who it is to be presented to and how frequently the review is to be conducted are all detailed in this section of the Governance Charter, as shown in the example Table 8.5. Again, like the meetings specification, a table similar to this should suffice but do not hesitate to do a more detailed specification if your contract situation warrants it.

Some parties have found it necessary to specify a detailed audit/review programme. Such an audit programme establishes:

- what audit technique might be employed – sampling, interviews, surveys, site inspections, and so on;

- how often the audit might be conducted – once a week, annually, near the end of the contract, and so on;

- what report will be created and to whom it will be distributed;

- what resources will be needed to conduct the audit – client, provider, external experts and the skill set required;

- what will be needed by the auditor – records, documents, access to personnel and management, site access.

Once you have established your review framework, either by a general table such as in the example or a more detailed audit programme, you will need to make sure that the contract has the necessary rights and obligations in it. For example, if you have identified that you want to conduct surprise audits of the provider, but have no rights to conduct them, the provider is well within its rights to refuse, charge for time and materials or limit the nature of the audit.

The types of provisions include:

- each party's obligations to retain specified records for a specified period;

- duty to provide the records upon request;

- notification obligations;

- duty to assist the audit;

- obligations to rectify audit findings.

Table 8.5   Example reviews table

Frequency	Review	Presented to	Conducted by	Scope of Review
Annually	1. Governance review	Client: • CEO • General Manager	Provider: • Managing Director • Account Manager	a. Analyze the parties' compliance with obligations b. Recommend better ways of working together c. Prepare actions and variations required
	2. Agreement Review Meeting	Provider • Account Manager • Service Delivery Manager	Client • General Manager • Contract Manager	a. Review of audit findings b. Variations c. Review and updating of documentation d. Cost and service level benchmarking
	3. Quality audit	Client • Contract Manager	Provider • Service Delivery Manager	a. Compliance with the Quality Plan b. Quality Plan improvement actions
Quarterly	1. SLA/ Contract Review	Client: • General Manager • Contract Manager	Provider: • Account Manager • Service Delivery Manager	a. Review of KPIs b. Variations c. Milestone planning d. Identification of improvement opportunities, technology refresh and consolidation
	2. Efficiency and cost reduction review	Client: • Contract Manager	Provider: • Account Manager • Service Delivery Manager	a. Identification of operational efficiencies b. Identification of cost reduction opportunities
Monthly	SLA performance review	Client: • Contract Manager	Provider: • Service Delivery Manager	a. Analyze overall performance of SLA b. Analyze performance against KPIs c. Prepare actions and variations required
As directed by the client	1. KPI calculation audit	Provider: • Service Delivery Manager	Client: • Contract Manager	a. Determine correct KPI calculations and source data of calculations
	2. Other	As directed by Client	As directed by Client	a. As directed by Client

Section 6: Issue Management

Neither party needs to, nor should, solve problems alone. Unresolved issues are disputes waiting to happen, so sound issue management can make or break a deal. This includes how either party can raise issues, how issues will be logged and tracked and what approvals are required for issue resolution – all of which are defined in this section.

Issue management in contracts is very similar to that for good project management. That is, there is a formal process for raising, recording and resolving issues that arise and these are logged and tracked. It is not unusual to find at least 300 open issues on any given day in a reasonable complex contract. Just think of all the people that have something to do with the deal in both parties, then think of the number of issues, large and small, each might be having. The challenge is to solve the important issues first.

Effective issue management allows for a visible decision-making process, typically by using some form of an issue sheet. An example of an issue sheet used in many contracts to record and resolve issues is given in Figure 8.5.

Note that the issue sheet is focused first on prioritizing the issue so that high priorities are solved first. Otherwise, people can lean towards solving the easy issues even if they are not that important in the scheme of things. Secondly, the focus is on solving the issue, as well as the implication of not solving it. This gives a way forward and also stops either party leaving an issue on the back burner for too long. Thirdly, the issue is assigned to an individual (which can be from either party) to solve it, not just a party. Individual accountability is crucial to getting it solved. Finally, the actual resolution is documented before the issue is closed out.

Like the term governance, the question of what an issue is and when an issue sheet should be raised will often arise. It is good practice is to raise an issue sheet:

- When anyone in either party wants something solved or a decision made by the other party – an issue sheet provides a systematic way to raise concerns. The underlying issue management processes then provide a prioritization mechanism (either as a classification scheme specification or by assigning the right to prioritize, in the first instance, to one of the parties).

- When any decision needs visibility – if you want a record that some form of understanding, agreement or resolution has occurred, raise

Issue Sheet		
Issue Sheet ID:	Raised by:	Date submitted: ____/____/____
Issue title:	Priority: ❑ High ❑ Medium ❑ Low	Governing documents affected: ❑ Conditions of Contract ❑ SLA ❑ Financial Schedule
Assigned to:	Priority rationale:	❑ Governance Charter ❑ Other Schedule: _____ ❑ Procedure: _____ ❑ Other _____
Description of Issue:		
Proposed resolution:		
Implication of not resolving Issue:		
Related Issues:		Information/background attachments:
Investigation/further work required:		Investigation assigned to:
Description of resolution:		
Resolution approved by: Client: _____ Provider: _____ (name, signature)		Date: ____/____/____ Date: ____/____/____
Comments:		

Figure 8.5   Example issue sheet

an issue sheet. In that sense, it does not matter whether something
is solved in 5 minutes, only whether you want a record made of it.

•   When something needs further investigation – issue management
      provides a tracking process for open items. Otherwise it is easy for
      these things to be forgotten until there is a crisis, which is what
      good issue management is designed to prevent.

- To raise a good idea – a way of improving something is also a good use of issue sheets; it does not just have to be about problems.

Having an issue management system has a key benefit besides the obvious one of getting things solved by the mere act of logging, tracking and assigning the issues. It also acts as a history of issues that faced the entire deal through its life that will offer lessons and solutions for other contracts as well as future generations of this contract. This history is also invaluable if key staff at either party leave and are replaced. New people can get quickly across the key issues – both past and current – by reading the issues log, resulting in handovers that are more efficient.

Section 7: Variation Management

Variations are a natural occurrence in most contracts. Variations do not need to be just about price – all the contractual documents should be 'living' and reflect the up-to-date practices. Not only does this serve to keep the documents reflective of the current agreement in practice, it also ensures that the next-generation deal will be based on, and operate with, current information.

There are many variations that can take place during the life of any deal, including:

- a change in scope – which can be increases or decreases in volume required, or the need to incorporate further work not originally foreseen or that was out-of-scope, but have been purchased so often that it should be in-scope;

- a desire to revise the pricing arrangement – to change a fixed lump sum to unit prices where demand has proven to be unpredictable, to change unit prices into fixed lump sums where demand is now predictable and stable, to clarify the reimbursables, and so on;

- a change of, or in, KPIs – either upgrade or downgrade based on the provider's performance, your organization's business requirements or new industry standards;

- the desire by the client to backsource certain work – either because the provider has not been performing adequately and your organization does not believe an emergency step-in will solve it, or because your organization wishes to rebuild the competence, or it believes the work should be performed internally for business reasons;

- the need to rectify defects or omissions – including accountability concerns (if actual operations have led to resources or activities being duplicated or omitted), poor or ambiguous specifications, or inclusion of schedules to form part of the legal framework;

- a desire to refresh the entirety of the agreement – either because there have been extensive variations or the agreement is not meeting the needs of either or both parties or to introduce good practice deemed necessary (that is, KPIs, incentives, and so on);

- a change in the structure of either party – merger, acquisition, divestment, reorganization, expansion, and so on, necessitating a contract overhaul.

Variation management is very similar to issue management. That is, there is a formal process for raising, recording and resolving variations that arise, and these are logged and tracked using variation requests. An example of a variation request form used in many contracts is given in Figure 8.6.

The reason a careful evaluation of variations needs to take place is that far too often they can get out of control, as the need for speed takes over everything else. The case below demonstrates just such an experience.

UNMANAGED SCOPE CREEP

As can be typical in a major ERP implementation, a bank suffered immeasurable scope creep driven by the numerous variations raised nearly daily. Eventually, the ERP project increased from $200 million to $800 million with only one module implemented in a test site. The bank called in an independent party to review how this was allowed to occur. At the end of the day, the bank's personnel did request the changes, formally and informally, and the supplier put them into the project, with neither party acting as a 'devil's advocate'. Eventually the project was brought back in-house and scaled down after both parties filed suits and the media generated much negative publicity.

Variation Request		
Variation Request ID #: _____ Variation Request title: _____	Raised by: Name of Representative _____ Signature_____	Date submitted: ___/___/___ Date Variation is to take effect:___/___/___
Priority: ❑ High ❑ Medium ❑ Low Priority rationale:	Documents to be varied: ❑ Contract ❑ SLA ❑ Financial schedule ❑ Governance Charter ❑ Other document _____ ❑ Procedure _____	
Description of proposed Variation:		
Business case for the Variation		
Benefit:	Risk:	Cost:
Implication of not making a Variation:		
Related Variation Requests (if applicable):		Information/background attachments
Investigation/further work required:		
Approved for investigation (Y/N) Investigation assigned to:_____ Investigation due date: _____		Investigation results:
Variation resolution: ❑ Rejected ❑ Deferred – until ___/___/___ ❑ Approved	Signatures: Client representative name _____ Signature _____ Date ___/___/___ Provider representative name _____ Signature _____ Date ___/___/___	
Description of approved Variation resolution (attach implementation schedule, if applicable):		

Figure 8.6   Example variation request

At some point, you may want to consider releasing a new version of the contract if the number of variations becomes so great as to make the contract no longer understandable. Never be afraid to release a new version incorporating the variations into the agreement and most certainly incorporate them into the next contract if good solutions occurred that were not foreseen as needed at the start. Otherwise, what tends to happen is the old contract, that did not work, is put back out to tender yet again. Then the whole variation cycle begins again, which means you waste your time reinventing the wheel over and over again.

VARIATIONS BECOME UNMANAGEABLE

A fourth-generation maintenance contract had one binder for the contract and three binders for the agreed variations. The variations evidence included in those three binders included copies of emails, correspondence and, on occasion, a signed variation agreement. However, it was nearly impossible to know the current conditions of contract as many of the variations related to previous variations but none of the documents were cross-referenced. Inevitably, the parties agreed to rewrite the contract and re-sign.

Section 8: Dispute Management

Too many contracts do not specify an internal inter-party escalation process, prior to getting third parties involved. With no agreed escalation, disputes can be dispatched to third parties far too quickly. While most contracts will state that the parties have a duty to try to resolve a dispute prior to seeking alternative dispute resolution (mediation or arbitration) or going to court, such contracts do not go far enough in specifying that process.

The first step is to outline who can raise disputes and the escalation from the governance structure in Section 2 of the Governance Charter (see Figure 8.2, page 184). Even if you do not like what the executives have resolved, whatever the resolution is – it will be far better and considerably less expensive than going to court. The next step is to specify the process, which follows a similar approach to that of issue sheets.

In fact, before either party is able to declare something a dispute, consider making it a requirement that it is first raised as an 'issue', at least to begin with. Just calling a problem an issue, rather than a dispute, can have a big impact. After all, most people would be less apprehensive about being invited to an 'issue brainstorming workshop' rather than a 'dispute negotiation.'

Then, if the issue cannot be resolved, dispute resolution can come into play. Generally speaking, disputes are not often arguments over fact, but over philosophical differences (contrasting opinions where there is no right answer) or interpretation of ambiguous requirements (different understandings on what was agreed). It can even be caused by perceptions and misinterpretations of the other party's behaviour, as illustrated in the case below.

A RAPID SPIRAL INTO A NIGHTMARE

A state government department and a service provider had just signed a 'partnering' Business Process Outsourcing (BPO) deal whereby the provider would not only maintain the facilities operated by the department, but also manage leases and other tenants as well.

On the first day of the contract, the provider's full-time account manager asked the client's director where his office would be. He had assumed that as it was a partnership, the two parties were to be colleagues, and he would have an office near the department director. It was a reasonable assumption, since that was the arrangement in other deals with other clients.

This request came as a surprise to the client's director for a number of reasons. First, the supplier's office was only a few blocks away so there was no logistical basis for the request. Second, he only expected to see the supplier if his help was needed in resolving issues. Third, there was a shortage of space that was known to the supplier.

But the director wasn't going to be ungracious and refuse to provide an office. Due to the space shortage, he had difficulty locating one but did track one down. It was in the basement and not particularly welcoming. He felt he was being quite congenial first by not refusing and, second, by not charging the provider for rent.

However, the account manager took the gesture as an overt signal that the relationship was not going to be a partnership at all. Quite clearly, the client intended a master–slave relationship and was going to try to take advantage of them. As a defensive move, he put the word out that the client wasn't to be trusted and the provider's staff were only to comply with the letter of the contract.

The first occasion to test the relationship happened in the first week, where something had to be done urgently, but was out of scope. The account manager refused until he had a signed purchase order from the client. He wasn't going to fall for the old trick of doing something without a PO, only to find out later that the client's accounts department would refuse to pay. When the director heard about this, his worst fears were confirmed. Partnering was just sales rhetoric; suppliers really do not implement it in practice. As his defensive move, he was going to make sure they complied with everything to the letter in the contract – it was the only way to manage suppliers.

Disputes soon began trickling in, raised by both parties regarding what the other wasn't doing in accordance with the contract. However, because of the original partnering approach taken, not much effort went into the contract and it was full of ambiguities, conflict and silent areas (where the contract said nothing). It was, in fact, a 'contract-light'. Since the contract wasn't of much help, it came down to who believed who said what during negotiations (for which minutes were not kept). Debates over who said what and mutual blaming kept going for a year until the supplier sold its business to another organization and the client and the new provider negotiated a 'real' contract.

The most critical dispute management skill is the ability to stay out of disputes in the first place, not by simply avoiding them but, rather, by carefully cultivating a problem-solving environment. This is skill in prevention, not in fighting.

Both parties are best served if disputes can be resolved using the inter-party structure described earlier in this section. Once third parties are involved (be they mediators, arbitrators, courts and/or the legal profession), a costly war that neither party wins is typically the result, and a mutually agreed compromise is generally harder to arrive at.

A DISPUTE ABOUT PROJECT COMPLETION

This case concerns a university and shows the need for clear acceptance criteria of deliverables. The parties couldn't agree as to whether a software development project was completed as there were no acceptance criteria on which to form an objective assessment. The provider believed it had completed the project and had already suffered a huge loss. The client believed many of the functions it was seeking were not operating in the way that they were supposed to.

The parties hired a consulting firm who reviewed the bid, the development processes and the understandings that were evidenced during the project. The documentation able to be provided by the parties was haphazard and incomplete. Numerous documents that could be reasonably expected to be available for observation and confirmation by the review team were unable to be provided by either party. After 6 months, the advisor resolved that the university should withhold payment only for items not delivered that were specifically identified as a function in the original request for tender, but the client had to pay for those functions that had been delivered but for which the quality was under dispute. There was no evidence supporting a specification of quality.

> Later the consulting firm and the university had their own dispute over the cost of the review. The bill exceeded the $200 000 quote due to extra work performed by the firm because of the lack of evidence the parties had to support their arguments, and the university refused to pay.

Dispute management is very similar to that of issue management. That is, there is a formal process for raising, recording and resolving disputes that arise, and these are logged and tracked using dispute notices. An example of a dispute notice form used in many contracts is given in Figure 8.7.

If the parties themselves cannot reach resolution, there are three types of alternative dispute resolution (ADR) that parties regularly use, and the contract often requires, prior to a party being able to go to court:

1.   arbitration;

2.   mediation;

3.   independent expert.

The history of these is quite interesting. Arbitration was originally created as an alternative to court to save both parties time and money. However, these days no one goes to arbitration without their team of lawyers, so it does not save much money. Therefore, mediation became the next form. Yet again, most organizations bring their lawyers to mediation as well, again substantially increasing the cost. Moreover, neither the arbitrator nor mediator may have a detailed understanding of either party's business, as they are usually legal or accounting professionals. Much of the time can be spent educating the arbitrator/mediator about the businesses and the issue, without even getting to the point of argument.

As a result, the independent expert alternative is becoming more popular. This is where the parties try to agree on an expert in the area (for example, an expert in facilities management) who acts akin to a marriage counsellor and will base their decision on industry norms and their own experience. A key part of this process is that neither party brings their lawyers. The goal is not to win, but rather to reach an objective compromise, a win–win situation.

As a side note regarding disputes, and one that will not enter into the Governance Charter, is what to do after a dispute has occurred. Most people,

DISPUTE NOTICE FORM		
Dispute ID:	Raised by:	Date submitted: / /
Dispute title:		Dispute to be resolved by: ❑ Independent expert
Assigned to: Client:_____ Provider:_____		❑ Mediation ❑ Arbitration ❑ Court ❑ Other _____
Description of dispute:		
Previous resolution attempts:		
Related Issues Sheets (attach copies):	Information/background attachments:	
Investigation/further work required:	Investigation assigned to:	
Description of dispute resolution:		
Resolution approved by: Client: _____, Date: ____/____/___ Provider:_____, Date: ___/____/___ <div align="center">(name, signature)</div>		
Comments:		

Figure 8.7   Example dispute notice

after believing that the other party won a dispute, immediately prepare for the next one – setting up better defences or even possibly seeking revenge; 'They got me the last time, but I'll get them back.' It is a rare individual that can quickly move on with no ill-will, and even rarer still to look at how they may have prevented the dispute in a proactive fashion.

If you cannot imagine ever saying you are sorry to the other party, you may not be able to recover from a dispute. If the parties still have to work together, small steps may be required. This involves just trying to do simple, non-controversial things together in an attempt to rebuild respect and, one day, trust. This can include just trying to conduct a normal operational meeting, have a normal reporting review or conduct a very basic forward planning session, the point of all this being learning to work together again.

However, it can occur that an individual in one or both parties cannot overcome the feelings of being betrayed, the belief the other party is untrustworthy or cannot overcome the urge for revenge (teaching them a lesson). In most cases, these individuals will need to be removed from their particular role on the contract and replaced by another. This is in the interests of expediency in re-forming a working relationship, and *not* about punishing that individual, who can hopefully be redeployed elsewhere to better effect.

Appendix: Example Governance Charter

SCHEDULE 6 – GOVERNANCE CHARTER
Power Plant Maintenance Contract

Contents

1 ABOUT THIS SCHEDULE

1.1 (**Purpose**) This schedule identifies the obligations of the parties with regard to the governance of the Contract and the Services.

1.2 (**Background**) This Governance Charter is one of many schedules to the Contract. An initial version of the Contract, and its schedules, were provided to the Contractor for bidding purposes. This Governance Charter represents the final agreed Governance Charter.

1.3 (**Definitions**) In this schedule, except where the context otherwise requires, all reserved words, phrases and terms are:

    a.   denoted with the first letter of each word being capitalized; and

    b.   specified in Schedule 1 – Definitions to the Contract.

2   ROLES AND RESPONSIBILITIES

2.1   (**Structure**) The structure of the management between the two parties is as follows:

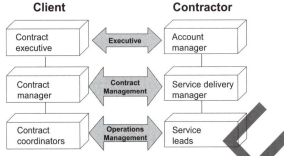

2.2   (**Responsibilities**) The responsibilities for each role are as follows:

Role	Organization Position	Responsibilities
Client		
Contract executive	General manager	1. Signatory to contract 2. Resolve escalated issues with Account manager 3. Planning and strategic management
Contract manager	Head, Contracts	1. Authorized Representative 2. Approve Variation Requests and Dispute Notices raised by Client 3. Accept or reject Contractor variations 4. Approve invoices 5. Approve performance reviews 6. Chair meetings and approve minutes
Contract coordinators	Team leads	1. Manage Client's day-to-day responsibilities 2. Approve work orders 3. Manage issues and variations 4. Audit invoices
Contractor		
Account manager	CEO	1. Signatory to contract 2. Resolve escalated issues with Contract executive 3. Planning and strategic management
Service delivery manager	Operations manager	1. Authorized Representative 2. Approve Variation Requests and Dispute Notices raised by Contractor 3. Accept or reject Client variations 4. Conduct reviews
Service leads	Line managers	1. Manage Contractor's day-to-day responsibilities 2. Prepare reports 3. Administrate meetings

2.3   (**Advisory Committee**) The parties may agree to have an advisory committee for the Contract. If so, that committee shall operate to:

    a.   facilitate stakeholder communication;

    b.   provide advice and feedback; and

    c.   assess risk and mitigation strategies.

3 CODE OF CONDUCT

3.1 Overview

3.1.1 **(Purpose)** This Code of Conduct identifies the behaviour that the parties agree to exhibit during the course of the Term of the Contract. The parties have agreed that if the Contract is to operate effectively, both parties must drive towards a 'partnering' style of relationship. To achieve this, the parties have set out their common goals in this Code of Conduct that are to operate during the Contract and shall use this as a process for relationship review and improvement.

3.1.2 **(No effect on legal relationship)** The parties agree that their legal relationship must always be governed by the Contract. Nevertheless, the parties have identified that this process needs to be implemented to enable both parties to operate effectively without the Contract being relied on in every instance.

3.2 Conduct to be demonstrated by the parties

Conduct	Description
1. Accuracy	Information provided; reporting; and data entered will be accurate.
2. Communication	The parties shall communicate frequently, openly, and honestly with each other. An environment of 'no surprises' shall be sought.
3. Continuous Improvement	The parties shall constantly search for better ways of doing things.
4. Financial	Both parties desire to apply the Profit Programme and not incur Work overruns. Each party shall achieve its financial goals: Organization – to reduce cost over time and have competitive pricing Contractor – to have reasonable profits
5. Industry Model	The parties desire the relationship to be seen as a leading model within the industry
6. Meet Needs	The parties shall be both proactive and reactive to each other's needs.
7. Perform Responsibilities	Each party will perform its responsibilities to the standard expected by the other party.
8. Problem Solving	The parties shall focus on rapid solutions to the problem, not apportioning blame or responsibility. Issues shall be resolved at the lowest level appropriate.
9. Resource Reinvestment	The parties wish to have recognized leadership in the Services through continuous reinvestment in human and capital assets.
10. Site Cleanliness	The parties shall maintain a clean and orderly Site environment.

3.3   Scoring the Code of Conduct

3.3.1   (**Survey**) Each party will conduct a survey of 50 per cent of its staff every six (6) months. The 50 per cent of staff not surveyed in the first survey shall be surveyed in the second survey. Each party shall conduct its survey at its expense.

3.3.2   (**Scoring**) The parties agree to score their perception of the other party according to the following.

1	2	3	4	5
Unacceptable	Below expectations	Adequate	Above expectations	Delighted

3.3.3   (**Target score**) The parties seek an average score for each party of at least four (4) for each period.

3.3.4   (**Analysis**) Each party shall provide the other with a justification of each score given, improvements deemed desirable, and proposed solution for incorporation into the Improvement Agenda.

3.3.5   (**Report**) The Contractor shall provide the combined trend analysis and report for each survey.

4 MEETINGS

4.1 (**Types**) The meetings listed below are a minimum requirement.

| Meeting | Agenda | Required attendees | | Timing |
		Client	Contractor	
1. Kick-off	Clarify Contract documents, roles, and protocols	• Contract executive • Contract manager	• Account manager • Service delivery manager	Following signing of Contract
2. Strategic	Present and discuss business directions of both parties	• Contract executive	• Account manager	Annually
3. Planning	Plan business changes affecting the services	• Contract manager • Contract coordinators	• Account manager • Service delivery manager • Service leads	Annually
4. Financial	Prepare cost projections	• Contract manager	• Service delivery manager	Quarterly
5. Operations	a. Propose procedural and staffing changes b. Assess variation requests c. Resolve issues	• Contract manager • Contract coordinators	• Service delivery manager • Service leads	Monthly
6. Closeout	a. Assess performance over Term b. Present and discuss lessons, challenges and recommendations	• Contract executive • Contract manager	• Account manager • Service delivery manager	Six months before Term expiry

4.2 (**Attendees**) The attendees listed in the table above must attend all meetings. Additional staff may be requested to attend these meetings from time to time. All additional attendees must be notified to the other party five (5) Business Days prior to the meeting.

4.3 (**Both parties**) Both parties will:

    a.   attend such meetings in good faith to discuss the topics and create a productive and satisfying relationship; and

    b.   arrange such other meetings as may be necessary in order to meet operational, financial, and strategic objectives.

4.4 (**Administration**) The Contractor shall organize, facilitate and minute all meetings. The minutes shall be distributed to the Client for approval no less than one (1) week following any meeting. Minute revisions can be directed by the Client up to, and including, the next meeting of that type.

5   REVIEWS AND AUDITS

5.1   (**Types**) The following reviews and audits shall be performed.

Review/audit	Topics	Performed by:	Presented to:	Frequency
1. Governance review	a. Analyze parties' compliance b. Recommend better ways of working together c. Prepare actions required	Contractor Account manager	Client Contract manager	Annually
2. Customer satisfaction survey	a. Summarize satisfaction survey b. Identify issues and trends c. Prepare actions required	Client Contract manager	Contractor Account manager	Annually
3. Cost reduction review	a. Identify operational efficiencies b. Identify cost reduction opportunities	Contractor Account manager	Client Contract manager and coordinators	Quarterly
4. SLA performance review	a. Analyze KPIs and overall SLA performance b. Prepare actions and variations required	Contractor Service delivery manager	Client Contract manager and coordinators	Monthly
5. KPI calculation audit	a. Determine correct KPI calculations and source data of calculations	Client Contract coordinators	Contractor Service delivery manager	At Client discretion

5.2   (**Contractor reviews and audits**) For all reviews conducted by the Contractor, the Contractor shall:

    a.   provide all required review information including, but not limited to:

        i.   scope and processes undertaken;

        ii.   review findings; and

        iii.   review substantiation and evidence as appropriate;

    b.   organize, facilitate, and minute all review meetings.

5.3   (**Client reviews and audits**) For all reviews or audits conducted by the Client, including any additional ones than that specified in 5.1 above, the Contractor shall:

    a.   provide unfettered assistance;

    b.   provide all information required by the Client by the date required and in the format required; and

    c.   organize, facilitate and minute all review meetings.

6   ISSUE MANAGEMENT

6.1   (**Raising**) Issues can be raised by the Authorized Representative in either party with regard to any matter via the Issue Sheet form (Appendix 1 – Example Issue Sheet). The parties recognize that raising issues is to be encouraged to foster a proactive and productive working relationship.

6.2   (**Administration**) The Contractor shall maintain the issues log and register all issues raised by either party, the log which shall be made available to the Client upon demand.

6.3   (**Procedures**) The following issue management procedures will be conducted:

   a.   the Authorized Representative raising the issue shall submit the Issue Sheet form, with as much information completed as possible, to the Authorized Representative of the other party;

   b.   the Contractor shall log the issue and complete all necessary items with the issuer;

   c.   the party assigned to resolving the issue will do so by the required time noted in the Issue Sheet; and

   d.   the Contractor shall report the progress of issues on a monthly basis.

6.4   (**Escalation**) Should any issue not be resolved by the due date, or the resolution not be able to be agreed at the time the issue is processed, the issue will be escalated to the Contract executives for resolution.

7   DISPUTE MANAGEMENT

7.1   (**Raising**) Disputes can be raised by the Client's Contract manager or the Contractor's Account manager via the Dispute Notice form (Appendix 2 – Example Dispute Notice). The parties recognize that solving disputes within the two parties is preferred than using the third-party dispute resolution provisions within the Contract.

7.2   (**Administration**) The Contractor shall maintain the disputes log and register all disputes raised by either party, the log which shall be made available to Client upon demand.

7.3   (**Procedures**) The following disputes management procedures will be conducted:

    a.   the Authorized Representative raising the dispute shall submit the Dispute Notice form, with as much information completed as possible, to the Authorized Representative of the other party;

    b.   the Contractor shall log the Dispute Notice and complete all necessary items with the issuer;

    c.   the individuals within the parties assigned to resolving the disputes will attempt to do so by the required time noted in the Dispute Notice; and

    d.   the Contractor shall report the progress of disputes on a monthly basis.

7.4   (**Escalation**) Should any disputes not be resolved by the due date, or the resolution not be able to be agreed at the time the disputes is processed, the disputes will be escalated to the Contract executives for resolution. If the Contract executives cannot resolve the dispute, the dispute provisions within the Contract shall be invoked.

8 VARIATIONS TO THE CONTRACT DOCUMENTS

8.1 (**Raising**) Requests to vary the Contract, and the Contract documents, can be raised by an Authorized Representative via the Variation Request Form (Appendix 3 – Example Variation Request). The parties recognize that either party may have valid reasons for raising variations and will work in good faith to reach agreement on such variations.

8.2 (**Administration**) The Contractor shall maintain a log and copies of all Variation Request Forms (in process, approved, and rejected) which shall be made available to the Client upon demand.

8.3 (**Take effect**) Variations shall not take effect until that variation is:

　　a.　agreed by the other party in writing and documented as a variation; and

　　b.　approved by the Authorized Representatives of both parties.

8.4 (**Document amendments**) The Client shall amend all documents as agreed in approved Variation Requests.

APPENDICES

8.5   Appendix 1 – Example Issue Sheet

Instructions: Shaded areas to be completed by Client

ISSUE SHEET		
Issue Sheet ID:	Raised by:	Date submitted: ____/____/____
Issue title:	Priority: ❑ High ❑ Medium ❑ Low	Governing documents affected: ❑ Conditions of Contract ❑ SLA ❑ Financial Schedule ❑ Governance Charter ❑ Other document: _____
Assigned to:	Priority rationale:	
Description of Issue:		
Proposed resolution:		
Implication of not resolving Issue:		
Related Issues:	Information/background attachments:	
Investigation/further work required:	Investigation assigned to:	
Description of resolution:		
Resolution approved by: Client: _____ Contractor: _____ <center>(name, signature)</center>	Date: ____/____/___ Date: ____/____/___	
Comments:		

This form shall be governed by the terms and conditions of the Contract.
Nothing in this form varies the rights and obligations of the parties unless specifically identified.

8.6 Appendix 2 – Example Dispute Notice

Instructions: Shaded areas to be completed by Client

DISPUTE NOTICE FORM		
Dispute ID:	Raised by:	Date submitted: ___/___/___
Dispute title: Assigned to: Client:_____, Contractor:_____		Dispute to be resolved by: ❑ Independent expert ❑ Mediation ❑ Arbitration ❑ Court ❑ Other _____
Description of dispute:		
Previous resolution attempts:		
Related Issues Sheets (attach copies):	Information/background attachments:	
Investigation/further work required:	Investigation assigned to:	
Description of dispute resolution:		
Resolution approved by: Client: _____ Date: ___/___/___ Contractor: _____ Date: ___/___/___ (name, signature)		
Comments:		

This form shall be governed by the terms and conditions of the Contract.
Nothing in this form varies the rights and obligations of the parties unless specifically identified.

8.7   Appendix 3 – Example Variation Request

Instructions: Shaded areas to be completed by Client

VARIATION REQUEST		
Variation Request ID #: _____ Variation Request title: _____	Raised by: Name of Representative _____ Signature_____	Date submitted: ___/___/___ Date Variation is to take effect:___/____/___
Priority: ❑ High ❑ Medium ❑ Low Priority rationale:	Documents to be varied: ❑ Contract ❑ SLA ❑ Financial Schedule ❑ Governance Charter ❑ Other document _____	
Description of proposed Variation:		
Business Case for the Variation:		
Benefit:	Risk:	Cost:
Implication of not making a Variation:		
Related Variation Requests (if applicable):	Information/background attachments:	
Investigation/further work required:		
Approved for investigation (Y/N) Investigation assigned to:_____ Investigation due date: _____	Investigation results:	
Variation resolution: ❑ Rejected ❑ Deferred - until ___/___/___ ❑ Approved	Signatures: Name of Client representative_____ Signature _____ Date ___/____/___ Name of Contractor representative_____ Signature _____ Date ___/____/___	
Description of approved Variation resolution (attach implementation schedule, if applicable):		

This form shall be governed by the terms and conditions of the Contract.
Nothing in this form varies the rights and obligations of the parties unless specifically identified.

GLOSSARY EXCERPT FROM THE CONTRACT

For purposes of this book on the Contract Scorecard and to be able to better understand this example Governance Charter, the following terms have been extracted from the example's contract.

8.8   Reserved words

Reserved word/phrase	Definition
Authorized Representative	The person authorized by a party to commit the party to, and act under, this Contract as specified in the FOA.
Business Day	Monday through Friday excluding public holidays in the state of Delaware.
Client	[Client name]
Commencement Date	The date the agreement officially begins: January 1, 2007.
Contract	This contract that includes this SLA and all other schedules that are incorporated into the Contract, as amended from time to time in accordance with the terms of the Contract.
Customer	Any individual that uses the Services.
Dispute Notice	The template form recording, tracking, and resolving disputes in Schedule 6 – Governance Charter
FOA	Form of Agreement, the first part of this Contract.
Issue Sheet	The template form for recording issues between the parties in Schedule 6 – Governance Charter.
Contractor	[Contractor name]
Services	The work performed by the Contractor under this SLA.
Term	The duration of the Contract from the Commencement Date to the Termination Date.
Variation Request	The template form for requesting, recording, and resolving variations in Schedule 6 – Governance Charter

9

The Strategic Specification – Unique Contract Schedules

'He that would be a leader must be a bridge.'

Welsh Proverb

About this Chapter and Strategic Schedules in General

Most deals have some form of anticipated strategic goals, but they often leave these unarticulated, perhaps only mentioning them in the background information contained in the tender documents. Strategic goals mentioned 'by-the-by' rarely have any chance of actually occurring. The strategic goals tend to be articulated in a number of places in the agreement depending upon what they are and how your organization wants to manage them, because each strategic goal can be fairly complex to detail in the appropriate business and legal language.

All of your organization's strategic goals are likely to be mentioned in the main terms and conditions of the contract (typically in a recital clause or in a strategic intent clause), but these tend to be quite high-level and are more to help a contract reader understand the context of the deal. Strategic goals that you are serious about achieving are best detailed in a separate contract schedule. For example, if your organization is in the public sector and has industry development requirements to be met by the provider, such as the development of a research facility or the use of regional contractors, the contract may have a separate schedule detailing those requirements.

Having a separate schedule that articulates the strategic goals of the deal and that details the provider's obligations in assisting your organization in achieving them also makes it easier to manage since the contract manager (and all the stakeholders to the deal) will not need to wade through the contract to discover what strategic obligations the provider has.

As these schedules can be large and varied, only a few examples have been included, one for each type of strategic goal (innovation, business contribution, alignment and underlying business practices). To give examples covering the vast range of strategic specification that take place in practice would require a document larger than this book!

Example Innovation Specification

The first example, Figure 9.1, reflects the desire by the client for the provider to help it discover innovation in the industry and the client's business – which is called environmental scanning. The client put the specification in the Conditions of Contract. The clause, as you will see, specified quarterly briefings and the KPIs covered both the frequency and quality of these briefings, as well as quarterly reporting.

Clause 17 Environmental scanning

17.1 **(Scanning)** The Contractor shall monitor developments in the industry and in the business environment of the Principal on an ongoing basis.

17.1 **(Briefing sessions)** The Contractor shall provide briefing sessions, on a quarterly or more frequent basis, addressing relevant and significant (in the Contractor's opinion) developments in the industry.

    a. Separate sessions will be conducted for business versus technological issues.

    b. All the Principal's persons attending briefing sessions shall be requested to complete an evaluation form that shall include ratings of the quality and effectiveness of the briefing session and their overall satisfaction with the Contractor's assessment of the impact on the efficiency or profitability of the Principal.

    c. Original completed evaluation forms are to be made available to the Principal, on request.

17.2 **(Performance indicators)** The performance indicators that will be used to assess the Provider's performance of this clause 17 are:

    a. **(Frequency)** Briefings are conducted at least quarterly.

    b. **(Rating)** Summary of the briefing evaluation by participants shows an overall satisfactory rating.

17.3 **(Effect of performance indicators failure)** Failure by the Contractor to provide to the Principal an acceptable level of service as described in Performance Indicators below may be referred to the Executive Committee for a suitable course of action.

17.4 **(Reports)** The Contractor shall provide a report quarterly to the Principal of any significant developments in the industry or business environment which have the potential to impact the efficiency or profitability of the Principal including:

    a. a summary of the evaluation of participants;

    b. ratings of the quality and effectiveness of the briefing session; and

    c. their overall satisfaction with the Contractor's assessment of the impact on the efficiency or profitability of the Principal.

Figure 9.1   Example innovation specification – scanning

Example Contribution Specification

I have included two examples of a contribution specification.

The first example, Figure 9.2, involves the specification of the range of knowledge transfer techniques that the provider was required to employ.

Schedule 11 Knowledge and skills transfer

1 **About the knowledge and skills transfer requirements**

1.1 **(Overview)** The Contractor will provide a range of mechanisms which enable the exchange and transfer of a range of knowledge and skills to the managers of the Principal. The mechanisms for achieving this shall include:

   a. annual secondment of a Business Analyst to the Contractor specified in provision 2;

   b. participation in training and professional development exercises specified in provision 3; and

   c. providing presenters to professional development programs arranged by the Principal specified in provision 4.

1.2 **(Reports)** The Contractor will provide a report on the outcome of the knowledge and skill transfer programme shall be provided by the Contractor on a quarterly basis.

1.3 **(Performance indicators)** No less than 'satisfactory' rating by:

   a. both the Business Analyst and the Contractor regarding each year's secondment,

   b. attendees of one party regarding the of training of the other party, and

   c. attendees of the Contractor's presenter specified in provision 4.

2 **Annual secondment of Business Analyst**

2.1 **(Provision of Business Analyst)** The Principal will supply the Contractor, on an annual basis beginning on the first Anniversary Date, one Business Analyst who will work under the Contractor.

2.2 **(Selection of individuals)** The Principal will propose suitably qualified persons from within the Principal's staff. The Contractor shall perform the final selection of the person to be appointed.

2.3 **(Conditions of employment)** The appointed person shall take leave from their current position for one year with the Principal and shall work under the Contractor's terms and conditions, but will at all times remain an employee of the Principal. The arrangements in clause 52 of the Contract (including indemnities from the Principal for acts and omissions of its employees on secondment to the Contractor) will apply.

2.4 **(Termination of secondment)** The Contractor shall have the discretion to terminate the secondment on the grounds of poor performance or inappropriate behaviour by the seconded Business Analyst. The Principal may offer a replacement for the residual period of the secondment, the acceptance of which is at the complete discretion of the Contractor. Such termination does not affect the next year's secondment.

3 **Training**

3.1 **(Internal courses by the Contractor)** The Principal shall provide a minimum of one place per year in each of the training programmes provided by the Contractor to its internal staff for:

   a. consultancy skills;

   b. leadership practices;

Figure 9.2   Example contribution specification #1 – knowledge transfer

c. managing organizations; and

d. sales.

3.2 (Internal courses by the Principal) The Principal shall make one place available to the Contractor on all training and professional development programmes which they conduct for their own staff.

3.3 (**Limitation regarding internal courses**) The requirement to make places on training courses and presentations available shall not apply where either party considers the programme to include commercially sensitive material which it is not appropriate to reveal to the other party. Parties will be so notified in these instances.

3.4 (**Public training**) Provide a minimum of two places for the Principal's personnel at any seminar or presentation facilitated by the Contractor, at which new technologies, or applications of technology, are discussed or reviewed.

3.5 (**Expenses**) Each party will meet all out of pocket expenses associated with its staff attending the other party's training programmes, including transport and accommodation.

4   Provision of presenters by the Contractor

4.1 (**Provision of presenters**) The Contractor shall provide at least one presenter at professional develop programmes arranged by the Principal.

4.2 (**Notification**) The Principal must notify the Contractor no less than two months in advance of the programme regarding the content and date/s.

4.3 (**Offer of presenters**) Three presenters shall be offered by the Contractor which the Principal may choose in its absolute discretion.

4.4 (**Substitution**) If the presenter cannot make the appearance due to illness or having left employment of the Contractor, a suitable replacement must be provided by the Contractor. No other conditions of substitution are permitted.

Figure 9.2   *Concluded*

The original intent of the client was just to let the provider offer whatever it wanted. However, the client had very clear ideas of what it wanted, as you will see in the example, and chose to make it a specification in the form of a schedule to the contract instead. As a result, they did get what they wanted within the fixed lump sum.

The second example of a contribution specification, Figure 9.3, involves the client requiring the provider to include the client in its proposals – not just for revenue, but also for branding purposes. The client, in this case, was a training institution and wanted the provider to use them with other clients, where appropriate, as part of their commercial relationship. However, since this type of business contribution with a provider was rather exploratory in nature, and ultimately at the discretion of the provider, KPIs were not deemed appropriate. The clause operated more as good-faith intent rather than a hard and fast requirement.

---

9. Recognition by the Provider of the Client as a preferred provider of training services

9.1 (**Duty to include in proposals**) In all proposals that have a general training component, or are seeking general training capabilities, the Provider will:

   a. for local clients, put the Client forward as the preferred provider of training services, and

   b. for overseas clients, provide the Client an opportunity to provide a training proposal for inclusion as the preferred provider of training services.

9.2 (**Pricing**) The costs of the training offered by the Client, and included in any offer documents to the Provider's clients, shall either be negotiated and agreed between the Contractor and the Client or shall be based on the Client's standard commercial rates.

9.3 (**Election**) The Provider may elect not to include the Client training proposal in any proposal it submits to overseas clients. Valid grounds for such exclusion from a proposal would include:

   a. lack of appropriate skills or qualifications by the Client,

   b. unavailability of the Client to conduct the training at the required dates and times, or

   c. if the Client does not represent best value for money in the opinion of the Provider.

9.4 (**Reports**) The Provider shall provide a quarterly report summarizing the:

   a. proposals using the Client's name during the quarter,

   b. training services delivered by the Provider to its clients during the quarter

     i. highlighting those delivered by the Client and

     ii. the reasons why the Client wasn't used in the other engagements,

   c. evaluation of the quality of training services delivered by the Client,

   d. any issues which need to be addressed by the Client, and

   e. possible future opportunities with the Client.

Figure 9.3　Example contribution specification #2 – brand exposure

Example Underlying Work Practices Specification

The example of an underlying work practices specification, Figure 9.4, required the provider to have a highly skilled and qualified workforce performing work for the client because of the client's regulatory obligations. To make this happen, the client specified the provider's obligations, which is where many organizations stop – thinking that it is merely enough to state the obligations.

However, this client was quite experienced, and knew much better. Accordingly, it required a detailed management plan regarding the workforce and the KPI involved the contract manager's perception as to how well the plan had been carried out each month.

G.5   Workforce Management

G.5.1   (**About this schedule**) This schedule provides for the Contractor's Workforce Management for provision of the Services in accordance with this Contract.

G.5.2   (**Qualifications of the Workforce**) In order to ensure the safety of the Workforce and the public, and to adhere to the principles as set out in the relevant legislation, all individuals working under this Contract (including the Contractor's employees, agents and Subcontractors) shall meet minimum requirements with regard to qualifications, competency and training, and have documentation to prove the same, as set out:

a)   Construction and Maintenance Competency Guidelines (or equivalent and as updated from time to time);

b)   Industry Commission Licensing arrangements;

c)   applicable enterprise competencies (as required by the Client); and

d)   other relevant competencies

that provides evidence of appropriate skill to deliver the Services safely and professional manner.

G.5.2   (**Contractor obligations**) The Contractor must ensure that all the Workforce carrying out the Services under this Contract:

a)   hold all applicable or necessary qualifications (including but not limited to trade qualifications and enterprise competencies) and permits, including those required by Law and those specified in the Workforce Management Plan attached to this schedule;

b)   are adequately trained (which includes ensuring that the Workforce have received the training set out in the Workforce Management Plan and are competent to carry out their duties in relation to the Services; and

c)   demonstrate current competencies in accordance with the Construction and Maintenance Competency Guidelines as amended from time to time.

G.5.3   (**Cost of training**) The Contractor shall be responsible for ensuring that all training has been received and shall meet all costs of such training.

G.5.4   (**New Workforce requirements**) Should any new Workforce be planned to be introduced on a Site by the Contractor:

a)   the Contractor must notify the Contractor Manager prior to the individual's commencement and provide a resumé, competency summary, training programme for the individual(s) and any other information the Contractor Manager deems appropriate; and

b)   any new Workforce must have completed the induction training specified in the Workforce Management Plan prior to commencement on any Service or Site.

G.5.5   (**Duty to provide evidence**) Within five (5) Business Days of receipt of a request from the Client, the Contractor must provide to the Contractor Manager evidence of

Figure 9.4   Example underlying practices specification – workforce management

the qualifications, competencies and permits held, and training completed, by any one or more of the Workforce providing the Services under this Contract.

G.5.6   (**Workforce Management Plan obligation**) The Contractor must establish and maintain a Workforce Management Plan to be attached to this schedule in respect of its operations that relate to the provision of the Services. The Workforce Management Plan comprises the approach to ensuring quality of the Workforce and the ability to meet the workload demand peaks regarding the Services.

G.5.7   (**Plan contents**) The Workforce Management Plan shall contain (but not be limited to) the following elements, noting if the element differs between the type of Workforce (e.g. employees, Subcontractor personnel)

   a)   Workforce and workload policies;

   b)   Workforce induction, competency and qualification standards, training and development programmes - include the standard workforce qualifications/training and specialised qualifications/training;

   c)   Workforce competency register (for all Workforce involved in the Services);

   d)   annual Workforce resource programme (high-level Works programme);

   e)   investment tactics regarding Workforce improvement and renewal;

   f)   peak (and trough) workload management plan;

   g)   contingency planning;

   h)   consultation and communication;

   i)   issue resolution; and

   j)   review and improvement.

G.5.7   (**Monthly performance evaluation**) The Contractor Performance Perception Evaluation represents the overall subjective perception of the Contractor's performance as perceived by the Contractor Manager, taking into account all items in this schedule and the attached Workforce Management Plan. The perceptions are those of the Contractor Manager in his or her absolute discretion.

KPI	KPI Minimum Standard	Data Source
Score out of 100 for the Workforce category	Score of 90	Monthly Contractor Performance Perception Evaluation Form prepared by the Client

Attachment: The Contractor's Workforce Management Plan (not attached for purposes of this example)

Figure 9.4   *Concluded*

Example Alignment with Corporate Initiatives Specification

The last example, Figure 9.5, is a big one and shows you the degree of specification that can occur with strategic Contract Scorecard goals. This was a longer schedule, given the specific economic objectives the client organization was trying to achieve with the provider. In this case, the client was a federal government agency that had a policy of choosing providers that would help the economics of the country as well as provide quality work at a good price. The economic benefits it sought included in-country employment, exporting and the use of local companies as subcontractors.

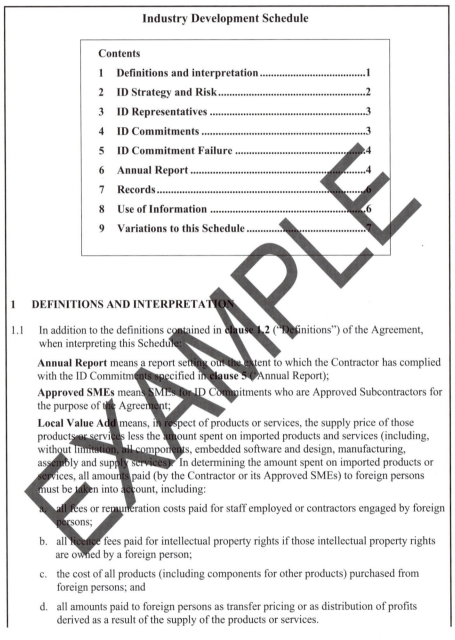

Industry Development Schedule

Contents

1   DEFINITIONS AND INTERPRETATION

1.1   In addition to the definitions contained in **clause 1.2** ("Definitions") of the Agreement, when interpreting this Schedule:

Annual Report means a report setting out the extent to which the Contractor has complied with the ID Commitments specified in **clause 5** ('Annual Report);

Approved SMEs means SMEs for ID Commitments who are Approved Subcontractors for the purpose of the Agreement;

Local Value Add means, in respect of products or services, the supply price of those products or services less the amount spent on imported products and services (including, without limitation, all components, embedded software and design, manufacturing, assembly and supply services). In determining the amount spent on imported products or services, all amounts paid (by the Contractor or its Approved SMEs) to foreign persons must be taken into account, including:

a.   all fees or remuneration costs paid for staff employed or contractors engaged by foreign persons;

b.   all licence fees paid for intellectual property rights if those intellectual property rights are owned by a foreign person;

c.   the cost of all products (including components for other products) purchased from foreign persons; and

d.   all amounts paid to foreign persons as transfer pricing or as distribution of profits derived as a result of the supply of the products or services.

Figure 9.5   Example alignment specification – industry development and employment

FTE means, in relation to a position of employment, Full Time Equivalent that will be calculated on an annual basis of average monthly figures;

ID Commitments means the obligations specified in **clause 4** ('ID Commitments');

ID Credits means credits against the Service Charges calculated in accordance with **clause 5** ('ID Commitment Failure');

ID Records means all information regarding the Contractor's and SMEs' operations relevant to this Schedule that will enable the Client to determine the extent and manner in which the Contractor has complied, or is complying, with this Schedule, including without limitation, the Contractor's fulfilment of each of the ID Commitments;

Net New Employment means the number of FTE jobs created over the relevant period in addition to base period employment numbers;

Parent Entity has the meaning given to that term by the Corporations Law;

Regional means any part of the country outside metropolitan areas of unless otherwise specified in this Schedule;

Related Body Corporate has the meaning given to that term by the Corporations Law;

SME (Small to Medium Enterprise) is a company that provides products and/or services and meets the following criteria at the signing of the Agreement:

a. together with its Related Bodies Corporate and Parent Entities has an aggregate annual revenue of less than $250 million; or

b. an annual revenue of less than $250 million together with its Related Bodies Corporate and Parent Entities has an aggregate annual revenue of more than $250 million

2 ID STRATEGY AND RISK

2.1 **(Desired outcomes)** The Client's desired outcomes from these key priorities are to:

a. maximize involvement of SMEs in delivering products and services;

b. achieve a substantial net increase in regional employment;

c. contribute to the development of technical skills in the local industry; and

d. not increase the Service Charges charged by the Contractor for the Services as a result of complying with this Schedule.

2.2 **(Risk)** The Contractor agrees:
a. to fulfil each of the ID Commitments completely as specified in this Schedule;

b. that it bears the risk for any change in industry circumstances that may impact on its ability to fulfil the ID Commitments or the cost of fulfilling those commitments; and

c. that it will not be released from any ID Commitment unless the Client agrees to a variation of this Schedule in writing.

Figure 9.5 *Continued*

2.3 (**Contractor warranties**) The Contractor warrants that:

    a. none of the ID Commitments has been claimed by the Contractor or any other person as part of any other agreement under which the Contractor, a Related Body Corporate, or a company with a substantial shareholding in the Contractor or a Related Body Corporate, has committed to undertake industry development.

    b. at the date of signing of the Agreement, appropriate contractual arrangements are in place with Approved SMEs to assure those entities' role in the provision of Services.

3 ID REPRESENTATIVES

3.1 (**Appointment**) Each party must appoint, and always have, an ID Representative to be its principal point of contact for all issues relating to this Schedule.

3.2 (**Meetings**) The ID Representatives must meet regularly (at least once annually, as soon as practicable after the Annual Report for the previous financial year is due to be submitted), and as otherwise requested by the Client, to discuss:

    a. the manner and extent of compliance with this Schedule (including as set out in the most recent Annual Report);

    b. if the Contractor has not fulfilled all of its ID Commitments for the year, a plan developed by the Contractor to improve its performance and remedy any shortfall; and

    c. any issues of concern to either party.

3.3 (**Replacement**) The Contractor must replace its ID Representative if requested by the Client or if the Contractor's ID Representative becomes unable or unwilling to fulfil the role. The Contractor must promptly appoint a replacement ID Representative, after obtaining the Client's approval.

4 ID COMMITMENTS

4.1 (**Regarding the Services**) The Contractor commits to maximize the Local Value Add, Net Employment, and involvement of SMEs in the provision of the Services. Without limiting this commitment, the Contractor must, as a minimum, provide the Services in compliance with the requirements set out below in Table 1.

Table 1

	Commitment
a. **Local Value Add** – as a percentage of annual Service Charges	77%
b. **Payment to Approved SMEs** – as a percentage of annual Service Charges	6%
c. **Total Net New Employment in performing the Services** – as the number of FTEs performing the Services	31
d. **Regional Net New Employment in performing the Services** – as the number of FTEs performing the Services	26

Figure 9.5   *Continued*

4.2   (**Sponsorship of students**) The Contractor commits to spending:

    a. $16,000 per annum in sponsoring two Honours Degree students in the Science faculties at a university approved by the Client; and

    b. $10,000 will be provided by the Contractor to sponsor prizes for tertiary students from these faculties.

5   ID COMMITMENT FAILURE

5.1   (**ID Credits**) Contractor does not achieve the ID Commitments specified in clause 4 above; the Contractor will be liable to pay the Client ID Credits as follows:

    a.   for ID Commitments 4.1.a and b – the amount of Services Charges represented by the percentage deficiency (or portion thereof);

    b.   for ID Commitments 4.1.c and d – $90,000 (representing average wage estimates) for each FTE deficiency (or portion thereof as applied to $90,000)

    c.   for ID Commitment 4.2.a and b – the actual dollar value deficiency which will be donated to one of more of the universities approved by the Client in clause 4.2.a.

5.2   (**Corrective action plan**) In addition to ID Credits, if the Contractor has notified the Client, or if the Client has become aware that the Contractor is not meeting, or is likely to not meet, one or more ID Commitments, the:

    a.   Client may require the Contractor to develop a corrective action plan to rectify the Contractor's failure or likely failure;

    b.   Contractor must propose the corrective action plan in accordance with the ID Variation Procedure and include in the plan sufficient information for the Client to be able to assess the financial and industry development impacts of the plan; and

    c.   If the Client approves of and signs the corrective action plan, it will form part of this Schedule.

5.3   (**Other remedies still available**) Nothing in this clause limits the remedies available to the Client under any other provision of the Agreement, including its right to terminate in accordance with clause 33 ('Termination') of the Agreement or to claim damages for any other breach of the Agreement:

6   ANNUAL REPORT

6.1   Provisions

    6.1.1   (**Due date**) The Annual Report must be delivered by the Contractor on or before 1 January each year regarding the previous year.

    6.1.2   (**Audit**) The annual report must be independently audited at the Contractor's expense.

Figure 9.5   *Continued*

6.1.3   (**Reporting information**) The information categories to be included in the Annual Report are listed below in clauses 6.2 to 6.5 and must contain at least all the information specified as well as

    a. both qualitative and quantitative information on the activities that the Contractor has committed to undertake to verify the compliance of this Schedule;

    b. descriptive material to reflect progress and achievements in implementing the ID Commitments; and

    c. substantiation on how each achievement has been calculated

6.1.4   (**Double counting**) No double counting is permitted when determining whether the Contractor has fulfilled its ID Commitments. That is:

    a. an activity will not be counted in assessing the achievement of more than one ID Commitment; and

    b. an activity that is claimed as part of any other Government industry development programme or under any other contract with the Client or a Government agency will be discounted to the extent that the activity has already been claimed for industry development.

6.1.5   (**Declassification as an SME**) A company will immediately cease to be an SME for the purposes of this Schedule if it is acquired at any time by the Contractor or any of the Contractor's Related Bodies Corporate.

6.1.6   (**Additional information**) The Client may request additional information where information in the report requires further clarification or is no adequate for the Client's needs.

6.2   (**Strategic overview section**) The Contractor must provide an overall summary/general descriptive information of

    a. the type and quantum of activity to which the Contractor has been contractually bound;

    b. the contribution these activities are making to improving the competitiveness of the local industry particularly the growth of SMEs; and

    c. how the activities align with the corporate strategies of the Contractor.

6.3   (**Level of Value-add section**) The Contractor must provide information on the type and quantum of Local Value Add activities.

6.4   (**SME participation section**) The Contractor must provide details on:

    a. the dollar value of the subcontract arrangement in terms of the work generated or sub-contracted to the SME;

    b. the type and nature of activities undertaken by the SME including the level of Local Value Add;

    c. how the Contractor has maximized the prospects for success in the relationship;

    d. a brief assessment by the SME on the quality of the alliance which may include:

        i. support for innovation provided by the Contractor;

        ii. access to global distribution opportunities;

Figure 9.5   *Continued*

    iii. assistance provided by the Contractor to improve managerial, business, marketing and financial skills; and

    iv. assistance provided by the Contractor to improve product and service quality.

6.5   (**Employment growth section**) The Contractor must provide details on:

    a. the increase in net employment and net regional employment over the Contractor, SMEs and Approved SMEs;

    b. location of employment;

    c. the skill levels of the employment created including entry level positions.

7   RECORDS

7.1   (**Retainage**) The Contractor must keep ID Records for **7** years following the Termination Date of this Agreement.

7.2   (**Access**) The Contractor must provide the Client's ID Representative with ID Records and all other information about the Contractor's fulfilment of the ID Commitments reasonably requested by the Client.

7.3   (**Form**) All ID Records provided by the Contractor must be:

    a. in written and electronic form, and otherwise in a form reasonably requested by the Client; and

    b. accompanied by sufficient supporting data to enable the Client to verify the manner and extent of compliance with this Schedule.

7.4   (**Audit rights**) The Client (through the Client's Audit Representatives) may conduct audits of the ID Records and the Contractor's (and its Approved SMEs and other SMEs used for the purpose of this Schedule) operations for the purpose of determining the manner and extent of compliance with this Schedule.

8   USE OF INFORMATION

8.1   (**Client rights**) The Client may:

    a. use any information made available to the Client under this Schedule for the purpose of assessing the Contractor's fulfilment of the ID Commitments:

    b. make public statements about the manner and extent of the Contractor's achievement of its ID Commitments, including information from the ID Reports and answers to any questions raised by the Client.

8.2   (**Consultation**) The Client will consult with the Contractor and obtain the prior written approval of the Contractor (which approval will not be unreasonably withheld) before using any information marked 'commercial in confidence', or before using any information in a public statement except where such use in public statements is necessary for the Client to comply with the obligations and duties of public accountability.

8.3   (**Contractor statements**) The Contractor may not make any statements about its fulfilment of the ID Commitments unless it has the prior written approval of the Client.

Figure 9.5   *Continued*

9   VARIATIONS TO THIS SCHEDULE

9.1   **(In writing)** This Schedule may only be varied in writing signed by each party.

9.2   **(Contractor requests to vary)** If the Contractor wishes (or if the Contractor is required) to change any aspect of this Schedule, it must:

    a.   notify the Client of the change;

    b.   substantiate the change and demonstrate that the change is at least as likely to promote the achievement of the Client's desired outcomes as set out in **clause 2.1** ('Desired outcomes'); and

    c.   specify the likely impact of the change (including, without limitation, the impact on the Contractor's ability to fulfil the ID Commitments in strict compliance with this Schedule);

9.3   **(Client acceptance)** the Client will within **30 days** after receipt of the notice (or such longer period as agreed by the parties), notify the Contractor whether it:

    a.   accepts the change, in which case the parties must agree to the change in writing;

    b.   wishes to negotiate the change, in which case the parties will use their reasonable efforts to promptly agree on the nature and extent of the change (if the parties cannot agree on the change, the Client may reject the change under paragraph (iii)); or

    c.   rejects the change, in which case the Schedule will continue in force unamended.

Figure 9.5   *Concluded*

10

Conclusion

'We are what we repeatedly do. Excellence, then, is not an act, but a habit.'

Aristotle

These days, the concept of using external organizations is generally considered an efficient and logical way to get things done. Yet there are many misconceptions about what contracting can, and cannot, do for you. Most of these lie in the almost ideological belief that contracts are a relatively simple transaction, that activities, assets and staff can more or less be easily provided by a supplier, and that inherent benefits will always follow. But contracts tend to be neither simple nor straightforward transactions. Rather than consider contracts to be something used to sue one another, consider contracts to be detailed strategies for managing what you need, how you want to get it, what you want to pay for and what you want to see as a result. Like all management strategies, the key lies in how you plan, implement and manage it.

Once an organization has made the decision to contract something out and the deal is signed, many people resort to the hands-off approach and just let the deal run its natural course, with only the occasional attempt at firefighting when some sort of operational issues arise. Running a contract in this reactionary mode, rather than a in a proactive one, never ensures that the desired outcomes are achieved – merely that failure is avoided. And the difference between these two states can sometimes add up to millions of dollars.

However, as contracting-out consumes an ever larger slice of an organization's annual spend, the ability to drive and demonstrate success becomes an increasing expectation of the management involved. The old way of just signing a deal and assuming it will all work out the way it was intended is no longer an acceptable practice within knowledgeable organizations.

A Contract Scorecard is one proactive tool that has proven successful and is worth contemplating, for a number of reasons. Firstly, it provides a key mechanism for capturing and articulating the particular outcomes your stakeholders are seeking from a contract/commercial relationship. The Contract Scorecard helps the parties not only establish how the quality will be evaluated, but also what the financial outcomes will be judged by, how the relationship is conducted and if the deal is achieving its strategic aims – in sum representing the overall success of the deal from an holistic view.

Then it helps guide the necessary detail within the contract documents, offering a logical way to construct and think about this suite of documents. In this way, the contract can become a constructive tool, to guide and achieve a successful deal, rather than confuse or complicate it.

Lastly, it provides an important tool for tracking, assessing and driving the results of the deal. The use of a Contract Scorecard does not imply less effort in managing contracts, only a different emphasis. The scorecard moves contract management from the more traditionally administrative role towards a direct role involved at a strategic level, to ensure the intended goals are achieved, whatever quadrants you have chosen.

Similar organizations that have contracted the same things have had very different results. Some have had cost savings; some have had cost explosions. Some have had deficient service delivery; some have had excellent service. Some have enviable supplier relationships; some have atrocious relations. Some have had outcomes that benefited the strategic goals of the organizations; others have not even got the basics of what they wanted.

The choice is yours.

References

Campbell, D. (1997) 'Socio-legal Analysis of Contracting' in P. Thomas (ed.) *Sociolegal Studies*, Aldershot: Dartmouth, 239–278.

Collins, H. (1996) 'Competing Norms of Contractual Behaviour' in D. Campbell and P. Vincent-Jones (eds.) *Contract and Economic Organization: Sociolegal Initiatives*, Aldershot: Dartmouth, 67–89.

Cullen, S. (2007) 'Outsourcing Success', *Sourcing and Vendor Relationships Executive Report*, 8:8, Cutter Consortium, December 2007.

Cullen, S., Seddon, P.B. and Willcocks, L.P. (2001) *IT Outsourcing Practices in Australia*, Sydney: Deloitte.

Cullen, S., Seddon, P.B. and Willcocks, L.P. (2005) 'Managing Outsourcing: The Lifecycle Imperative', *MIS Quarterly Executive*, 4:1, March, 229–246.

Cullen, S. and Willcocks, L.P. (2003) *Intelligent IT Outsourcing: Eight Building Blocks to Success*, Chichester: Elsevier.

Deakin, S. and Wilkinson, F. (2000) 'Contract Law and the Economics of Interorganizational Trust' in C. Land and R. Bachman (eds) *Trust Within and Between Organizations: Conceptual Issues and Empirical Applications*, Oxford: Oxford University Press.

Domberger, S., Fernandez, P. and Fiebeg, D. (2002) 'Modelling the Price, Performance and Contract Characteristics of IT Outsourcing', *Journal of Information Technology*, 15, 107–118.

Kaplan, R. and Norton, D. (1992) 'The Balanced Scorecard: Measures that Drive Performance', *Harvard Business Review*, Jan–Feb, 71–79.

Kaplan, R. and Norton, D. (1996) 'Using the Balanced Scorecard as a Strategic Management System', *Harvard Business Review*, Jan, 75–85.

Kern, T. and Willcocks, L.P. (2001) *The Relationship Advantage: Information Technologies, Sourcing and Management*, Oxford: Oxford University Press.

Nagel, T.W and Murphy, M.T (1996) 'Structuring Technology Outsourcing Relationships: Customer Concerns, Strategies and Processes', *International Journal of Law and Information Technology*, 4:2, 151–175.

Stinchcombe, A. and Heimer, C. (1985) *Organizational Theory and Project Management: Administrative Uncertainty in Norwegian Offshore Oil*, Oxford: Oxford University Press.

Vincent-Jones, P. (2000) 'Contractual Governance: Institutional and Organizational Analysis', *Oxford Journal of Legal Studies*, 20:3, 317–351.

Willcocks, L. and Fitzgerald, G. (1994) *A Business Guide to Information Technology Outsourcing*, London: Business Intelligence.

Index

About the Author

 Dr Cullen is the Managing Director of The Cullen Group, a specialist organization offering consulting, training and methodologies regarding commercial agreements. Sara was formerly a partner at Deloitte where she ran the contract consulting division, and her PhD from Melbourne University is in the field of outsourcing. She has consulted to over 110 private and public sector organizations, spanning 51 countries, in over 140 contracts with values up to $1.5 billion per year.

She has facilitated contracts in a large variety of organizational areas including call centres, claims management, construction, equipment supply and commissioning, facilities management, finance, food services, HR, logistics, IT, maintenance, recreational services, sales and security. She has designed partnering arrangements, franchise-type agreements, shared risk/reward structures and incentive programs as well as traditional arrangements.

Her consulting services include sourcing strategies and approaches; tendering, contract design and drafting; design of KPIs and incentive/recourse schemes; relationship/contract management; pricing; negotiation, remediation; market assessments, audits, risk assessment and mitigation, and mobilization and disengagement planning.

Ms. Cullen has been featured numerous times in such publications as *ABIE Source*, the *Australian Financial Review*, *BRW*, the *Bulletin*, *Computerworld*, *Directions in Government*, *European Journal of Information Systems*, *Information Economics Journal (UK)*, *Insurance Directions*, *Journal of Strategic Information Systems*, *MISQ Executive*, *New Accountant*, *Outlook India*, *Oxford Handbook* and *Strategic Asset Management*.

She has written 75 publications, conducted many reviews for governments in Australia, New Zealand and Hong Kong, featured in more than 60 articles and presented in more than 300 major conferences, in addition to research with the London School of Economics, and Oxford, Warwick and Melbourne

Universities since 1994. Her in-depth knowledge has been globally recognized, resulting in reviews of outsourcing research for the *California Management Review, MIS Quarterly Executive,* the *Journal of Information Technology* and the European Conference on Information Systems.

Dr. Cullen has lectured at many universities including Melbourne University, Monash University, Swinburne University, the Queensland University of Technology, the Royal Melbourne University of Technology and Seoul University.

Dr. Cullen earned a Bachelor of Science in accounting from St. Cloud State University (US); she was awarded a Masters of Management (Technology) from Melbourne Business School and earned her PhD from the University of Melbourne where she is an Honorary Research Fellow. She is also a US-qualified CPA.

She can be reached at scullen@cullengroup.com.au and www.cullengroup. com.au.

If you have found this resource useful you may be interested in other titles from Gower

The Bid Manager's Handbook
David Nickson
244 x 172 mm 234 pages Hardback: 978-0-566-08847-6

Law for Project Managers
David Wright
244 x 172 mm 176 pages Hardback: 978-0-566-08601-4

Outsourcing IT
Rachel Burnett
244 x 172 mm 276 pages Hardback 978-0-566-08597-0

Project Reviews, Assurance and Governance
Graham Oakes
244 x 172 mm 288 pages Hardback: 978-0-566-08807-0
e-book: 978-0-7546-8146-5

Purchasing Performance
Derek Roylance
234 x 156 mm 192 pages Hardback: 978-0-566-08678-6
e-book: 978-0-7546-8308-7

The Relationship Driven Supply Chain
Stuart Emmett and Barry Crocker
244 x 172 mm 208 pages Hardback: 978-0-566-08684-7
e-book: 978-0-7546-8778-8

GOWER